Soldier of the Sixth

The Reith brothers and Pennisular war medals.

Soldier of the Sixth

Major Jim Pickering

The Pentland Press Limited
Edinburgh · Cambridge · Durham

First published in 1993 by
The Pentland Press Ltd.
1 Hutton Close
South Church
Bishop Auckland
Durham

ISBN 1 85821 010 0

Typeset by Elite Typesetting Techniques, Southampton.
Printed and bound by Antony Rowe Ltd., Chippenham.

Soldier of the Sixth
is dedicated to
All ranks of the Regiment,
past and present,
and, in particular,
those of the Regiment
who have given their lives
to the country

Acknowledgements

With gratitude to Miss Cynthia Clark, without whose generosity this book would not have been published.
With grateful thanks to all those who have in some way or another contributed to the production of the book.

Contents

Preface

At the outset I must state in all honesty that I have never aspired to be an author. 'In that case,' I can hear you say, 'Why are you writing this book?' My motive for doing so is, to me, so overwhelming that to shrink from the task would be to fail in a duty to posterity.

Among those of us who have served as soldiers during the the first fifty years or so of the twentieth century, few would dispute the fact that in the entire history of the British Army no period has been more momentous. These are the years that cover the fighting in the heat and sand of the Sudan, in the bush and veldt of South Africa, in the mud of Flanders during the First World War, in Europe, Italy, North Africa, Burmah and Malaya during the Second – and all this under conditions of service that have altered swiftly and dramatically. As one surveys the changes that have taken place in peacetime and wartime conditions alike over the period in question, one realises that they have been nothing short of phenomenal.

With such considerations in mind, the author has sought to provide a permanent record of the experiences of one soldier serving in one particular regiment during that period.

Obviously similar stories could be written about soldiers serving in any one of the seventy British infantry regiments of the line that were in existence at the end of World War I. Nevertheless I am sure that any soldier, whatever his regiment, will find in the following narrative much to interest and amuse him – perhaps even something to inspire him.

As with all soldiers' stories, the possibility of occasional inaccuracies or exaggerations cannot be excluded. However, I hope sincerely that due allowance will be made for these in view of the fact that the book covers a period of close on seventy years and has been written chiefly from memory. I thank God for those minute cells of the brain which have stored so vast an amount of information.

Most of the background history has been gleaned from records held in the Regimental Museum at Warwick, to which I am indebted, and the same is true of some of the pictures.

Let me conclude by dedicating this book to the whole 'family of the Regiment', past and present, not forgetting my father (who served in it for 24 years) or my mother, for the influence which both of them exercised over me has been truly profound.

Foreword

by Lieutenant General Sir Jeremy Reilly KCB DSO
Colonel, the Royal Regiment of Fusiliers
and
late of the Royal Warwickshire Regiment

This is a fascinating little book which brings together parental recollection, contemporary regimental 'talk' and personal memories to provide a most readable account of life 'in one particular Regiment during a momentous period for the British Army during which the changes which have taken place in peacetime and wartime conditions have been nothing short of phenomenal'.

Humour, pathos and the detail of events, relationships and places, are captured by the author's autobiographical, albeit third person style, which makes for compulsive reading for anyone with an interest in the times or locations concerned, these being mainly military stations at home and abroad during the inter-war years. However, the reader is also able to track the relationship of two generations of 'Pickerwings' with, initially Lieutenant (in Peshawar), and finally Field Marshal (in the office of the Chief of the Imperial General Staff) Montgomery – or 'Monty' as he was always known in the Regiment.

Number 5102774 Boy (soldier) Pickering J.H. enlisted into the Royal Warwickshire Regiment, 6th Foot, in a barracks at Shorncliffe in 1925; Major J.H. Pickering retired from the regular army in 1961, having been commissioned from the rank of sergeant in 1940. But Pickering's recall of life in his Regiment runs much further back than his own thirty-six years of service might suggest. He was an 'Army Brat' and followed his father into the Royal Warwickshires. His father enlisted in 1898, in which year the 1st Battalion of the Regiment participated in Kitchener's campaign in the Sudan (Omdurman and Khartoum), and in due course was promoted to be the Officers' Mess Sergeant of the same battalion whilst Captain B.L.

Montgomery rose to be its Adjutant. Two decades afterwards, Lance Corporal Jim Pickering found himself serving as a clerk in the Orderly Room of the 1st Battalion throughout the time that 'Monty' commanded it in Palestine, Egypt and Poona; experiencing the delights of what is now called the Corbett National Park and the pitfalls of setting up a first family home at Fyzabad.

Jim Pickering has made excellent use of the resultant collection of experiences and stories in creating this book which will bring pleasure to members and friends of the Regiment and interest to others. It conveys well the aroma and flavour of life in a Regiment as noted by an observant participant with a retentive memory and an evident sense of humour. As such it will undoubtedly provide a welcome supplement to more formal histories of the period.

Regimental Headquarters,
The Royal Regiment of Fusiliers,
H.M. Tower of London

October 1992

Chapter 1

The Origins and History of the 'Saucy Sixth'

Three hundred years and more have elapsed since many of our now famous regiments were formed. There can be very few of our living contemporaries who have not, at some point, been associated with one or other of them, fewer still who have not heard or read of their exploits. To realise how true this is we have only to recall such legendary episodes as the Charge of the Light Brigade, the Battle of Waterloo, the Thin Red Line, the Relief of Lucknow, Rorke's Drift or the Retreat from Mons. In recent times Dunkirk, the Battle of Alamein, Arnhem, Goose Green and Stanley have become no less widely known. In all these battles British soldiers have fought gloriously to preserve freedom and honour. Thousands of them have shed their blood and the soil of countless countries and continents throughout the world has thereby been hallowed and enriched: the Peninsula, Flanders, Egypt, Italy, France, Germany and the Falklands – the list is endless.

Volumes have been written about the campaigns waged in these countries and the commanders who conducted them. Wellington, Gordon, Montgomery, Colonel 'H' and many others besides have become household names. The histories of individual regiments have been written, re-written and brought up to date with each succeeding campaign. Each has some special battle to commemorate, such as Martinique, Minden or Ladysmith; or they may record some memorable achievement of the regiment such as the March from Kabul to Kandahar or the Storming of the Heights of Abraham.

Other regimental historians remember with pride the nicknames associated with past glories: 'Pontius Pilate's Body Guard' (The First Foot, Royal Scots), 'The Fighting Fifth' (The Royal Northumberland Fusiliers),

'The Saucy Sixth' (The Royal Warwickshire Regiment), 'The Naughty Nineth' (The Royal Norfolk Regiment) or 'The Death and Glory Boys' (The 17/21st Lancers). All are steeped in tradition and immensely proud of the Battle Honours that grace the Colours of their respective regiments. They are proud too of the badges adorning their own headgear and, in particular, of their own regimental heroes – none more so than the Lancashire Fusiliers (20th Foot), which can boast of having won, in the course of that never-to-be-forgotten landing at Gallipoli, six Victoria Crosses before breakfast. To a lesser degree, perhaps, the boast of the 39th Foot (the Dorsetshire Regiment) is worthy of record: they are 'Primus in Indus', the first British regiment in India.

Perhaps as so much will be said in the pages which follow about 'The Regiment' (namely The Royal Warwickshire Regiment), it will be helpful to give some brief survey of its origins and subsequent history. In view of the distinguished officers it has produced, all of them serving in the Regiment at the same time, this history may surely be accounted unique.

It was during the reign of Queen Elizabeth I of England that some of her soldiers found themselves in Holland in the service of the States General during the Dutch War of Independence. However, in 1665 war broke out between England and Holland, with the result that these troops were recalled to their homeland. One of the officers returning at this time was Sir Walter Vane, a Captain in Russell's Regiment. This was later to become the Grenadier Guards.

In 1668 Sir Walter Vane became Colonel of the Holland Regiment, which itself later became 'The Buffs' (3rd. Regiment Foot). In 1674, at the end of the war with Holland, Sir Walter was given the rank of Major-General and was commissioned to form a force of ten companies of troops. Shortly afterwards he was killed and the force he had mustered was formed into four regiments, one Irish, one Scottish and the remaining two English. The first of these latter was the 5th. Foot, later to become the now famous Royal Northumberland Fusiliers. The second regiment was the 6th. Foot. The numbers derive from the order of their return to England in 1685. Neither of the two English regiments arrived back in time to take part in the suppression of Monmouth's Rebellion. In 1688, just three years later, they both returned to Holland with William, Prince of Orange. It was at this point that the 6th. Foot was given the nickname of 'The Dutch Guards' and that the Regiment adopted as its colours the royal blue and orange of the House of Nassau. The orange was in fact known as 'old gold'.

The Regimental Badge is the figure of an antelope, and two conflicting explanations of the origins of this are on record. The first is that when Sir

Walter Vane formed his original twelve companies of troops, the 12th. Company, from which the 6th. Foot was formed, had as its badge the crest of the antelope ducally gorged and chained. It is this crest, it is alleged, that appears in later years as the Regiment's badge.

The second account suggests that the antelope badge originated in the course of the Peninsular War. On 20th. August 1810, during the Battle of Saragossa, the Regiment captured, among other trophies of war, a standard bearing the figure of an antelope, the ancient and royal emblem of the Moorish regiment to which it had belonged. Queen Anne (so the tradition goes) was pleased to bestow upon the 6th. Foot the honour of forthwith adopting the antelope badge as its own in recognition of its courage and its outstanding achievements.

The Regiment fought at the Battle of the Boyne in Ireland and later against the French in Flanders. Its first Battle Honour was *Namur*, 1695. Then in the early part of the 18th. century we find it in Spain, where it was taking part in the War of the Spanish Succession. In 1742 the 6th. Foot went to the West Indies, only to find itself suffering severely from tropical diseases. Yet after no more than a brief respite it was ordered north to Scotland to help in quelling the 1745 Rebellion.

It was during this period that a woman named Hannah Snell, born in Worcester in 1723, enlisted in the Regiment under the pretence of being a man. She enlisted at Coventry in 1745, giving as her name 'James Grey', and marched with the Regiment on its way to deal with the Rebellion as far as Carlisle. Here, however, she got into trouble and was sentenced to 500 lashes. At this point, realising that her masquerade was at an end, she deserted. However, there was to be no suppressing either her wantonness or her will to serve the Crown. She enlisted afresh, this time in the Marines, and sailed to the West Indies in the sloop *Swallow*. She ended her career serving as a 'Pensioner' at the Royal Hospital, Chelsea, where she died.

It was not until 1782 that the Regiment came to be associated with the county of Warwickshire. The Army had decreed that every regiment would thenceforward recruit from a specific county. The Sixth Foot thus came to bear the title of the Sixth or First Warwickshire Regiment. In that same year it adopted as its Regimental March 'The Warwickshire Lads'. Although the words were written by the famous actor David Garrick, the music was composed by Charles Dibdin. He is reputed to have sung it at the Shakespeare Centenary Celebrations at Stratford-upon-Avon on the 6th. September 1769. The refrain runs:

Ye Warwickshire lads and ye lasses,
See what at our jubilee passes.
Come revel away, rejoice and be glad,
For the lad of all lads was a Warwickshire lad,
Warwickshire lad, ever be glad,
For the lad of all lads was a Warwickshire lad.

Of course, as is the way of all soldiers, those belonging to the Regiment down the years have opened the song with a version of their own:

The Warwickshire lads and their lasses
With petticoats up to their asses.

On the day following the inauguration of this song the air was played by the fifes and drums of the Warwickshire militia outside the Stratford-upon-Avon town hall. So popular did it become that it later became the Regiment's 'quickstep'.

The Regiment's second Battle Honour, that of *Martinique* won in 1794, was awarded during the period when it was serving in the West Indies in the wars of the French Revolution. Upon its return to England in 1795 the Duke of Gloucester (Prince William Frederick) was appointed Colonel of the Regiment, and to mark the occasion it was given permission to bear on its buttons and appointments '. . . the Antelope within a crowned Garter surrounded by the motto, "Honi Soit Qui Mal Y Pense" '. It was not until 1930 that the Garter was borne on the Colours of the Regiment. This honour was granted by King George V on the submission of General Sir Robert Whigham, the then Colonel of the Regiment.

The Sixth Foot then spent seven years in Canada before once again returning to the Iberian Peninsula to fight in the Peninsular War. Here it gained two more Battle Honours, those of *Rolica* and *Vimera*, subsequently returning to England for a short period of rehabilitation. Thereafter it returned to Spain to fight under the Duke of Wellington, gaining the further Battle Honours of *Vittoria* and the *Pyrenees*. After one particular battle the Duke of Wellington commended the Regiment, saying after the attack that it had been the finest he had seen. The Battle Honours of *Nivelle* and *Orthes* were then added to the Regiment's collection, after which they were again commended by General Walker, who stated: 'I can hardly sufficiently praise the gallantry and steadiness with which the Sixth Regiment performed this severe duty'.

One of the Regiment's most treasured possessions is a small snuff box now preserved in the Regimental Museum at Warwick. It was given by

Lieut.-Colonel Hedges of the 48th. Regiment (later the Northamptonshire Regiment) in 1785. On either side of it words have been scratched: 'Seek glory' on one side and 'Huzza for the Sixth Regiment, Now keep glory' on the other. The first inscription is the work of the donor, Lieut.-Colonel Hedges. Tradition has it, however, that the second was executed by the Duke of Wellington himself while dining with the Regiment after the Battle of Orthes.

In 1814 some regiments from the Peninsular War were sent to Canada to take part in the war with the United States and the Sixth was one of these. It was at this time that it acquired the Battle Honour of *Niagara.* However, its travels were not yet finished, for it went on first to South Africa and then, for the first time in its history, to India. It was in 1832, whilst it was stationed at Kirkee, near Poona, that King William IV directed that 'The Sixth Regiment of Foot shall be permitted to bear the appellation of "Royal" and that it should thenceforward be styled, "The Sixth or Royal (1st.) Warwickshire Regiment" '. From that point onwards its facings were changed from orange to blue.

It was during the Irish Rebellion of 1798 (a hundred and twenty-four years after the Regiment had been formed) that a small force of militia fencibles and yeomanry, together with about 120 men of the Sixth Foot under Major MacBean, was sent to oppose the French force under General Humber which had landed at *Killali* in May. On the 27th. August the French drove our forces back at *Castlebar.* The little band of the Sixth did what it could to cover the retreat and to such purpose that Lord Cornwallis, the Viceroy of Ireland, afterwards wrote: 'The Sixth behaved well and had the rest done the same, the day had been ours'.

Many of the older regiments have had particular families associated with them over a period of many years, with fathers, sons and brothers all serving in the same regiment. The Royal Warwickshire Regiment has its families too and the present book is concerned with just such a family, namely the Pickerings. However, of all the families which have served in The Regiment, perhaps the most famous was that of the Reiths, who emerge into prominence in connection with this retreat at Castlebar. In the course of this action Sergeant Archibald Reith and also his son James (a drummer boy aged twelve), particularly distinguished themselves. Sergeant Reith's father is said to have been a Dutchman who joined The Regiment in the reign of William III and fought at Prestonpans. The boy James served all through the Peninsular War, retiring in 1819 with the rank of Drum Major. He left his Peninsular War medal (which had eight bars) to the Regiment. His younger brother Alexander enlisted in the Regiment in 1801, also as a twelve year-old drummer boy. He too served throughout the Peninsular War, rising to the rank of Colour Sergeant. He died in December 1882 aged 94, likewise leaving his Peninsular War medal (with seven bars) to the Regiment. Both of the medals, together with a photograph of their holders, are proudly displayed in the Regimental Museum at St. John's House, Warwick. We must now turn to the story of that other regimental family the Pickerings, members of which have served in the Regiment from 1898 to 1961.

Chapter 2

Sergeant Howard Pickering and his Family

William Howard Pickering, known to all his family as 'Howard', was born at Balsall Heath in Birmingham in 1879. Orphaned at an early age, he was placed in the Gordon Boys' Home in that city. On leaving school he was given a job as an assistant in a greengrocer's shop belonging to his aunt in Stoney Lane, Sparkhill. In the course of delivering groceries he met Florence Perrigo, the eldest child of a family of nine. 'Florie' was at that time working at the Birmingham Small Arms Factory in Small Heath, where she helped to assemble one of the first three–speed cycles to be made there. While in the Gordon Boys' Home, Howard had learned to play the cornet, and now, since he could not otherwise afford to get married, he joined the Royal Warwickshire Regiment as a bandsman.

At that time the 1st. Battalion of the Regiment, commanded by Lieut.-Colonel W. E. Forbes, was serving under General Gordon in the Sudan, where it took part in the battles of Omdurman and Khartoum. In September 1898 the Battalion was moving down the River Nile on a steamer when the boat grounded and stuck fast in the mud. The soldiers of the Battalion attempted to push her off but tragically one of them was drowned.

On 8th. September the Battalion left Atbara by train en route for Alexandia in Egypt. Thence it proceeded on 18th. October to Suez (again by train) in order to embark on a troopship bound for India. Ten days later it arrived at Bombay, whence it continued its journey by train via Poona to Bellary. Strangely enough, the Battalion had already been stationed in Poona in 1826 and was to repeat the same journey as far as Poona in 1934. Some time after its arrival in 1898, however, it moved to Fort St. George at Madras.

Soldiering in those days was tough indeed. The trains were far from comfortable, being little better than cattle trucks and of course devoid of air conditioning. The soldiers sat on wooden slatted seats, though naturally the officers did fare a little better. The troopships were even worse, and below decks the stench, especially in hot weather, was such that even the most hardened of 'old sweats' found it almost unbearable. It was on the troopships that the game of 'Housey housey' (now known as Bingo) was introduced. It was officially permitted but always had to be controlled by the P.R.I. (President Regimental Institutes), who levied a percentage of the takings for the Regimental Fund. The game of 'Crown and Anchor', though forbidden, was nevertheless played from time to time by illicit gangs. They used to pay look–out men to watch for the approach of the Regimental Police just as nowadays 'spivs' plying their illicit trade on the pavements of Oxford Street pay look–outs to watch for the civil police.

The Battalion spent about six years in South India, its final station being Belgaum. In 1902, in the presence of the Viceroy, Battalion Headquarters and four companies, together with the Band, took part in the ceremonial installation of His Highness the Maharajah of Mysore. It was, perhaps, one of the most colourful ceremonies ever attended by the Regiment. Mysore ranked among the most beautiful and historic cities in that part of India and during the eighteenth century, in the time of Tippoo Sultan, many battles had taken place there. The history of those battles of South India used to be proudly commemorated by many of the Irish regiments which were disbanded in the early twenties. On the Colours of The Royal Dublin Fusiliers, for example, were emblazoned the Battle Honours of Carnatic, Mysore, Condore, Wandiwash, Pondicherry, Guzerat, Sholinghur, Nundy Droog, Amboyna, Ternate, Banda, Seringapatam, Kirkee, Mahaidapoor, Beni Boo Ali, Ava, Mooltan, Goojerat and Lucknow. It seems tragic that regiments such as these, which have made so tremendous a contribution under the British in the past, should have ceased to exist. The records of those early days of the British Army in India make fascinating reading.

Whilst the 1st. Battalion of the Regiment was serving in India, the 2nd. Battalion was making its contribution in South Africa, being immersed in the Boer War. Subsequently it was allotted the ignominious task of guarding Boer prisoners in Bermuda. After all the fighting in South Africa, the 2nd. Battalion had been looking forward to returning to England. To be sent to Bermuda instead, and on such a task, was a great disappointment. On their arrival, however, the colonists were determined to give the Regiment the warmest possible welcome and to show their appreciation of its achievements in the war which had just ended.

Howard Pickering was then a bandsman and by this time the Band, which until then had remained in England, had joined the 2nd. Battalion and was able to take part in the Victory Celebrations, including the march past, at which the Governor of the Colony took the salute. After the ceremony the Regiment was presented with silver purses. In October 1902, at the end of their stay in Bermuda, another celebration took place and one which all the troops taking part remembered and spoke of for many years after. After the march past on this occasion, the whole Battalion sat down to a most sumptuous meal which had been prepared and provided by 'the Ladies of the Colony'. Drink was to be had in abundance. The soldiers were given pipes and plenty of tobacco and for non–smokers half-pound slabs of chocolate were provided. Finally, as the troops descended the steps of the Civic Hall with, as one soldier put it, 'liquor running out of their ears', they were all told to have their mugs ready to receive a last drink for the road. On either side of the steps stood two large cauldrons filled with rum with which further to 'wet their whistles'. At that point an order emanated from the lips of the C.O., Lieut.-Colonel Quale Jones (himself as happy and bubbling as any of his soldiers), which was perhaps the most gentlemanly ever to be issued to a body of troops. He summoned the R.S.M. and directed that the men should 'fall in leisurely'! This they did, and one can visualize the scene: the red-coated soldiers linking arms in fours in order to maintain some semblance of dignity and then moving forward calypso-style as the Band played the regimental marches, 'The Saucy Sixth' and 'Warwickshire Lads'.

On its return to England the 2nd. Battalion was stationed at Devonport, and it was here that Howard Pickering, then a lance-corporal, began to make a name for himself on the field of sport. He was selected to play soccer as an amateur for Plymouth Argyle. He also won the West of England Marathon Championship. In 1905 Howard was promoted to the rank of sergeant and appointed Officers' Mess Sergeant at the Regimental Depot at Warwick. It was on Christmas Day of that year that he married Florence Perrigo (It also happened to be her birthday!) at St. John's Church, Sparkhill, Birmingham. He was then aged twenty-six and was thus entitled to 'live on the strength' in married quarters. For until reaching that age a soldier could not benefit as a married man. An officer was unable to receive corresponding benefits until he was thirty. Howard's married quarter was above the Officers' Mess at Budbrooke Barracks, and it was in this small but homely flat that Frances (Cissy) was born on 24th. February, 1909.

During their stay at Budbrooke Barracks an incident occurred which afterwards caused great amusement. Out of it, however, developed a lasting family friendship which continues to this day. Situated on the side of the barrack square was a life-size 'rocking horse' used to give officers riding practice. During such training it was customary for an officer to be properly dressed in white breeches and frockcoat. As the horse was not far from the troops' barrack room, it was inevitable that these latter should observe from afar, peering out of the windows without letting themselves be seen. One day a prank was hatched. That evening, under cover of darkness, a couple of soldiers surreptitiously painted the saddle of the horse with black lead. The following afternoon they watched in impish anticipation as one of the subalterns, immaculately attired and complete with whiter-than-white breeches, approached the horse. He was, of course, wholly unaware of the dastardly prank that had been played upon him. Only after returning to his room in the Officers' Mess did he realise his fate. Naturally he took a poor view of the troops' 'fun' and speedily sought the help of the R.S.M. in tracking down the culprits. They were duly discovered, charged, under the appropriate section of the Army Act, with conduct to the detriment of good order and military discipline, and sentenced to a number of days' C.B.

One of the erring soldiers was a certain Private George Kingsbury and as part of his punishment he was ordered to report to the Officers' Mess to carry out 'fatigues' in the kitchen; it entailed washing up after meals and performing other menial chores. At that time Howard Pickering's wife Florie was supervising the preparation of the officers' meals. Now, on seeing the gaunt looking young soldier, she exclaimed, 'Poor chap! He is in need of some nourishment'. Thereupon, in Howard's absence, she gave him a meal the like of which he had not had since joining the Army. However, she did afterwards tell her husband of her 'good' deed. Soon after this, George Kingsbury decided to turn a new leaf and became a good soldier. From then onwards the Pickerings and the Kingsburys became lifelong friends.

Chapter 3

Service in India before the First World War

During the trooping season of 1909/10 Howard and Florie Pickering, together with their infant daughter Cissy, sailed by troopship to join the 1st. Battalion, The Royal Warwickshire Regiment, then stationed at Peshawar on the North-West Frontier of India. Just one year before the Pickerings arrived, a young second lieutenant had also joined the Battalion from Sandhurst. His name was Bernard Montgomery. Apart from being good at games in general and a member of the Battalion hockey team, he was soon to show signs of becoming an accomplished horseman. He had arrived in India, however, just too late to receive his baptism of fire, for the Battalion had been engaged in operations on the North-West Frontier and had only just completed them. All who had taken part were awarded the India General Service Medal and 1908 clasp. During the operations Major Waterworth had been awarded the D.S.O.

In those days conditions for a soldier's family were pretty primitive. For a period the Pickering family's married quarter consisted of part of the Quartermaster's Stores. In fact the only form of division separating their principal room from the Clothing Store was a pair of blankets. During their time at Peshawar the married families moved up to one of the hill stations in the foothills of the western Himalayas, and here the Pickerings' married quarter was even more primitive, consisting of nothing more than a typical army bell tent. For part of this period Howard was able to join his family.

One of the hazards of life here was the prevalence of 'loose wallahs', the term applied to the typical Indian burglar who constantly raided the lines by night. It was Howard's practice to keep in readiness a long bamboo stick, one end of which was weighted with a metal ring while the other had a leather wrist-strap attached. Known as a 'lakri', it was the type of weapon commonly used by the police whenever trouble was expected. One night Florie, who was a light sleeper, was disturbed by a noise, and naturally concluded that a loose wallah was prowling nearby. Giving Howard a dig in the ribs she whispered: 'Howard, there's a loose wallah outside'. Seizing the lakri and clad only in his nightshirt, Howard immediately sallied forth to meet the intruder. The night was pitch dark and all he could see was the silhouette of a figure on two legs with its back to him moving a few yards ahead. Being a well-trained soldier, he lost no time in 'appreciating the situation' and going in to the attack. Grasping the lakri by its thong, he swung it with all his strength at the dim outline before him. There was an almighty thud followed by an awe-inspiring growl. Only then did he realise what he had hit. No loose wallah this, but a full-grown Himalayan bear! Fortunately the blow was enough to drive the animal off, for it straightway vanished into the darkness. On later occasions, whenever Florie recalled this episode, she used to say: 'If ever a bear had a sore backside it was that one'.

Another of her stories was so extraordinary that it might be thought fictitious were it not so well authenticated, even though, strangely enough, it does not appear to have been recorded in any of the official diaries of the Regiment. At the time of the incident in question the Battalion was stationed at Belgaum, one of the most lovely cantonments in South India, sheltered under the lee of the Western Ghats only a short distance inland from the ancient Portuguese port of Goa.

It was a couple of hours' train journey north of Bangalore, on the narrow gauge line of the railway known as the Mahratta and South Indian Railway, which connects Bombay and Madras via Bangalore. It was also the Depot of that famous South Indian Regiment, The Mahratta Light Infantry. In those days, as is still so often the case, when on parade the Adjutant was an officer to be feared. The particular Adjutant of the time of which I am speaking was no exception to this rule. Certainly he was no friend to any slovenly soldier. The weekly Adjutant's Parade was invariably held on the morning following the day when the soldiers received their meagre pay. Soldiers being what they are, many of them would have spent the previous evening in the 'wet' canteen and would be suffering from 'the morning after the night before'. On such occasions even the slightest lack of alertness on parade brought an immediate sharp rebuke from either the R.S.M. (who was always prowling in the rear) or from the officious and bewhiskered officer sitting on his *ghorra* (horse) with his face buried under his topee. Among the troops, the Adjutant concerned had the reputation of being 'a real b . . .'. Furthermore, he appeared to have an uncanny ability to see out of the back of his head. Any defect, however slight, in any of a soldier's drill movements would evoke a rebuke and in many cases would earn that soldier punishment without trial. In the words of the R.S.M., he would spend 'a few days where the flies won't get at you', the soldiers' argot for detention.

The incident which I am about to relate happened in 1906, the fourth year of King Edward's reign, at the end of a long period of exceptionally hot weather, when the spirits of even the toughest soldier might be expected to flag. On the night before the Adjutant's Parade it was the custom among many of the 'old sweats' to resort to the 'wet' canteen (usually a ground-floor room of the regimental canteen) in order to drown their sorrows and refresh themselves. I should explain at this point that the canteen was incorporated into one of the double-storied barrack-type blocks, but situated at some distance from the troops' sleeping quarters. At one end there would be a sparsely furnished bar, whilst the rest of the room contained a number of small tables with seats around for the drinkers. The room was invariably lit by oil lamps of the hurricane type suspended from the ceiling. On either side of the canteen was a wide verandah screened by large plants. Here, during the hot nights, imbibers could sit at their ease. Outside the main door the native 'punkah wallah' would be reclining with his back to the wall, having attached to his big toe a cord running over pulleys to a hook on the punkah frame. Hanging from the frame would be a series of strips of rush matting so that so long as the punkah wallah was awake and jerking his toe to and fro, the punkah frames would be kept moving forwards and backwards causing the strips of matting to act like large fans. Above the screeching of the punkah frames and the voices of many of the 'swaddies', by this time 'well oiled', the monotonous clicking of the crickets could be heard.

On the night in question three hardened 'old sweats', regular frequenters of the 'wet' canteen, were sitting drinking round one of the tables. Amid the rising din of increasingly drunken voices the conversation of this group turned on the following morning's Adjutant's Parade. Probably at least one, if not all three, had served in the South African War and had already spent several years abroad, so that they would have been feeling generally at the end of their tether. Suddenly one of them launched into a bitter tirade of abuse against 'that b...d on his *ghorra*', by which he meant the unloved Adjutant. 'One of these days I'll shoot the b...!' he exclaimed. This evoked an immediate response. 'You're too much of a b...funk,' retorted his two companions. 'Right,' said the first speaker, 'We'll soon see who's the funk.

We'll cut cards and the loser will shoot the b... on his *ghorra* tomorrow morning.

At 6.30 hours the following morning the Battalion was formed up 'in line of companies', and on this occasion the troops were dressed in non-ceremonial order. In other words they were wearing khaki drill shorts and shirts with hose tops, pith helmets instead of the ceremonial solar topees, and the usual highly polished leather belts with no less highly polished leather slings on their rifles. On the left side of the 'puggaris' adorning their pith helmets each man sported a neatly fastened silk-corded 'flash' in the regimental colours. Every regiment had its own distinctive 'flash', of which there were many variations. It was worn on the pith helmet or topee in place of the badge, which was worn on the forage cap.

On the morning of this particular Adjutant's Parade the soldier who had lost the 'cut of cards' the night before was suffering from an even thicker head than usual when he got up, and because of this he began to allow his thoughts to wander, probably dreaming of a visit to 'The Dun Cow' at Warwick or possibly, if he was a Birmingham man, to one of the popular pubs in the Bull Ring. By that time he had, for the time being, forgotten about the round of .303 which he had put 'up the spout' of his rifle before going on parade. So drowsy did he feel that he was quite unaware of the Adjutant who was, as usual, sauntering along the front rank of the parade on his *ghorra*. Suddenly, with a jerk of his reins, he brought his charger abruptly to a halt opposite the dozy soldier. Next the air was rent by the familiar loud voice shouting: 'Sergeant Major...Take this man's name. He's fast asleep!'

At this, with the speed of any normally trained soldier who has made a plan for a given situation, the 'old sweat' brought his rifle up to the 'on guard' position, cocked the bolt and, almost in the same motion, raised it to his shoulder and pressed the trigger. As the rifle cracked, the Adjutant dropped to the ground and his horse, frightened at the noise, bolted off with his startled 'syce' in pursuit. For a moment pandemonium broke out but in a trice the erring soldier was dispatched to the Guardroom under armed escort whilst the body of the Adjutant was conveyed to the mortuary to await a full military funeral that same evening. The soldier was later tried by Courts Martial and sentenced to be shot by a firing squad of the Regiment.

In 1946, forty years after this incident and just after the end of World War II, Jim, by this time an officer, was travelling on a tram in Bombay. Sitting opposite to him he noticed an elderly European gentleman who was wearing the medal ribbons of the South African War on his waistcoat.

Leaning forward towards the old soldier, Jim asked: 'Can you tell me which regiment you served with?' 'The Warwicks, of course,' replied the old gentleman, never noticing that Jim was himself wearing the antelope cap badge, 'I left them here in Bombay in 1912.' 'So, you must have served in Belgaum, Sir,' was Jim's next query. 'And what do you know about Belgaum – that was long before your time?' retorted the old man. 'Isn't that where the three soldiers cut cards to shoot the Adjutant in 1906?', replied Jim, not to be outdone. The old soldier's eyebrows lifted in surprise. Obviously he had forgotten that tragic episode in the Regiment's history. Nevertheless he was able to confirm the truth of the story told to Jim by his mother so many years before.

Since no record of the incident appears in the Regiment's official records of the time, it is just possible that the men concerned were not in the Royal Warwickshires but in another regiment which was stationed at Belgaum during the same period. However that may be, of the fact that it did happen Jim has no doubt whatever. The veracity of his mother's story was amply corroborated during his chance encounter with the old soldier.

In 1911 the Battalion moved to Bombay. Colaba Barracks, where it was stationed, was situated on the Causeway Peninsula at the entrance to Bombay Harbour. This was the year of the famous Delhi Durbar when King George and Queen Mary visited India to review both the British and the Indian Armies. The ensuing ceremonials called for what was, perhaps, the greatest gathering of British and Indian troops ever to take part in a single act of homage. In and around the city of Delhi vast camps were erected and the centrepiece for the ceremony itself was an enormous covered dais. From this the King and Queen presided as the troops marched past, attended by the Viceroy and a host of colourful dignitaries. What a sight it must have been! Taking part were detachments from every British regiment then stationed in India as well as from all the famous Indian regiments, all wearing their full ceremonial dress. Among them were Indian infantry, Punjabis, Maharratas, Dodgas, Jats etc., and Indian cavalry such as the Bengal Lancers, Skinner's Horse, Guides' Cavalry and many more. Others taking part in the march past were detachments of the Bombay and Madras Pioneers, the Gurkhas, Pathans and the like. All the participants were given the Delhi Durbar Medal with its ribbon striped in blue and red. Those from the Regiment receiving it were, of course, immensely proud of the honour.

In the course of his visit the King unveiled a monument on the quayside in Bombay which became known as 'The Gateway to India', and which was erected to commemorate the royal visit itself. At the unveiling ceremony the

1st. Battalion provided part of the Guard of Honour. Although Howard was not fortunate enough to go to Delhi for the Durbar, that same year he and Florie had another occasion to celebrate. On 18th. May 1911 their first son was born in the Married Families' Hospital, Colaba. He was christened James Howard and it was decreed there and then that as soon as he reached the age of fourteen years he would join the Regiment as a 'Boy'. Unfortunately, through some oversight, the notification of his birth never reached Somerset House. Evidently the appropriate army form (Form A.2, if I remember rightly) failed to arrive at its destination. However, twenty or so years later, when Jim was stationed in Poona, he went to the Registrar's Office in Bombay and discovered that a record of his birth did exist, though all it stated was: '18th. May, 1911. Male child born to Florence and Howard Pickering.' Naturally he obtained a copy of that certificate for future reference. Of those early years in India Jim can, of course, remember nothing, but a photo is extant, at which he often looks, of his sister Cissy and himself in the arms of his ayah, Luxshambai.

On the 12th. December 1912 the Battalion left Bombay by troopship en route for the United Kingdom. Not a few of the soldiers had been overseas since the start of the South African War and the excitement was so intense that some of them burst into song:

Bless 'em all,
Bless 'em all,
The young and the short and the tall.
You'll get no promotion this side of the ocean,
So cheer up, my lads, bless 'em all!

The troopship came up the English Channel on New Year's Day 1913 and after disembarkation the Battalion proceeded to its new station at Risborough Barracks, Shorncliffe. All the buildings were constructed of corrugated iron so that it was known to all as 'Tin Town'.

At that time Howard was the Officers' Mess Sergeant while Lieutenant B. L. Montgomery, who had already acquired the nickname of 'Monty', was the Adjutant. To those who knew him he had already shown signs of becoming an outstandingly good soldier. In later years, when he had won world-wide repute and had become Chief of the Imperial General Staff with the rank of Field Marshal, he attributed his success in no small measure to his early years of training in the Warwickshire Regiment.

Chapter 4

The 'Saucy Sixth' during the First World War

Within twenty months of its return to England the 1st. Battalion found itself having to leave the homeland once more. In August 1914 war had been declared against Germany. The Battalion had been mobilized and was en route to join the British Expeditionary Force in Flanders. On that memorable day of departure the khaki-clad 'Tommies' marched out of Risborough Barracks behind the Regimental Band and Drums with Antelope leading and Colours flying, to the stirring music of 'The Saucy Sixth'. The soldiers' wives, families and sweethearts were lining the road at the barracks entrance.

Each soldier was equipped in 'full marching order'. That meant that he had on his back his 'large pack' containing his greatcoat, spare pair of boots and a change of clothing, and slung beneath it his mess tin, ground sheet and entrenching tool. He also carried his haversack containing 'small kit': his 'housewife', holdall, knife, fork and spoon, comb, razor and lather brush, button stick and button brush. On his right hip the soldier carried his filled water bottle, while in his ammunition pouches he had 50 rounds of .303 live ammunition. In addition, of course, each soldier carried his personal weapon, be it Lee Enfield rifle, Lewis gun or, in the case of officers, sword and revolver.

All bandsmen were already wearing on their arms the white armband with red cross that signified their role, for once in the theatre of operations they would be acting as stretcher bearers. Following in the rear of the marching troops were the horse-drawn G.S. waggons loaded with additional equipment, blankets etc., and also limbers and field kitchens. The Transport Section, as it was known, was under the command of a subaltern and the Transport Sergeant.

Before long the Battalion was in the thick of the fighting and it took part in the retreat from Mons. During this early part of the War an extremely sad episode has to be recorded. As a result of a confused situation the Battalion became split up. Part of it, under the command of the C.O., Lt.-Colonel 'Johnny' Elkington, reached St. Quentin with the men exhausted and in need of food. The mayor, fearful of his town being shelled, pressed Colonel Elkington to sign an agreement to surrender, whereby if the enemy advanced to occupy the place whilst his troops were still there, they would lay down their arms. Only on that condition would he supply them with any food. In view of the exhaustion of his men and the great loss to civilians and property which would result from any bombardment, Colonel Elkington, in an unwise moment, assented. Happily what was feared never came to reality, but for his error Colonel Elkington was tried by Court Marshal and cashiered. Determined to restore his good name, he enlisted in the French Foreign Legion and after 18 months service in it, during which he was seriously wounded, he was awarded the Medaille Militaire and Croix de Guerre. In recognition of his gallant conduct the British authorities then restored him to his former rank and position in the Army and he was awarded the D.S.O. by King George V.

It was shortly after this incident that Monty, still a subaltern, won the D.S.O. in an incident which took place at Meteren. He often used to relate how he came face to face with a German who was on the point of shooting him. In all his training as an officer, he declared, he had never been taught to use his sword other than in its ceremonial function for saluting. He knew how to use the bayonet but what good was that to him when an officer's personal weapons were the sword and the revolver? Nevertheless Monty, alert to any situation, chose a moment when he was within striking distance of the Hun and used his jackboot on him to good effect. He buried his right foot in his opponent's crutch, disarmed him and took him prisoner. Shortly after this encounter Monty was severely wounded and returned to England to recuperate.

Much has been written about the British Tommy during those terrible years of World War I, in which, as has been said, thousands lost their lives as cannon fodder. They fought in the mud of Flanders, on the beaches of Gallipoli, in the sands of Mesopotamia and on the road to Jerusalem. During the period 1914–18 hundreds of battalions were savagely decimated; some were almost wiped out. To take one instance of many, one well-known regiment, The Duke of Cambridge's Own (57th. Foot, Middlesex Regiment) had two battalions which lost a total of 95 officers and 948 other ranks. Each individual casualty was a soldier who loved his country and gave his life's blood for it.

During those years the Sixth Foot, Royal Warwickshire Regiment mustered a total of eighteen battalions. It can proudly record that no less than six Victoria Crosses were awarded to members of it for bravery on the field of battle. The citations are as follows:–

Private A. Vickers – 2nd. Battalion.

On the 25th September, 1915, during the Battle of Loos, the 2nd. Battalion attacked at 6.30 a.m. In the face of terrific fire they reached the first line of trenches to find that the wire was not cut. Private Vickers, on his own initiative and with the utmost bravery, ran forward in front of his Company and, standing up in broad daylight, cut two gaps in the wire. His gallant action contributed largely to the success of the assault.

Lieutenant-Colonel Henderson – 9th. Battalion.

The 9th. Battalion formed part of the 13th. Division, which was engaged in operations against the Turks before Kut. On the 25th. January, 1917 a Turkish counter-attack forced two neighbouring battalions from part of their position and threatened to overwhelm them. The situation was critical and Colonel Henderson, the Commanding Officer, who had been wounded a short time before, jumped onto the parapet of his trench and, shouting to his men to follow him, advanced alone some distance in front of the whole Battalion, cheering them on under the most intense fire over 500 yards of open ground until the objective was secured from end to end. Lieutenant-Colonel Henderson, having been wounded three times, died later in the day.

Captain R. E. Phillips, 9th. Battalion.

On the same day that Colonel Henderson won his award, Captain Phillips, who had shewn great courage in the attack on the Turks, went out under very heavy fire and, with the help of a comrade, brought Colonel Henderson, who was lying wounded in the open, back to our trenches.

Private A. Hutt – 7th. Battalion.

On the 4th. October, 1917, during the attack by the 48th. Division before St. Julien, the 7th. Battalion had as their objective Tweed House. 'A' company captured their first objective but when they continued their advance, all the officers and non-commissioned officers in Pte. Hutt's platoon were hit. Pte. Hutt thereupon took command and led forward the platoon. He was held up by a strong point on his right, but immediately ran forward alone, shot the officer and three men in the post and caused forty or fifty others to surrender. Presently realising that he had pushed too far forward, Hutt withdrew his party. He personally covered the withdrawal, sniping at the enemy and killing a number of them. Then he carried back a comrade who had been badly wounded and put him under shelter. After he had organised and consolidated his position, he learnt that some wounded men still lay out in the open, where they were likely to be taken prisoners. As no stretcher bearers were available, Hutt went out himself and carried in four men under heavy fire.

Captain J. R. Gribble – 10th. Battalion.

On the 21st. March, 1918 the 10th. Battalion was put under 154 Brigade of the 51st. Division at a position north-east of Velu with orders to hold on to the last in the face of very heavy German attacks. The next day was one of constant shelling for the 10th. Battalion, but elsewhere the line was gradually forced back. On the 23rd., in the morning, the Germans broke through at Beatumetz, one unit after another was forced to give ground, but The Royal Warwickshires not until the afternoon. Even then Captain Gribble, with his Company on the right, would not yield. His orders were to hold on, and he did not withdraw, though he might easily have done so when the rest of the Battalion was forced back to the secondary position. When his right flank was 'in the air' owing to the withdrawal of the neighbouring troops, he sent a runner to the left with a message that he would stay till ordered to retire; this resolution he inspired his men to accomplish and when last seen he was still fighting, surrounded by the enemy at close range. By this splendid example Captain Gribble was instrumental in preventing the enemy from obtaining a complete mastery of the crest of the ridge for some hours, and by his magnificent self-sacrifice he enabled the remainder of his own Brigade to be withdrawn. Captain Gribble was wounded and taken prisoner; he died at Mayance on 24th. November, 1918 before he could be repatriated.

Lance-Corporal W. Amey – 1/8th. Battalion.

On 4th. November, 1918 the 75th. Brigade attacked at Landrecies in order to secure the bridgehead on the Sambre. The 1/8th. Battalion on the left met with stiff opposition near Faubourge Soyer. The day was foggy, and many hostile machine gun posts were in consequence missed by the advancing troops. Lance-Corporal Amey, on his own initiative, led his section under heavy fire to attack one of these points. He drove the garrison into a neighbouring farm, and captured about 50 prisoners and several machine guns. Then, single-handed, he attacked another machine gun post, killed two of the garrison, and, driving the rest into the cellar, held them there until help arrived. Finally, again single-handed, he rushed a strongly held post and took thirty prisoners. Throughout the day he had displayed the highest degree of valour and determination.

Among other officers of The Regiment who became well known was Bruce Bairnsfather, the comic artist who became famous for his drawings depicting life on the Western Front, as well as being the creator of the character 'Old Bill', the typical 'old sweat' of the British Army, who later figured in a play, 'The Better 'Ole'. At that time he was serving as a captain in the Royal Warwickshire Regiment, 6th Foot.

At the outbreak of war Jim himself was, of course, only a very young child, living at Folkestone with his mother and family while his father was away fighting the Germans. Yet he vividly remembers watching the train-loads of soldiers from many parts of the Empire as they approached Folkestone Harbour en route for the Front. Such patriotic songs as 'Pack up Your Troubles in Your Old Kit Bag', 'Goodbye Dolly, I Must Leave You' and many others could be heard as the trains passed by. One night, after going to bed and then being awakened by the air raid warning siren, Jim looked out of the window to see in the searchlights a German zeppelin which, to his great delight, was shot down in flames.

It was on 16th. May, 1916 that he had his first personal experience of the anger of war. He was taken shopping with an elderly friend in Folkestone, and was at the western end of Tontine Street when suddenly he heard the low drone of an aeroplane. Soon everyone in the street was looking upwards. The German Iron Cross markings on the plane could be clearly seen and it was quite clear that it was on no mercy mission. Within seconds policemen were blowing their whistles and cries of 'Take cover!' could be heard. The only cover available, however, appeared to be the doorways of the shops and a policeman suddenly pushed Jim and his friend into one of these. However, everyone still continued to gaze up at the small plane, which was so slow in flight that it seemed almost stationary. Then in a moment several explosions took place in the vicinity of Stokes' fruit shop and debris flew in all directions. The Germans had made their first daylight bombing raid. Contrary to what might have been expected, there was no pandemonium – only quiet bewilderment. In this raid five civilians were killed.

Chapter 5

Jim Becomes a Boy Soldier

During the years immediately following the cessation of hostilities many famous regiments were disbanded. The Machine Gun Corps vanished, as did all the famous Irish regiments, The Connaught Rangers, The Dublin Fusiliers, The Leinsters, The Royal Irish Regiment (18th. Foot) and The Royal Irish Rifles. Most of these had seen service in the days of the East India Company, which blazed the trail for the British Army in India.

Jim's father had been an early victim of the Germans' first gas attack. So badly gassed had he been that he had been brought home from the Front. Although he had hoped to soldier on for some time after the War, the notorious 'Geddes Act' was brought in approving drastic reductions in the Army, and in 1921 Howard himself was discharged. After 24 years of service in the Army it is not surprising that he should have chosen to live close to the military garrison of Shorncliffe Camp.

Although at this time Jim was still at school, he used to take a lively interest in the many activities of the regiments stationed at Shorncliffe only a few yards from his home. He would watch the thrilling mounted sports of the cavalry regiments, including those of the 13/18th. Hussars, known as 'The Lily Whites' and of the 11th. Hussars ('The Cherry Pickers'). He could also see the regimental teams playing football and rugby. Although he had never played rugby himself, he often watched The King's Own (Lancaster Regiment, 4th. Foot), the winners of the Army Rugby Cup, when they were at their best. Their team included a certain Lieutenant A. R. Aslett, who played for England. This famous regiment, one of the most senior Infantry Regiments of the Line, took part in the Battle of Waterloo, a fact which was brought to Jim's remembrance many years later when he was given a 'Waterloo Medal' that had been awarded to a soldier of the 4th. Foot. It had been found at Maresfield Camp in 1957. Apart from the 'ribbon ring', for which Jim had a replacement made, it was in almost perfect condition.

One of the highlights of Jim's pre-Army days occurred when his Dad's old Battalion football team reached the semi-final of the Army Cup after their return from duty in Southern Ireland. They were to play 'The Queen's', Royal West Surrey Regiment (2nd. Foot) on the Folkestone Road ground. For Jim's father, to miss watching such a match was too much to expect. As for Jim himself, as soon as he heard about it he persuaded his father to manufacture an excuse for him to miss school so that he too could watch the match. His initiation to the Army soccer scene was a thriller indeed. At full time the score was 2–2 and there was more drama to follow. During the second period of extra time the Queen's were awarded a penalty. Their star player, a soldier named Woodard, took the 'spot kick' only to call forth a fantastic save from the Warwicks' keeper, 'Doddy' (Sgt. Dodd). Alas, in making the save he pushed the ball to the feet of the penalty taker, and with his second shot he made no mistake. The Queen's went on to win the Army Cup quite easily.

Later in that same year, 1925, the Battalion moved from Chatham, being posted once again to Shorncliffe, where it was stationed at Napier Barracks at the north–west corner of the famous Sir John Moore's Plain. Jim's fourteenth birthday fell in May of that year, and his parents lost no time in applying for him to join the Regiment as a band boy. Unfortunately, Jim's vital statistics fell far short of the standard required. Instead of the minimum height of 4 ft. 10 inches, he was only 4 ft. 7 inches and his weight too, of 72 pounds, fell far short of the standard laid down. However, the Commanding Officer, Lieut.-Colonel C. R. Macdonald, C.M.G. knew Jim's father well and at this juncture he was not to be deterred. He submitted to the War Office for special consideration an application in which he stated that he was sure the boy would develop once he was in the Service. Certainly he was showing faith in the diet and way of life of the Army! To the family's great joy, the War Office conceded, and on 4th. July, 1925, seventeen days after Jim's fourteenth birthday, he was invited to enlist.

At the time the Battalion was under canvas on the Hythe Rifle Ranges, where it was engaged in firing the annual rifle course. At the appointed hour Jim was conducted to a marquee to meet Captain P. A. M. Eldin, who was to perform the formalities of 'swearing in'. 'P.A.M.', who was later destined to become a parson, handed Jim a bible upon which he took the oath to serve King and Country. After this he was duly handed the 'King's shilling' as a mark of acceptance. The dignified little ceremony was something which Jim always remembered with pride. His contract was to serve nine years with the Colours and three on the Reserve. To this, of course, had to be added the four years of 'Boy service', which did not count. Thus Jim was now committed to serve in the Army for thirteen years in all. From that day onwards his full title was: Number 5102774 Boy J. H. Pickering.

One of the most important of all the duties of a new recruit was to report to the Regimental Clothing Stores to be clothed and equipped. The Regimental Storeman at that time was 'Timber' Woodward, a man of character revered by all ranks in the Regiment including the officers. He was a typical 'old sweat' and rather corpulent. His left arm appeared to be all but covered with chevrons, indicating many years of service, while his left chest bore a row of campaign ribbons which included that of the 1908 Indian General Service Medal as well as the L.S. and G.C. for Long Service and Good Conduct.

When, shortly after his enlistment, Jim reported to Timber Woodward he found himself welcomed almost as a son, for in the course of his service in India Timber had known both Jim's father and his mother. Timber proceeded to give Jim a truly fatherly talk, emphasising the need for the boy to keep himself to himself. After issuing the schedule of kit, Timber then went across to a large box which he kept beneath his bed in the corner of the store and took from it a ten shilling note. 'There,' he said, 'Don't spend it all at once or you'll have your mother after you.' He went on to tell Jim that once he had saved five pounds in the bank he would double it. As Jim's pay came to only one shilling a day, that would be no easy feat. Moreover, in Jim's case, of the five shillings which he actually received at the 'pay table', he gave his mother four, keeping the remainder for cleaning kit and perhaps an occasional 'char and wad' from the canteen. The two shillings kept back from a boy's weekly wage were intended to cover that most ambiguous of all charges, 'barrack room damages', for from this the Quartermaster Sergeant used to pay such barrack damages as could not be attributed to any individual soldier.

Timber also had an unofficial job; he was known to all ranks as the 'regimental bookie'. In fact the kit box from which he gave Jim the ten shillings was his 'safe'. Officers as well as many other ranks used to deposit their betting slips at the Clothing Store. Hence it came as no surprise when, after serving in the Regiment for 27 years, Timber took advantage of his vocational training in the Army to become an official bookie in civilian life. His clerk was Mrs. Ada Baxter, the widow of Tom Baxter, who had served for 21 years in the Regiment as an 'officer's servant'. Another 'old sweat' of that time was the Regimental Barber. He appeared to be even more decorated on the arms than Timber. On top of his long row of chevrons were several badges indicating his outstanding skill at arms; he was one of the best rifle and Lewis gun shots in the Battalion.

To many a lad of Jim's age enlistment in the Army might have come as a shock. It meant few home comforts and a meagre diet, accompanied by strict discipline and hard work. Jim himself, however, had been brought up in a Service atmosphere, always strictly controlled by his parents and being taught to respect his superiors. Thus it was a way of life which he readily accepted. On enlistment, his father's advice was as follows: 'Keep yourself to yourself; keep your "nose clean" and you won't go far wrong'. His father also emphasised the importance of obtaining the required Army Certificate of Education, without which no real progress could be made. It was compulsory for all boys to go to school each day. In addition, they had one hour's P.T. and one hour's drill; the rest of the day was taken up with band practice.

No soldier could ever qualify for 'proficiency pay' without obtaining a 2nd. Class Certificate of Education and no N.C.O. could be promoted beyond the rank of Colour Sergeant without holding a 1st. Class Certificate. At that time the number of other ranks holding a 2nd. Class Certificate was probably about 80%. About 50% would have obtained a 1st. Class Certificate, the remaining 15% would have only a 3rd. Class Certificate.

Jim has a vivid recollection of a certain lance–corporal who, though otherwise an outstandingly good soldier and worthy of promotion, simply could not pass his 2nd. Class Certificate of Education. However, a couple of his friends happened to be instructors at the Regimental School and they were determined that 'Tich' would get his Certificate no matter what the cost. He was about to sit the examination for the thirteenth time. The classroom was so arranged that the invigilating officer (who, incidentally, was the N.C.O.'s Company Commander, also known as 'Tich') was conveniently positioned with his back to two large cupboards. These had been strategically placed so as to leave a convenient gap between them. As soon as the exam. commenced, Tich's friends began holding up boards in the gap between the cupboards displaying enough data to enable him to arrive at the correct answers to each question as it arose. At the end of the time appointed Tich took his papers up to the invigilating officer. After making a quick perusal of them, the officer handed the papers back to him, telling him to return to his seat and think over some of his answers. At the same time he all but told him what to put down. Even then, after all this co–ordinated effort on the part of those concerned, he once again just failed to reach the pass mark. However, at this point the School Warrant Officer came to the rescue; he recommended to the Adjudicating Board that Tich should be treated as a borderline case and awarded the Certificate accordingly. This was agreed upon. The last time Jim saw Tich was at the

Regimental Depot after World War II. By that time Tich had reached the rank of W.O.II.

To return to Jim's own early days in the Regiment. Having enlisted, he joined fifteen other band boys and a dozen drummer boys at Napier Barracks, Shorncliffe. In construction the barracks were typical of their time. Most of the barracks of those days had been built towards the end of the nineteenth or the beginning of the twentieth centuries, and conformed to a set pattern. All the administrative buildings, including the N.A.A.F.I. and Guard Room, were situated on one side of the barrack square, with the troops' living quarters on the other. Each of the blocks of living quarters consisted of two separate rooms with ablution rooms between.

The accommodation, though of course primitive by today's standards, was in fact quite adequate. All barrack rooms were of a standard design and the furniture with which they were equipped was likewise laid down in a standard schedule. The schedule might appear to have a grandiose ring to it but the furniture itself was in fact quite primitive. The floors were left uncovered and the plain wooden planks had to be scrubbed once a week with cold water and a long instrument known as a 'dry scrubber'. The beds were of iron and made in two parts in such a way that when not in use their bottom halves could be pushed in so as to resemble chairs. Mattresses were composed of three 'biscuits' of coir. Behind and above each bed space was a double shelf upon which was placed the occupant's large pack, water bottle and mess tin. The lower shelf, made of a wooden board, contained the soldier's bible and prayerbook, both ends of which had to be polished! Nailed to the middle of this shelf was the soldier's brass name plate suitably engraved and surmounted by a regimental cap badge which was soldered onto it. Under the bottom shelf two pegs projected from the wall and on these hung the neatly folded greatcoat and gas respirator. For inspections the soldier's second pair of boots was placed at the foot of the bed with soles facing upwards to reveal the highly polished studs and heeltips. At inspections all barrack room utensils had to be scrupulously clean. The 'tubs, bath, 6-gallon' were in fact only big enough to bath a baby, but were obviously provided to carry water for washing the floors. However, since they had to be kept in a highly burnished state for inspections, they were rarely used for this purpose.

The ablution room was equipped with a long slate slab, above which six cold water taps (hot water there was none!) projected at regular intervals. On the floor in front of the washing slab extended two long duckboards for the troops to stand upon while washing. Such at least was the theory! In fact the boards were placed in position only for inspections. They were scrubbed white and at all other times were kept safely on one side together with the washing basins. These latter were burnished and likewise kept only for inspections.

Just outside each barrack room door was a raised plynth such as might have been used for a statue of a famous soldier. Its real function, however, was far removed from any such exalted purpose. The lavatory blocks were always situated some distance away from the troops' sleeping quarters. Each evening, at approximately 21.30 hours, three quarters of an hour before lights out, the Room Orderly of the day was required to proceed to an allotted space at the rear of these lavatory blocks to collect an item described in military vocabulary as 'tubs, urine, soldiers, for the use of'. The receptacle thus designated was then placed on the plynth ready to be used during the night by the occupants of the barrack room concerned. Immediately after Reveille the following morning it had to be emptied by the Room Orderly. For so small a man as Jim, to stagger out carrying a full tub was no mean feat. Yet when it was his turn of duty he had to do it.

In connection with these urine tubs an amusing incident once occurred. A band boy by the name of Jerry had the reputation of being simple; he was susceptible to pranks played on him by the other boys. The first time Jerry's turn as Room Orderly came he was duly instructed in his duties by one of the other boys. He was told that immediately after Reveille he must report to the Provost Sergeant at the Guard Room to collect the 'defaulters' milk'. Sure enough, next morning after Reveille George Humphreys the Provost Sergeant noticed him staggering across the barrack square holding the tub with both hands. All the other boys, of course, were watching discreetly from afar. As soon as Jerry reached the Guard Room verandah the onlookers saw George apparently waving his stick in the air and pointing in the direction of the Boys' Room. Almost immediately he himself made steps in that direction, but by the time he arrived all the boys had 'gone to ground'. Nevertheless it was George who had the last laugh. That evening when, according to custom, all the boys reported to the Guard Room for roll call, they were each ordered to report to him a quarter of an hour after Reveille the following morning to perform some particularly nasty chores.

An N.C.O. was always appointed to be in charge of each barrack room. At the time of Jim's enlistment the N.C.O. i/c The Boys' Room was a corporal whose nickname was 'Biddy'. When sober he was a real friend to the boys. Unfortunately he was addicted to periodic bouts of heavy drinking and the effects of these could be highly alarming. In the words of the boys, he was a 'real demon' at such times, being prone to strange hallucinations. One particular night, when Biddy had had a thorough skinful, he returned to the barrack room in the early hours crawling on all fours and making a noise like a rabid dog. Thoroughly frightened, the boys dared not move in their beds, for the slightest movement seemed to enrage him. The moment he sensed any he would drag the poor boy concerned out of bed and douse him with water. Strangely enough, for all his night-time marauding, at the first note of the bugle call at Reveille the following morning Biddy would spring out of bed and in a trice would run the whole length of the room, lifting each bed up at the foot as he went so as to tip the occupant onto the floor.

The Army food was frugal indeed. Breakfast, at 7.20 a.m. usually consisted of a slice of dry bread, a sausage and a mere 'showing' of baked beans, or perhaps a thoroughly smelly kipper, together with a plate of sugarless porridge and a thimbleful of watered milk. The tea was likewise sugarless and, to judge from its colour, almost devoid of milk as well. The only other hot meal was served at 12.45 p.m. It invariably conformed to the same unattractive stereotype, for it consisted of bully beef served in a variety of ways, together with potatoes and revoltingly cooked cabbage. The sweet would consist of boiled rice with neither sugar nor milk, or possibly jam roll. For the 'tea meal' the menu would include tea, a slice of bread and margarine and a spoonful of jam. The Boys were, in one respect, given preferential treatment in the form of an extra meal, namely supper at 6.30 p.m. It took the form of 'leftovers' from the earlier meals of the day. On Fridays bread was replaced by 'bully biscuits' and margarine by dripping. Despite all this poor food, however, the soldier of those days appeared no less fit than his counterpart of the present day, who is able to choose from a variety of dishes at his meals.

Chapter 6

A Soldier's Life in the Twenties

It will be remembered that as well as having the antelope as a cap badge, it was always the custom for the two battalions of the Regiment to have live antelope as their mascots. The antelope on the Moorish standard which the Regiment captured during the Peninsula War was obviously an African one. Nevertheless, the antelopes used as mascots were of the Black Buck species from India. Traditionally, the 1st. Battalion's antelope was always named Billy, while that belonging to the 2nd. Battalion was Bobby. Not long after joining the 1st. Battalion at Shorncliffe Jim was appointed one of its antelope leaders. This meant that on all Regimental parades on which the Band and Drums were leading, he would have to lead the antelope at the head of them. Naturally it was a proud responsibility. Just as a soldier has his ceremonial uniform, so also did the antelope. He had a coat of navy blue cloth with a rose and crown embroidered on each of its front corners and gold braid along either edge. On either tip of the antelope's horns were silver caps and around his neck was a white buff collar with silver discs bearing the dates of previous antelopes. It was to this collar that the leads were attached.

On parade the antelope was generally well behaved, though he did appear to resent having a horse near him and would always strain at the leash if any passed by.

One particular Church Parade is indelibly imprinted on Jim's memory. It was at Shorncliffe Garrison Church early in October 1925. In those days families of the Regiment and their friends, together with many other local people, would gather to attend the Church Parade and afterwards watch the March Past. On this particular occasion Jim's sister Cissy was there with her Brownie Box camera to take photographs, especially ones of Jim leading the antelope. After the Parade old soldiers of the Regiment would resort, if they were corporals or below, to the 'wet' canteen, while the sergeants and their wives and the officers' ladies would make their way to their respective messes for drinks.

As for Jim, after the Parade he walked the short distance to his home for Sunday dinner. Since his Dad had been to the Sergeants' Mess to have a drink with some of his old pals, it was a little delayed.

The following morning, just as Jim was about to commence band practice, he noticed Tom Baxter, his family's next-door neighbour, talking to the Band Sergeant, 'Cabby' Hanson. They appeared engrossed in serious conversation. After a few moments Cabby called Jim aside and told him to put his instrument away; he was wanted at home and must go there immediately.

As he rounded the corner approaching his home he noticed that the blinds of the front room were drawn. Then as he entered the door the news was broken to him that a short while before his father had suddenly collapsed and died. It was a truly terrible blow to him. He had always idolised his Dad and the feeling had been reciprocated. It did not take long for the sad news to be conveyed to all ranks of the Battalion and on the following Thursday afternoon 'Pick', as he was known in the Regiment, was buried in the Shorncliffe Garrison Churchyard with military honours. That was the first time that Jim had ever walked behind a gun carriage with the Union Jack covering the coffin and with the solemn strains of the Dead March sounding in his ears. It was here too, at the funeral of his own father, that he first heard the Last Post and Reveille sounded at the graveside.

After these sad events he lost no time in accepting the responsibility of becoming his mother's chief support. She had been left with seven children to bring up on twenty-seven shillings a week. Yet even then she always somehow found enough to spare for the ingredients of a bread pudding or some other tasty snack for Jim to take up to the barrack room to share with the other boys.

Those were the days when Jim was at his most impressionable. Whilst the hour spent each day on the drill parade was never a time for relaxation, it nevertheless had its place in the forming of character and the inculcating of discipline. The R.S.M., known as 'Big Bill', had come to the Regiment from the Scots Guards, where he had been a drill sergeant. In addition to the campaign medals of World War I, he wore on his chest the D.C.M. and Croix de Guerre, both of which were awarded for bravery on the battlefield. Although, like most R.S.M.s, he had a very loud voice, his bark was, as the saying goes, a good deal worse than his bite and he was always ready to give the boys sound, fatherly advice.

Many other 'characters' enriched life in the Battalion at that time. One of them was the Quartermaster, a Major Jimmy Handley. He was a short and decidedly rotund figure who had enlisted in the ranks about the year 1885. Thus he had served for a period of about forty years, a fact which was to some degree manifest from the medals he wore. He had fought at Atbara and Khartoum in General Gordon's campaign in the Sudan, and also in India and Flanders. His wife was regarded as 'Mum' by all ranks; Jim came to know her well. However, one day when he was passing her garden she called out: 'Jimmy, will you tell those other band boys that if they want any apples they must come and ask for them – not pinch them at night. One of these nights I'll be waiting for them and they'll feel my hand across their backsides. That won't be pleasant, I can tell you!'

Throughout the Battalion at that time a truly amazing range of campaign medals was to be found. Among them was one Ashanti Star, one China Rebellion Medal (1900), several Sudan Medals and a number of South African Campaign Medals, together with innumerable First World War medals. The decorations for bravery included at least two D.S.O.s and numerous M.C.s and M.M.s. It was strange to see an 'other rank' with an M.C. It was held by 'Pot' Baker, the C.S.M. of Headquarter Company, who had been given the award during the time he held a temporary commission. He relinquished it after the War. The C.O., Colonel Macdonald, had been awarded the C.M.G.

During the year 1926/27 the Battalion Boys' Football Team did outstandingly well for they reached the final of the Boys' Army Cup. They were narrowly beaten by the Army Apprentices' School from Chepstow. The performance was all the more creditable in view of the fact that whereas the Apprentices' School was an establishment of several hundred boys, The Royal Warwickshire boys had only two dozen to pick from. One of the stars of the 'Warwicks' team was 'Tiny' Newett. Though only sixteen, he was an incredible 6 feet 5 inches tall. If ever there was a real 'Brummy' it was Tiny, for he came from one of the less salubrious quarters of Birmingham, known as Garrison Lane. Despite his lanky physique, on the football field he was a wizard. Often he would have the entire crowd of spectators in hysterics as he swayed and jigged, dribbling the ball in a manner that was nothing short of uncanny. If Jim, who was only four feet seven inches tall, happened to get in Tiny's way on the field, the latter would simply swing his foot over Jim's head!

It is interesting to record the names of some of the officers serving in the 1st. Battalion, The Royal Warwickshire Regiment in the year 1925. The Company Commander of 'A' Company was none other than Major B. L.

Montgomery D.S.O., the now legendary Field Marshal Lord Montgomery of Alamein, K.G., G.C.B., D.S.O. One of the subalterns was Lieutenant A. E. Nye, M.C., who graduated from The Duke of York's Royal Military School at Dover, was commissioned into the Leinster Regiment and then transferred to the Royal Warwickshire Regiment on the disbandment of the Irish regiments in 1922. After the Second World War he was appointed High Commissioner in India and Canada, and it was generally assumed that had the British stayed in India, he would have become Viceroy. He reached the rank of Lieut.-General and held the appointment of Vice-Chief of the Imperial General Staff with the following decorations:– G.C.S.I., G.C.M.G., G.C.I.E., K.C.B., K.B.E., M.C.

The Adjutant during those years of the twenties was Lieut. G. C. Evans who also became a Lieut.-General. He was knighted and awarded three D.S.O.s during the War. It is interesting to record that Field Marshal 'Bill' Slim had also served in the Regiment, in which he was a lance-corporal during the First World War. What an outstanding record for any regiment of the British Army!

One of the most revered men in the Regiment, and a familiar figure to all, was the Bandmaster. Inevitably, Jim made his acquaintance at a very early stage in his career. He walked with a slow, deliberate step and with his feet splayed at an unusually pronounced angle, a trait which had earned him the nickname of 'Dabber'. He was grey haired, as well he might be, for in his 42 years of Army life he had served under Queen Victoria, King Edward VII and King George V. This was apparent from the medals which he wore; they included those of the South African War as well as the Durbar Medal of 1911. That he was more than capable of looking after the Band Boys can readily be understood; he was the father of no less than eighteen children and his family occupied two large Warrant Officer's married quarters.

It was not long before Jim became closely acquainted with Dabber's family. One day his regular batman, Tommy Thompson (another 'old sweat'), went on leave and Jim was detailed to take his place. In addition to having the Bandmaster's uniform buttons etc. to clean, his chores included the cleaning of an extremely long row of boots and shoes of multifarious shapes and sizes, belonging to all the members of the family. However he never minded this in the least for he was rewarded with a few extra snacks and also the large sum of half a crown as 'extra duty pay'. Dabber's wife was a truly wonderful woman; she seemed to take all her family duties in her stride. Just as among the Band Boys Dabber's word was law, so within their domestic household her word was no whit less respected.

Few bandmasters could have been more dedicated to their work than Dabber. To the task of training the Band Boys in particular he gave high priority, devoting considerable time to giving individual tuition to each of them. He was fatherly in more ways than one. One remarkable instance of this trait was an occasion in the barrack room which Jim witnessed at relatively close quarters. Dabber was supervising the musical studies of one boy, a cornet player, who had the reputation of being a handful. Dabber was, as usual, wielding his baton to beat out the time when he became aware that the young cornet player was allowing his thoughts to wander. Thereupon Dabber lunged out with his unoccupied hand and gave the dozy boy such a swipe that it catapulted him across a nearby bed. It will readily be understood from this that when Dabber was about the boys were invariably on their toes. 'I will not waste time putting you on a charge,' he would say, and then it was. . . WALLOP! At the beginning of May, 1926 the Band and Drums of the Regiment proceeded to Birmingham to take part in a Tattoo due to take place on the Horse Show Grounds at King's Heath. Here they were accommodated under canvas. Unfortunately, however, shortly after they arrived the General Strike took place, which put an abrupt end to the activities that had been planned. Nevertheless the episode was not without its compensations; many of the contingent had relatives in the Birmingham area. Jim was able to visit his grandmother and many other relatives living in the Sparkbrook and Small Heath areas, whom he would never have had any possibility of seeing but for the Tattoo.

Chapter 7

Transfer to Inkerman Barracks in Surrey

In 1927 the Battalion departed from Shorncliffe. Shortly before this move Jim had been sent on a course to the Royal Military School of Music at Kneller Hall. Unfortunately, however, he had developed a slight heart flutter, the consequence of which was that he had to give up playing his instrument. In circumstances such as these the normal course of events would have been for him to be discharged. In his case, however, the M.O. gave it as his opinion that he would probably grow out of the weakness. On these grounds he was permitted to remain in the Army and was given a job in the Orderly Room as 'runner'; it entailed distributing mail throughout the Battalion.

By this time the Battalion had arrived at Inkerman Barracks, Woking. This was an old prison building which had been condemned. It comprised a particularly large main block, at the centre of which stood a watch tower, and it was surrounded by the old prison wall. It certainly had the appearance of many other famous prisons throughout the country, and at that time few, if any, improvements had been effected, apart from converting the cells into accomodation for the troops. The lavatory blocks were situated out in the open at some distance from the troops' barrack rooms and during the winter months they were invariably frozen up. Certainly it was necessary to put a greatcoat on when nature called at night! The buildings were, of course, devoid of central heating in any form; nor did they have running hot water or even slipper baths. Showers were the order of the day and even they were usually cold.

The basement of the main building was infested with rats. So much so that no sooner had the last soldier left the dining room after a meal than the rats would move in to scavenge and raid the bread cupboards. Hence rat hunting was a sport widely indulged in by the boys in the evenings. All holes in the dining room floor would be sealed with the exception of one, which was just below the window. The doors would then be closed and one boy, known as the 'blocker', would stand on a barrack room form holding a 'mop, woollen headed, soldiers, for the use of'. As soon as he could see sufficient rats running about the room, he would ram the mop into the hole, thereby cutting off their last line of retreat. Immediately all the beaters would rush into the room for the kill. More than once a cornered rat was known to attack a beater at this stage. At the end of the kill all the carcases would be lined up on the verandah to be counted before being taken to the incinerator for a ritual burning.

Whenever a soldier died it was customary for the coffin to be placed in the detention cell of the Guard Room to await a military funeral at Brookwood Cemetery nearby. Since Jim and a couple of other clerks used to work in the Orderly Room just adjacent to this cell, they normally had to walk through it in order to reach the ablution room. This would happen several times a day. However, whenever the detention cell was being used to house a coffin, he and his pals would walk two hundred yards to another ablution room rather than walk past it.

Inkerman Barracks was only about two miles from the famous Bisley Rifle Ranges. Consequently, whenever the annual Army and National Rifle Championships were held, all ranks of the Battalion would be called upon to perform range-marking duties. For this they would receive 'extra duty pay' at an hourly rate. During the Battalion's final stint at Bisley, just prior to their departure, they had the great pleasure of seeing one of their own officers, Lieutenant Norman Boyer, winning the King's Medal at his first attempt. It was a truly magnificent achievement.

In the previous chapter I have touched upon a number of characters to be found in the Battalion at that time. One of the characters at Inkerman Barracks was a private soldier known to all ranks as 'Cockney George'. As his nickname suggests, he hailed from the metropolis and was one of those individuals who invariably kept up a jovial spirit; it never seemed to flag. With the exception of the boys, he was the shortest soldier in the Battalion and was a carpenter in the Pioneer Platoon. It was always said that he had learned his trade as an 'apprentice' in one of the less reputable 'hostels' of London, which were akin to Inkerman Barracks itself.

Cockney was never cut out to be a soldier, and more often than not he would get away with doing just what he wanted in his own time. He was never happier than when sitting down to a game of cards, and wherever a gambling school was in session Cockney was bound to be in the thick of it. Often at weekends the Pioneers' Shop would be converted into a casino. Being in the basement of the main building, it was all too easy to exclude any signs of life within by the use of army blankets. Electric lights were never used while gaming was in progress. Candles would be stuck in jam jars and the suffused glow they gave off would be quite sufficient for the needs of the players. However, as in all walks of life, the 'law', in this case in the person of the Provost Sergeant, was bound periodically to be on the prowl precisely in order to sniff out such erring soldiery. Sometimes he would be successful and would be seen escorting the law-breakers to the Guard Room, where they would have to spend the rest of the weekend incarcerated until brought before the 'Assizes' on Monday morning.

After one such episode, Tich Edwards, the Company Commander of H.Q. Company, had sentenced several members of his Company to varying periods of C.B. After the proceedings were over he remarked to his batman, a west country man named Joiner: 'I hope you do not associate with the gamblers I have just dealt with'. 'Sirrr,' replied Joiner, 'that's a mug's game'. Famous last words indeed! That very night he in turn found it impossible to resist his old pal Cockney's invitation to 'have a few hands' in the basement after lights out. The players had convinced themselves that George, the Provost Sergeant, would not strike twice on consecutive nights. Alas for them, George had read the culprits' minds all too well! The outcome was that both Cockney and Joiner found themselves in the bag along with several other gamblers.

When the accused were arraigned before him at Orders the next morning, Tich's surprise, as well as anger, may be imagined. Fortunately it was his batman's first offence and he merely received an 'admonition'. Cockney, on the other hand, as an 'unrepentant criminal', was awarded 7 days C.B. and was remanded to be dealt with further by the C.O. From him he later received a further sentence of 14 days C.B. to run consecutively with the sentence already passed upon him.

It should be explained to the uninitiated that an award of either five or seven days C.B. was recorded on a soldier's Company Conduct Sheet and such entries could only be expunged after the Sheet had been clear of any further entry for three years. Punishment in excess of 7 days C.B., or in the form of detention, could be awarded only by the C.O., and any such punishments remained on the soldier's Regimental Conduct Sheet for the rest of his service. It was laid down that once a soldier had a 'Regimental entry', he could not qualify for either the Long Service or the Good Conduct medals.

One particular episode Jim will never forget. It was the rule that for inspection every Saturday morning a soldier's gas respirator had to be taken out of its haversack so as to keep it fresh and free from distortion. One particular Saturday morning, unfortunately, Jim went off to work in the Orderly Room without having taken out his respirator. As he found out afterwards, quite a number of soldiers had committed the same 'crime'. However, unknown to Jim, his pals had taken it out for him. Even so, to pull his leg they told him that he was one of those whose names had been taken for the offence. On Monday morning, according to custom, all offenders were ordered to parade outside the C.S.M.'s office for 'Orders'. Jim attended too and when the C.S.M. arrived he asked him what he was doing there. 'I did not leave my gas mask out for inspection on Saturday morning, Sir,' replied Jim. 'Oh didn't you?' retorted the C.S.M., 'In that case you had better stay here and march in with the rest'. All this despite the fact that his name had never been entered on the charge sheet! All the offenders were awarded three days 'extra fatigues', a punishment which was not entered on conduct sheets. It was only after he had completed this punishment that Jim learned of the prank which his pals had played upon him. Of course they gave him a loud cheer as he sauntered forth at 6.30 a.m. each morning dressed in full marching order, to be inspected by the Battalion Orderly Sergeant.

Inevitably some incidents were unforgettable and were recalled and talked of long after they had taken place. One such was 'spicy' enough to warrant repeating even at this length of time. The chief protagonist in the drama (for such it became) was one of the most popular members of the Sergeants' Mess. He went by the name of 'Teddy' and, with his striking good looks and natural charm, was known not only as a very fine soldier but as a bit of a dandy too. The wife of another sergeant was considered to be one of the most attractive women in the Regiment, and not surprisingly she developed a soft spot for Teddy, a feeling which was evidently reciprocated. The friendship between the two had not escaped the eye of 'Chippy', the R.S.M. At the time the lady's husband was out of station on a course and now, to adapt the old adage, 'While the cat was away the mice were playing.'

One night Teddy made his way surreptitiously to the married quarter where his attractive lady friend was waiting and found himself eagerly welcomed. Unfortunately for him, Chippy had posted 'spies' who had alerted him. For all his care, the entry of the culprit to the married quarter had not gone unnoticed. Immediately, as part of a pre-laid plan, an ambush was set up. Sentinels were placed unobtrusively at strategic points so as to cut off every possible line of escape.

After a prolonged wait it was at length observed that every vestige of light in the married quarter had been extinguished. By this time, no doubt, those keeping vigil outside were conjuring up vivid pictures in their imaginations as to what was being enacted inside, where the lovers were snugly ensconced. While all this was taking place, however, Teddy had somehow become aware of his predicament and had realised that the enemy lay in siege outside. Being an exceptionally acute and experienced soldier, in true military fashion he had 'appreciated the situation' and, 'having taken all the factors into consideration', had 'made his own plan of escape'. It is clear from subsequent events that the time factor played an important part in his plan. He calculated that as the night wore on the 'sentinels' would grow tired and their alertness would be diminished. Perhaps they would even conclude that the bird had already flown. Also included in Teddy's plan, as will be seen, was an element of 'diversion and surprise'.

Suddenly, about an hour before 'first light', the lady of the house, clad in a pair of her husband's trousers, one of his great coats and an old forage cap, flung open the back door, knocking over the dustbin as she did so in order to make as much noise as possible. Then, to create a further diversion, she ran off in a direction opposite to that which led to the barracks. The ruse appeared to take the cordon completely by surprise. Almost immediately whistles were blown and the whole posse, including those who had been keeping watch at the front of the house, gave chase after the 'phantom' Teddy.

Thus far Teddy's plan was certainly working, for no sooner had the last 'sentry' disappeared from the front door than the wily old soldier slipped away towards barracks by a preconceived line of retreat. Naturally it was not long before his ruse became clear. Almost as one, the whole cordon pounced on the khaki-clad figure they were pursuing, only to find that they were in fact embracing the lovely lady of the house instead of the real Teddy. Wasting no time in interrogating their captive, they turned to pursue the real enemy, who by this time had made good his escape – or so he thought. Alas, he had reckoned without Chippy! The R.S.M. had also prepared for every eventuality and, as a last measure, had placed yet another 'sentry' to cut off the final dash he had calculated that Teddy would make back to the safety of his own bunk in the Single Sergeants' Quarters. In a few moments the drama had ended. A crestfallen Teddy was forced to suffer the ignominy of being captured while hiding behind the doors to the yard of the Q.M 's Store.

It goes without saying that he was immediately placed under close arrest and the following day he was charged with contravening the appropriate section of the Army Act. Naturally all the pundits concluded that after the customary 'summary of evidence' Teddy would have to face a Court Martial. However, the local District Commander, obviously taking into account his previously exemplary character, gave him the choice of either being dealt with summarily or facing a Court Martial. He wisely accepted the former and the outcome was that he was reduced to the rank of corporal. So ended one of those sagas, spiced with a vestige of romance, which from time to time create so much excitement and drama in the Regiment. In this case, unhappily, it tarnished the reputation of the erring soldier who had played the principal role in the play.

Yet another episode which remains in Jim's memory concerns a soldier who was known in the Regiment as 'Dandy Desmond'. One Saturday, when Jim was Duty Clerk in the Orderly Room, he received a telephone call from Scotland Yard saying that the police had apprehended a deserter from the Regiment by the name of Desmond. Although at that time Jim was Documents Clerk, and as such responsible for maintaining all the documents of every soldier in the Battalion, that name did not ring any bell. However, when he enquired of 'Hoppy', the Orderly Room Corporal, Hoppy's face lit up. 'Of course he's ours,' said Hoppy. Almost immediately an escort was sent to the 'Yard' to bring the prisoner back. Only then, as the news was spreading all round the Battalion, did the whole story unfold. Some eight or nine years before, in the early twenties, the Battalion had been stationed in Southern Ireland in the midst of the Uprising. Dandy had been an officer's servant. On Christmas day, while his boss was celebrating in common with most of the other officers and other ranks, he had 'borrowed' one of his own officer's uniforms, put it on, and then walked brazenly past the Guard Room and out of Camp, not to be seen again until that day long afterwards when he returned to the Battalion under escort.

After his desertion rumours had circulated that he had joined the Foreign Legion and these were now proved to be correct. Yet even now he appeared to have lost none of that penchant for immaculate turnout for which he was famous. He arrived in a smart pin-striped suit, white shirt with stiff collar and suede gloves. He was a dandy to his fingertips and in the truest sense of the word. Furthermore he could, as Hoppy put it, 'talk the hind leg off a donkey'. At this juncture his gift must have stood him in particularly good stead for, to the surprise of all ranks, the only punishment he received was 14 days detention. Some said that it was because he, like the C.O., was a Freemason. That, I am sure, was merely soldiers' talk.

All this, however, was far from being the end of Dandy's ignominious exploits. Before long he had managed to convince everyone that he had turned over a new leaf and was really dedicating himself to becoming a good and trustworthy soldier once more. Then, to the consternation of all concerned, he produced one of his old tricks, proving the truth of the adage that the leopard cannot change his spots. It was strange how he had managed to persuade those in authority of the sincerity of his reform. He had actually been given another job as officer's servant, this time to one of the senior officers of the Battalion, known to all ranks as 'Tight Boots'. The nickname was a rhyming play on his real name of Knight-Bruce.

For a while Dandy carried out his duties with dignity and decorum and the Major treated him almost as one of his own family. During his first leave period he applied for, and was granted, permission to visit France where his wife and family were living. He returned safely, thereby adding to the general conviction that his reformation was genuine and that he really was a 'good boy'. In the light of after events, however, that venture was thought to have been a mere 'sprat to catch a mackerel'. His next leave was conveniently arranged so as to coincide with the Major's own. When the latter returned, however, it was only to discover that for the second time the bird had flown, this time taking with him a number of his boss's personal belongings and items of value from his home. This time Dandy disappeared for good and, so far as is known, has never been heard of since.

'Tight-Boots' was a character indeed. His appearance and manner were such as few who served with him could ever forget. Tall and angular, when not actually on parade he was rarely seen without his monacle, pipe and deer-stalker hat, and was always accompanied by a posse of small dogs. These he used to control shepherd-like by means of a shrill whistle hung on a cord round his neck. The distinctive sound it made invariably heralded his approach. He was also known for his conservative habits and pursuits. Almost every Monday morning his first port of call on entering barracks would be the Orderly Room, where he would enter his name in the Officers' Leave Book to cover the days on which he wished to go hunting during the week. This was never less than three days of the working week. Like all good soldiers, he would return later in the day to ensure that the C.O. had approved his absence. So highly did he value his hunting, it used to be said, that the day it was not approved, Tight-Boots would resign his commission.

The name of Tight-Boots, coupled with that of Dabber, calls to mind a very special occasion in the calendar of social events which took place while the Battalion was stationed at Woking. It was the annual football match between the officers and sergeants, when all other ranks and their wives, together with the officers and their ladies, would turn out to witness a never-to-be-forgotten spectacle.

What an affair it was! It was the custom for the officers to pick the sergeants' team and vice versa. The sergeants' team, accompanied by their supporters, asssembled at the Mess. Although the Regiment was Infantry of the Line, it was nevertheless decreed that on this auspicious occasion the sergeants' team would be escorted to the Sports Field by their own mounted band. This in itself was no mean feat for the animals used were none other than the Transport Section's pack mules, which at the best of times resented anybody or anything being placed on their backs. George Humphrey the Provost Sergeant was suitably attired for his role as mounted Drum Major. He led the procession, which was followed by the team, clad in the Regimental colours of royal blue and gold and riding in one of the mule-drawn G.S. wagons.

Their arrival on the Sports Field evoked a tremendous volume of cheering from the crowd. Dabber, the veteran of the team, was to guard the sergeants' goal against every onslaught from the enemy and was suitably attired for the purpose with cricket pads to preserve his ageing pins and a fencing mask to protect his face, for it was considered that the officers would have no respect for age or rank. Many of them, after all, had fought in campaigns all over the world and had been decorated. Whilst awaiting the arrival of the officers' team, the sergeants lost no time in 'oiling' themselves in preparation for the fray.

Suddenly a fanfare of trumpets sounded the 'Advance' from the Officers' Mess, which overlooked the Sports Field, and all eyes turned in that direction. Tight-Boots was the first to emerge. He was clad in full hunting pink, his crop in one hand and a hunting horn in the other. At the first sound of the horn the local pack of hounds advanced in full cry upon the football pitch. A moment's silence followed before the main door of the Mess opened. True to tradition, the officers were determined that their team should be led by the antelope. In fact, however,the creature to emerge from the Mess was a most peculiar looking beast. True enough, it had an antelope's head, but its body was forty-five feet long, covered with the Ante Room carpet, and propelled by twenty legs covered with striped football stockings and, of course, shod with football boots. To the sound of beating tom-toms, baying hounds and persistent notes on the hunting horn, the antelope-centipede made its way towards the pitch. As it advanced, the sergeants' team formed itself into a guard of honour to greet it. After their tortuous journey beneath the weighty carpet the officers' team demanded further liquid refreshment before they would take the field.

At length the game got under way, but only with frequent interruptions for smelling salts or whisky to be applied to the many players who feigned injury. Their real purpose was to gain time or perhaps to force a draw.

However, the final result was destined to be far less tame. The final minute of play was full of drama. During it the referee awarded a penalty to the sergeants for abusive language on the part of one of the officers' full backs. Immediately the captain of the sergeants' team summoned Dabber to take the spot kick. For the first time in his entire military career he was seen, for all his encumbrances, to break into a gentle trot as, to the accompaniment of loud cheers, he made his way towards the officers' goal. Before the kick was taken, however, Tight-Boots, complete with pipe, summoned an 'O' Group and while this was in session someone ordered a smoke canister to be lit. Before the smoke had a chance to obscure the goal area, Dabber, urged on by his entire team as well as their supporters, moved slowly and deliberately towards the ball. Then, with the identical technique which he had so often used on the band-boys' backsides, he let fly with his right foot. Never before had a penalty been taken with such venom or such deadly accuracy. Straight and true flew the ball towards Tight-Boots, the officers' goalkeeper. He took evasive action but it was too late. It hit him clean in the 'breadbasket', whereupon, to the wild jubilation of all the sergeants, their wives and supporters, he and the ball rolled over the line together. At that moment the referee blew the final whistle. It had previously been agreed that the losers were to entertain the victors, together with their supporters, and so all made their way to the Officers' Mess to celebrate. Despite the hilarity of the whole affair, one indirect consequence of the match proved to be tragic. For 'Topper' Brown, the C.Q.M.S. of Headquarter Company, who had served in the Regiment continuously for twenty-seven years, that had been the first football match in which he had ever played in his life. Immediately after it he went back to the office to complete the accounts, omitting to have a bath and a change of clothing before doing so. As a result, he caught a severe chill which developed into pneumonia and in the end led to his death.

In connection with sporting activities within the Regiment, Jim recalls another memorable occasion, this time in the field of boxing. An event which never failed to arouse the utmost interest was the Battalion Individual Boxing Championship. The reigning champions always received the loudest acclaim when they appeared to defend their titles, and the particular evening in question was no exception. As Private 'Topper' Brown of the Q.M.'s staff entered the ring as welter-weight champion, the ovation he received from his many supporters was nothing short of tumultuous. His opponent was a new recruit by the name of 'Ben' Cecil. Ben was an ex-miner from the town of Tredegar in the Welsh Valleys. Obviously because of the depression in Wales, he had turned to the security which the

Army could provide. He was a little older than his contemporaries. His blond hair was sparse and, when not on duty, he was rarely seen without a clay pipe in his mouth.

Once the two opponents had entered the ring, Topper (the 'Champ.') began dancing up and down and shadow boxing in his corner as champions do. By contrast, in the corner opposite Ben sat motionless, his face devoid of expression except perhaps for a slight frown as his piercing blue eyes stared across the ring. At the sound of the bell Topper moved quickly into the centre, feinting and weaving, head jerking from side to side, and exuding snorts from behind his gum-shield. Ben, having adopted a rigid 'southpaw' stance, hardly moved. As Topper bobbed and weaved around him he seemed to be becoming impatient for the 'kill'. Once more he feinted and then moved in. As he did so Ben's left fist shot forward like the stroke of a piston. Its speed and power were awe-inspiring and it landed with an audible thud right on the point of Topper's jaw. Falling flat on his back as if pole-axed, the ex-champion never moved while the referee counted him out. For a moment, as Topper was carried to his corner, there was a deathly hush. Then the sound of singing broke out as the voices of a few Welshmen launched into 'Land of our Fathers'.

The next bout also caused something of a stir, for it was the Battalion Heavyweight Title. Here again the reigning champion had a reputation for despatching his opponent at an early stage in the fight. On this occasion the challenger was a brawny young Australian subaltern who had already acquired the nickname of 'Nick'. Strangely enough, he too was a 'south-paw'. Soldiers always seem to relish the spectacle of one of the other ranks humiliating an officer, and as the bout commenced the spectators were rubbing their hands in anticipation of the slaughter to come. However, the night was full of surprises. In a manner almost identical to that of the previous fighter, the underdog confounded the form-book and yet another title-holder was laid flat on his back to be counted out.

From that moment onwards Nick was respected by all ranks. As the years passed by he became a highly popular and much-loved officer. Quite early in World War II he proved himself on the field of battle as well, being awarded the Military Cross for bravery. Before this, however, he served for some years with the 1st. Battalion in Poona and here Jim remembers another incident in which he was involved. It took place in the early thirties. Whilst waiting for a parade to commence Nick turned to a soldier of the Transport Platoon who was not his own syce (groom) and said: 'Smith, go and fetch my *gorrhah* (horse). 'Which one is it, Sir?' replied Smith, loking at a small group of chargers some little distance away. Nick pointed to one particular animal which happened to be a stallion. 'The one with the big balls!' he said with a wry smile. That was enough for Smith to identify Nick's charger!

Particular sporting events in a Regiment often come to be associated with particular individuals. This was certainly the case during the period 1928 to 1934, when the Battalion excelled at tug-o'-war, a sport which is not often much raved about. A newly commissioned subaltern by the name of 'Pat' aspired to raise a team to enter for the Army Tug-o'-war Championships later in the year. To obtain volunteers for his team he advertised in Battalion Orders under 'Notices'. From the outset he was determined that only dedicated enthusiasts should be trained, and when two or three dozen men came forward, the physical tests to which he subjected them were so gruelling that most of the 'goats' dropped out. Finally a small, elite and dedicated band survived and these made up his squad.

The training apparatus consisted of a tripod of scaffold poles with a pulley fixed to the top. Over this ran an extra long tug-o'-war rope to which was attached a large specimen of 'boxes, coal, barrack room, soldiers, for the use of'. It was filled with large slabs of concrete. The team had to pull the 'tub' to the top of the pulley, lower it under control until it had almost reached the ground, then check it and then pull it back up to the top again. The process was repeated until the men were fit to drop. The result was that a very high standard indeed was achieved. On several occasions the Battalion Lightweight Team (110 stone) reached the last four in the Army Championships, and once they were runners-up. In Alexandria the Battalion team took on a team from the pick of the Mediterranean Fleet and beat them. One pull lasted six minutes, which in tug-o'-war circles is a lifetime.

Pat later became Adjutant and was an officer universally loved by all the troops. It was he who recommended Jim for a commission shortly after the outbreak of World War II. Later he went to France with the 2nd. Battalion and had the misfortune to be wounded and made a prisoner of war. However, he was awarded the Military Cross and after the War rose to the rank of Colonel.

At the age of sixteen, Jim had the honour of playing cricket for the Regiment, and the Regimental scorebook (still in existence) records the names of Major B. L. Montgomery and Boy Pickering, together with that of Lieut. G. C. Evans (later to become Lieut.-General Sir Geoffrey Evans). In one particular match these two officers opened the innings with a stand of one hundred and eighty runs. About the same time Jim too had a remarkable innings. He was at Aldershot at the time, being attached to the R.A.S.C. Depot at Buller Barracks while undergoing a course of instruction. He was invited to play for the Corps team in their annual match against the R.A.O.C. The first wicket fell at 3 and at that point Jim joined the opener, Lieut. Kekewitch. Jim was instructed to keep his end up, which he did to such good effect that the score reached 182 for one wicket and he was still not out. By this time Lieut. Kekewich had made well over a century, while Jim had achieved a worthy 53, not out.

One day when Jim happened to be on leave at Hythe in Kent, he was walking near the Small Arms School there when he noticed an officer in mufti. He recognised him as Colonel Taylor, the Commandant of the S.A.S., who was also in the Regiment. Accordingly, following the correct drill for such an encounter, he placed his walking-out cane beneath his left arm and, after the requisite number of paces, saluted the Colonel with his right hand. The Colonel's immediate reaction was to stop Jim, ask for his name, and congratulate him on his turn-out and alertness. Jim thought no more of the incident until after his leave had expired and he had returned to barracks. He was then summoned to the C.O.'s office where he was informed that Colonel Taylor had written a congratulatory letter to the C.O. That day Jim was promoted to lance-corporal (unpaid), the very first step up the promotion ladder. In those days much significance was attached to even the most junior of ranks. Orders given by a lance-corporal had to be obeyed to the letter. It was often said that a lance-corporal was the 'dogsbody' who was at the beck and call of all and sundry. Promotion was extremely slow and it was usual for a lance-corporal to have to wait three years before he was paid for the rank. Often it was seven to ten years before he reached the rank of sergeant, and it was rare for an N.C.O. to reach the rank of W.O. in under fifteen years.

Chapter 8

Service in Palestine

Between the Wars each infantry regiment had two battalions, one of which served at home while the other was posted to one of the many colonial stations such as India, Malaya, China, Palestine, Egypt or countless other smaller countries. At that time there were (not counting the Brigade of Guards) about 120 battalions in the British Army, though of course, as a result of losing the Irish regiments in 1922, the number had been reduced.

As already related, the 1st. Battalion had left India in 1912 and now, in 1930, the time was approaching for the 2nd. Battalion to end its foreign tour. They were serving at Khartoum in the Sudan, where the Regiment had fought at the end of the previous century. In the Spring of 1930, therefore, all ranks of the 1st. Battalion were awaiting the publication of Army Council Instructions to learn where it would be posted during the following trooping season. Naturally there was much speculation. Then one afternoon a smartly dressed Indian gentleman arrived at the Orderly Room requesting to see the C.O., who, he asserted, was his 'friend'. It did not take long for word to buzz round that 'Mo' (Mohamed Ali), the Regiment's Contractor from India, was in the C.O.'s Office. The tom-toms must have been beating with a vengeance for word had already reached Bombay, where 'Mo' had his headquarters, as to which part of the Empire the Battalion was being posted to. Naturally it was widely assumed that it would be India. 'No doubt he's brought gold, frankincense and myrrh,' said the troops as Mo paid his respects to his old 'sahib'. Mo, however, was already aware of the true facts of the case: the Battalion's real destination was Moascar on the Suez Canal. Due, however, to a deteriorating situation in the Middle East, the initial plan was changed and the Battalion was ordered to move to Jerusalem in the following January.

Further exciting news was now noised abroad. When the Battalion sailed, 'Monty' was to take command. Later in his career Monty was to gain a reputation for being original. Already at this stage he manifested this trait by arranging that some time before departure all ranks would march to a local cinema in Woking to see a film of the Holy Land. It was to be introduced by the C.O. designate himself. He also arranged to be present at the fitting-out parade of all ranks, when Mo and his staff would measure and fit the requisite khaki drill clothing together with topees and pith helmets according to the regulations of those days.

At this time the average age of the soldiers in the Battalion could have been little more than twenty years; many were considerably younger. The majority were destined to remain abroad for six or seven years – most, in other words, of what are generally considered 'the best years of a man's life' – before returning to their homeland.

One of Jim's daily chores in the Orderly Room was to clean the offices of the C.O. and the Adjutant. In the course of this duty he observed on the wall a list of all officers in order of seniority and beside each officer's name was a brief record of service which had been prepared by 'Hoppy', the Orderly Room Corporal, for the benefit of the C.O. One day, shortly before Monty's arrival, Jim was tidying the tables while Hoppy was changing the name of the outgoing C.O. for that of Monty, 'Major, Brevet Lieut.-Colonel B. L. Montgomery, D.S.O'. Pointing to the name, Hoppy remarked to Jim: 'This chap will go to the top of the tree'. Those words were spoken in November, 1930 and how prophetic they proved to be! Hoppy had often played cricket with Monty and from past service together he knew him well. Obviously he had good reason to make so profound a statement. Many years later, when Monty had become Field Marshal, Jim found an opportunity to tell him of Hoppy's prophecy. 'He knew what he was saying, didn't he Pickering?' was Monty's reply.

On 31st. December, 1930 Jim and his brother Cecil said goodbye to his mother and family at the end of their embarkation leave. It was a very sad day for them, for they knew that it might well be six long years before they saw them again. On the 16th. January, 1931 the two brothers spent their last night in England in Bisley at the home of Mr. and Mrs. Lay and their family of six girls. Mr. Lay was the groundsman at Inkerman Barracks. That was nearly sixty years ago and still to this day Jim maintains contact with the family.

Next day the Battalion entrained at Brookwood Station en route for Southampton to embark on the H.T. *Neuralia*. By any standards it was a foul day, with a south-westerly gale blowing up the Channel. Nevertheless, of all the days in Jim's life this one turned out to be one of the most momentous, for ultimately it affected its entire course. After stowing his sea kit bag and other belongings on the appropriate mess deck below, he wandered back on deck to catch a final glimpse of old England. On the quayside had gathered a considerable number of friends, wives and sweethearts and the Regimental Band was playing. At that point Jim noticed, at some little distance from him on the deck, a small knot of soldiers gathered round a khaki-clad figure with a bible in his hand. The badge on the man's cap bore the insignia 'A.S.R.', indicating that he was an Army Scripture Reader. Content for the present to 'listen afar off', Jim did not approach. He heard the Reader quote part of Psalm 34, verse 8: 'O taste and see that the Lord is good'. The Reader went on to say that the Christian life is like a pie with a crust on top. 'You don't know what it's like until you have broken the pie-crust, put your finger inside and pulled out a plum'. Just at that moment the ship's bell sounded, warning all visitors to leave the ship. As he was packing up his belongings, the Scripture Reader hurried over to Jim whom he had noticed listening. 'Are you a Christian?' he asked. The forthrightness of the question took Jim aback. After a moment's thought he replied: 'Well I do read a New Testament that my mother gave me, and I say a few prayers under the bedclothes each night, but I must confess, I'm not a real Christian'. Hurriedly the Reader went on to warn him that on going abroad he would meet many temptations; there was only one Person who would be able to help him when he was tempted and that was the Lord Jesus Christ. As he left he begged Jim to commit his life to Christ. 'Why not trust Him now?' he said.

With these words still ringing in his ears and with a heart heavy with homesickness, Jim made his way below. However, the impression which that conversation had made upon him was indelible. That very night, after climbing up into his hammock, he resolved that henceforth he would endeavour to live a Christian life.

No sooner had the ship sailed than she ran into the teeth of a considerable gale. Hatches were battened down and all ranks were confined to their quarters below. Life there was anything but pleasant, for conditions were cramped to a degree and once the old tub began to toss and roll, they deteriorated even further. It was not long before most of the landlubbers had lost the meal they had eaten earlier. In those days, of course, air conditioning as we now know it did not exist and the air became ever more foul. To make matters worse, the smell from the galley of kippers being cooked for the following morning's breakfast drifted through the mess decks and added fuel to the flames of sea-sickness already raging. Throughout the night the storm continued without abatement, yet despite all that they were having to endure, when morning came all ranks had to 'stand to' their lifeboat stations to await inspection by the ship's Captain and the O.C. Troops. Jim's particular station happened to be outside the detention cell, which, to the discomfort of any of its inmates, was situated on the lowest deck, adjacent to the hold and almost in the bows of the ship. For those suffering from sea-sickness it must have been the worst part of the ship. As for Jim, even though normally a good sailor, every time he took up his position for 'lifeboat stations' he felt his stomach being turned, and the call of the bugler sounding 'stand down' was welcome indeed. As intimated, his brother Nank was somewhere on board too, but although he enquired after him no one seemed to have seen him from the moment the ship sailed. Eventually he was found huddled in a blanket at the back of a lifeboat box looking almost as green as the sea itself.

By the third day, which happened to be a Sunday, the ship had already passed through the Bay of Biscay and was moving along the coast of the Iberian Peninsula. Being an ardent churchgoer, Monty lost no time in ordering a 'Drum-head Service' to be held on one of the upper decks. During the afternoon he summoned all W.O.s and N.C.O.s to assemble in one of the lounges for a 'conference' with the object of expounding his plans for future promotion examinations. True to form, he said that he was going to revolutionise the promotion system in the Battalion by instituting his own set code of exams., which would be in addition to the normal standard ones laid down in the Army. He would announce the syllabuses on arrival in Jerusalem. He explained all this in that emphatic tone of voice of his, now so familiar to thousands of servicemen as well as to civilians all over the world. Then his bright penetrating blue eyes fastened on some of the older N.C.O.s sitting immediately in front of him. 'For the moment,' he went on, 'all promotion vacancies will be held in abeyance for three months so as to give every N.C.O. the same fair chance. At the end of that period, only those who have passed my promotion exams. will be considered for promotion. If the older N.C.O.s fail to pass, they will not be promoted. This will give the younger N.C.O.s scope for acceleration in climbing the ladder. I hope that this is clearly understood by you all – what?' Then, as though to add spice to what he had said, he added: 'Remember, every soldier carries a baton in his knapsack'. Certainly that talk created a tremendous stir; for several days it was the central topic of conversation on the boat. A number of the 'old sweats' who had hitherto considered promotion almost automatic had already resigned themselves to handing in their tapes rather than be bothered with swotting for promotion.

In the course of the voyage Jim saw for the first time the forbidden gambling game of Crown and Anchor being played by his fellow soldiers.

The alternative game of 'Housey, Housey' (now known as Bingo) was permitted, but it was statutory for a percentage of the profits to go to the P.R.I. Fund. The 'spivs' who ran the Crown and and Anchor games would place look-outs just as 'spivs' do on the pavements of Oxford Street when carrying on their illicit trading. These gambling scenes recalled to Jim's mind something that Fred Savory had told him some time before. He was showing him his medals, which included The Ashanti Star, the two Sudan Campaign Medals, the King and Queen South African Medals and the Delhi Durbar Medal. In all they numbered ten, yet despite all his years of service Fred had no Long Service and Good Conduct Medal. 'I lost that playing Crown and Anchor on the voyage home from India', he explained. It transpired that he was caught playing the forbidden game on the troopship and was awarded 96 hours detention, thereby forfeiting his chance of qualifying for the medal. He added jokingly that the 'roti medal' (as it was called by the troops) was awarded only for eighteen years of undetected crime.

The rest of the voyage passed swiftly, being devoid of any happenings of significance unless one counts brief calls at Gibraltar and Malta. Ten days after leaving England the ship arrived at Port Said, affording all ranks their first glimpse of the 'Glorious East'. Naturally it evoked much excitement. The ship was soon surrounded by miriads of small native boats, known to servicemen as 'bum boats', with the natives in their galabiahs selling their wares. Above the din the cry 'What do you want, George?' could constantly be heard and here and there traders could be seen holding above their heads an example of the typical Egyptian leather pouffe. 'You give me five pounds for dis!' they would shout, to which the soldier addressed would reply: 'Ten bob or nothing . . .' Despite the disparity in value, the native would invariably place the object in his raffia basket, throw the rope up to the deck so that the soldier could pull it up, and then lower it again with the ten shillings in it.

Whilst all this was going on, a ramp had been placed between the hold of the ship and the first of several coal barges which had drawn alongside. Within minutes a long procession of native coolies of both sexes could be seen carrying baskets of coal on their heads to fill the bunkers for the next stage of the ship's journey. As the ant-like procession advanced the natives kept up a constant chant, and whenever their efforts began to flag they would receive a prod in the side from one of the gang leaders, producing a louder chanting and an increase in the tempo of their work. Here for the first time the troops could hear from the gang leaders words which were later to become familiar: 'Igari, igari, IGARI!', 'faster, faster, FASTER!' They themselves would soon be using those words to any native who was slothful. Those soldiers who, all unsuspecting, had remained on deck soon found themselves becoming almost as black as the coolies themselves as the ship became permeated in every crack by a dense cloud of coal dust. As in most Eastern countries, it was not long before a 'gullie-gullie man' appeared, attracting small gatherings of troops around him as, at the touch of a magic wand, he produced live chicks out of his tarbush. As this performance was being enacted a small galabiah-clad boy ran around the deck with English newspapers under his arm. 'News of the Next World' he would shout, this being his version of the title of a certain well-known Sunday newspaper. Another cry which was later to become familiar to the troops was that of the egg seller: 'Eggs-a-bread!'. His eggs, however, were no bigger than those of an ordinary pigeon – no wonder that they cost only half a piastre (one penny) apiece! As for the small rolls of bread he sold to accompany them, he had carted them round in the sun so long that they were like concrete.

By this time the troops had changed from serge to khaki drill trousers and shirts and were preparing to disembark. Large lighter-type craft pulled alongside and in these the troops were ferried to the quay where a train was waiting to take them along the Suez Canal to Kantara West. The journey did not commence until after dark, and just before midnight they were again ferried across the Canal to Kantara East, where the Battalion was to entrain for the journey up to Jerusalem. Although by this time the troops were very tired, there was still much to maintain their interest and keep them awake. Shortly after first light the train stopped just outside the town of Gaza, where groups of local Arabs could be seen squatting idly or swilling their faces with water from their cupped hands. Their camels too were being watered before the commencement of the day's work.

The Battalion arrived at Jerusalem Station, which is about a mile outside the walls of the Old City on the Bethlehem Road. Thence they marched to Talavera Barracks, a newly constructed hutted camp. Its name derived from the fact that the first regiment to occupy it was The Northamptonshire Regiment (48th Foot), whose principal battle honour was Talavera.

Of course once they had arrived in Jerusalem, it did not take the 'old sweats' long to set out exploring the 'night life' of the city. The Jaffa Road, which was a part of it that lay outside the city walls, contained many bars and other haunts where there was a fairly large cosmopolitan community. Much had been heard about arrack, the potent drink of the East, and it goes without saying that the topers were eager to sample it. Many were no less eager to meet the local girls or 'bints', to use the argot of the place.

At that time Palestine was a non-family station. All the soldiers' families had been left behind in England and before long a number of the 'grass widowers', finding themselves off the leash, began to kick over the traces. On the first Friday evening after arrival a certain corporal of the drums named Charlie, together with some of his pals, visited some of the bars in the Jaffa Road area. Normally Charlie could hold his own with most drinkers, relying on a cup of 'gunfire' tea to clear his head the following morning. This time, however, he had not allowed for the effects of arrack. Although he managed to get to bed that night with a skinful, the following morning he discovered that the 'gunfire' tea, so far from clearing his head, had the opposite effect, making him quite drunk again. So bad was he, in fact, that he was completely incapable of going on Adjutant's Parade and was charged with being drunk at 8 o'clock in the morning. It was a sharp lesson indeed to many of the more ardent 'boozers' to beware of the deadly effects of arrack.

Another 'grass widower' who had an unsalutary experience was 'Fitz', a member of the Quartermaster's staff who lived in Jim's barrack room. He had gone out with other pals to the small village of Talpioth, situated only a few yards from the Camp along the Bethlehem Road. Fitz returned to Camp very late with a real skinful. Normally he was one of those soldiers who would crawl out of his 'flea pit' (the name given to a soldier's bed) just in time for work or parade. On the 'morning after' this episode, however, he caused astonishment throughout the barrack room by getting up at the sound of Reveille and putting on his blue gym shorts and shoes, apparently to go for a run. Off he went, jogging up the path towards Talpioth. It was some time before he was seen returning, and he was holding a handkerchief in front of his face as he slunk into the barrack room. It later transpired that the night before, after leaving one of the bars, poor Fitz had been violently sick a couple of times, and when he awoke he had discovered that his false teeth were missing. Unfortunately his search for the missing dentures had been in vain and quite naturally he was chided by all his pals, one of whom declared that he had left his false teeth in the neck of one of the 'bints' he had been seen 'gum-sucking' in the bar the night before.

Many incidents of this kind had the flavour of arrack about them. Our old friend Cockney George had planned to visit some of the 'dens of iniquity' of the Jaffa Road. Although he did not reveal his intention to Jim, he asked him if he could borrow his walking-out shoes for the evening. 'Mind where you go with my shoes, Cockney,' said Jim, to which the little man replied: 'You know me, Jim. I'll never let you down. 'With these words he went off like a dog with two tails. The following morning as he approached Jim, Cockney hung his head as if in shame. By the look of Jim's shoes he seemed to have been on a route march; they were covered in dust. 'Jimmy,' said Cockney, 'I'll tell the truth and shame the devil. Every time we came to a bar I would turn to go in, but your shoes would not let me; they went straight on. Then when I passed a church your blessed shoes would turn in even though I wanted to go past. However, Jimmy, I promise you that they would not let me go into one of the brothels.' 'But how did you get my shoes in that state?' asked Jim. Cockney then went on to relate that when he and his pals decided to return home, there was only one 'Victoria Carriage' available, but when they all went to get inside there was no room for him. In consequence he agreed that he would ride on the axle at the rear as he used to when he was a boy in London. It was obvious that he had spent most of the journey home running behind the cab rather than leaning over the axle.

Whenever British troops served abroad it was customary for them to have one day in the middle of each week as a holiday. It was a custom that had been instituted during the reign of Queen Victoria for her troops serving in India. This day was commonly known as 'Old Soldiers' Day' and in that part of the Empire it was always a Thursday. However, to be different as always, Monty decreed that in Palestine it would be a Wednesday. In consequence, Taffy the Orderly Room Sergeant delegated Jim to organise a rota, so that each clerk in turn would have to perform the tasks of 'duty clerk' in case of an emergency. Jim, not desiring to be officious over the matter, gathered all the clerks together in the barrack room and suggested that they should draw lots to see who would commence the rota. Thereupon Topper Brown (the one whom Ben Cecil had 'put to sleep' in the Regimental Boxing Championship at Woking some time before) said: 'You can cut me out. I'm not going to do duty tomorrow (the first Wednesday) whatever the draw.'

For the first time in his career as an N.C.O. Jim was faced with a difficult situation which needed firm but careful handling. His reply was: 'I'm afraid that whoever is drawn first will carry out the duty'. Then, as he went to walk past Topper to get some paper and a pencil, the latter threw a punch which landed on Jim's face. At that psychological moment Jock, one of the more senior N.C.O.s, happened to walk into the barrack room. He saw what had happened and immediately informed Topper that he was under close arrest. It did not take him more than a minute or two to detail an escort to march Topper to the Guard Room where, in the troops' language, he was 'put inside'.

The following morning his Company Commander decided that he should be remanded to appear before the C.O. In such cases of a soldier being charged with striking an N.C.O. Monty always gave short shrift. As soon as the charge had been read and the evidence given there was a moment's pause. Then, cocking his head on one side in the distinctive Montgomery manner, Monty said with his customary firmness: 'Well, Brown, and what have you to say – what? Striking an N.C.O. is a very serious matter – what?' Before Topper could reply, Monty went on: 'There's nothing you can say, is there?' After a further brief pause he continued: 'Will you accept my punishment or be tried by Court Martial?' 'Your punishment, Sir,' murmured Topper. 'Twenty-eight days' detention,' said Monty, 'March him out, Sergeant-Major'. Thus, within no more than a couple of hours, Topper left Jerusalem under escort on a train journey to the 'Glass House' (Detention Barracks) at Cairo, where all such offenders carried out their punishment. In the words of the troops, 'to sample the flesh pots of Egypt'.

Topper was not the last soldier to proceed on this unpleasant journey. A soldier in 'A' Company, known to all as 'Flash Harry', had the reputation of being particularly truculent. Having committed some quite minor offence he was marched before his Company Commander, who bore the nickname of 'The Swine'. Strangely enough, both Flash and The Swine were unfortunate enough to have stammers. 'W-w-w-w-what have you to say?' demanded the Major after the charge had been read out. After a pause an obviously agitated Flash started to stammer in reply. Before he could finish, however, the Major exploded in fury. 'I won't be mocked!' he began angrily, but before he could finish his pronouncement, Flash suddenly leapt forward, put his hand beneath the table and tipped it on top of the Swine. For a moment pandemonium reigned. Then Flash was whisked away to the cells and later the C.O. ordered that he should be tried by Court Martial. The upshot was that he followed Topper to the 'Glass House', there to sojourn for a far longer period. Unfortunately this was only the first in a whole series of such episodes in the service of this unruly soldier over the course of the next few years. He had an intense hatred of the Army and was bent on obtaining his discharge at all costs. Later, when stationed at Poona, he faced a series of Courts Martial culminating in a sentence of five years penal servitude. That was the last seen of him in the Regiment.

To most men, however, soldiering in Palestine was highly enjoyable. There were very few real restrictions and those who wished could travel freely to all the neighbouring countries. Perhaps the only real restriction was in the use of water, which at that time was very scarce. For a soldier to waste water in any way was an offence. No washing under running taps was permitted and after use the small bowls of dirty water had to be placed in large drums to be used first for the washing of clothes and after that for the watering of gardens. A mandatory punishment of 96 hours detention was laid down for the first offence of wasting water, with heavier sentences for subsequent offences. Unlike India, there were no dhobies to do the troops' washing, so one afternoon each week was set aside for the troops to do their own laundering, and this without any hot water or irons! It was some time before contractors were arranged to perform this service.

Many thousands of soldiers who served with Monty during the 1939/45 War will remember his famous 'keep fit' campaign, when he ordered all ranks to take part in P.T. exercises as well as to do a cross-country run each week. Only those, however, who served with him in the 1st. Battalion, The Royal Warwickshire Regiment will remember the origin of such campaigns. One afternoon each week, usually on Thursdays, every soldier, including officers (except for a handful of 'duty personnel') had to run round a selected course of about three miles. The C.O. himself followed the run on his charger, and riding beside him would be a groom carrying a green flag. The object of this was that when Monty arrived at the finishing point, all the 'dawdlers' behind the green flag were ordered to do an additional run the following afternoon. No wonder there used to be a general stampede to get past the green flag in a last desperate attempt to avoid an extra run.

Another of Monty's innovations was to arrange all ranks' dances on Friday nights. Realising that there was quite a shortage of 'local talent', he gave prizes for the best fancy-dressed 'females' to act as partners. This was always amusing. At the first dance Cockney George and several other chaps dressed up as 'hoola hoola girls', which gave the C.O. and all present a good deal of fun. However, it was surprising how many girls did turn up; there were Greeks, Armenians, Italians, French, as well as some Jewesses.

Monty always spent a considerable time chatting to the troops and their friends and in this way he acquired a considerable store of knowledge about individual soldiers. He always prided himself on his ability to get to know and understand the soldiers under his command. 'The greatest single factor in winning a war,' he once said, 'is the understanding of man management. Officers are trained to lead soldiers in battle, but unless they fully understand all their problems and gain their confidence, the battle will be lost. It is the soldier who really fights the battle and is able to hold that which he has won.'

One of the most enjoyable weekends Jim spent during his year in Palestine was a trip to Amman to play cricket against the local R.A.F. Squadron stationed there. The journey was made in 30 cwt. trucks travelling along the old road from Jerusalem past Bethany and the Good Samaritan

Inn, through Jericho over the Allenby Bridge, thence up the dusty gorge to Es Salt, and so finally on to Amman. This was wild and barren countryside indeed, the only signs of vegetation being the pomegranate trees laden with fruit which seemed to grow out of the very rocks. During the weekend one of the R.A.F. officers appeared to be involved in almost every activity taking place. He was a Flight-Lieutenant Atcherley, known to all ranks as 'Batchy', and at one time renowned for his exploits as a pilot in the British team that won the Schneider Trophy in the famous Super-Marine planes.

Some time later a Christian doctor and his family took Jim along the Jerusalem-Jericho Road again, this time for a picnic beside the River Jordan. On the way back they passed some other friends from Jerusalem who were just going down to Jericho. Shortly after their return to Jerusalem the Doctor received a telephone call asking whether he had got back safely without incident. As in biblical days, the road to Jericho was still beset with 'highwaymen' and it transpired that the other car-load of friends had been stopped by bandits and dispossessed of their jewellery and any other valuable items they were carrying. In retrospect, the Doctor was convinced that the bandits had also seen them, but because they saw a soldier in uniform in the front of the car, they had been dissuaded from attacking them. Such incidents were far from uncommon at the time.

One great advantage enjoyed by the soldiers serving in the Holy Land was that fruit was exceedingly cheap. Each day one of the picturesque women from Bethlehem, dressed in a finely embroidered blouse and white head covering adorned with gold coins, would bring a large basket of grapes for sale. She would give a couple of pounds of grapes for only a piastre, equivalent to twopence-halfpenny in English money. Again, for a piastre a soldier could buy twelve to fifteen of the largest Jaffa oranges or a large water melon.

The Battalion was widely dispersed, with detachments at Hebron, Sarafand, Nablus and Beit Vegan (near Jaffa) and Headquarters at Jerusalem. Hence it was not possible for combined military training to be carried out. However, as he had previously decreed, Monty had ensured that all N.C.O.s would prepare for his own promotion examinations, which were to be held about Whitsuntide. Jim was absolutely thrilled to learn that he was one of only a handful of lance-corporals to pass the exam. in its entirety. Another achievement worth recording was that he obtained the highest score in the rifle classification tests at Beit Vegan. This far exceeded his wildest dreams. However, the magnitude of the achievement was later attributed to the markers' pencils. They had realised that this was Jim's first classification course, upon which depended his award of proficiency pay, and their enthusiasm had been on a very generous scale. It goes without saying that despite the excellence of his score, it did not merit him being selected for the Battalion Rifle Team.

Monty's command in Jerusalem was not without its ups and downs. In April a draft of about four hundred reinforcements joined the Battalion. Many of these soldiers had already spent up to five years in India and Sudan with the 2nd. Battalion, but as they had not completed the statutory tour of six years abroad, instead of returning to England they had disembarked at Port Said to join the 1st. Battalion in Palestine. Most of them were tough, seasoned soldiers who were unhappy not to be returning to 'Blighty' with their own Battalion. Many of them were heavy drinkers who had even been used to drinking toddy, the local Indian liquor, and it was not surprising that they soon aspired to drown their sorrows in a few noggins of arrack, not realising the devastating effects of this local Middle Eastern beverage. A number of them who were on detachment at Sarafend went on the binge one night and returned to Camp in truculent mood. They became rowdy and aggressive and when confronted failed to respond to their C.S.M.'s orders to return to their billets. After what became a miniature battle, about twenty ringleaders were 'put inside'. That week every cell of the Guard Room was occupied. Monty, however, was in no mood to allow these 'old sweats' to lower the good name of his Battalion and he showed no mercy. He ordered all the culprits to face a Court Martial, which resulted in sentences of from 28 to 112 days' detention to be served in the 'Glass House' at Cairo. This certainly had a sobering effect upon those bent on trouble.

Some little time before the Battalion was due to leave Jerusalem, a member of the Transport Platoon, one of the many soldiers with the name of Brown, was walking along the Bethlehem Road in the vicinity of the Camp when he witnessed an accident in which a passing motor collided with a she ass. Unfortunately the poor animal died, but before doing so she gave birth to a foal. Topper Brown immediately took the little orphan into his care and commenced to feed it on a bottle. As it was a female he gave it the name of Mary. It became a great pet and would follow its 'step-mother' wherever he went. Sadly enough, Mary was ultimately killed by kindness. Someone gave her green fodder which resulted in her death from colic.

Another tragedy in the Battalion took place on its last day in the Holy Land just as it was leaving Jerusalem. True to tradition, Bobby the antelope, which had earlier that year arrived from the Sudan with a draft from the 2nd. Battalion, was leading the Band and Drums on the Battalion's march to the station before departing for Egypt. Suddenly it collapsed and died. As was the custom, it was taken back to Talavera Barracks and buried with due ceremony. 'Jamie' Wright of the Pioneer Platoon, who was a member of the 'Rear Party' and who at one time had been employed by the Imperial War Graves Commission as a stone mason, carved an appropriate headstone for Bobby's grave. There was a sequel to this for some fifteen years later, when the 2nd. Battalion was serving in Palestine during the Israeli War of 1946, the headstone was recovered and brought back to England, where it was placed in the Regimental Museum in perpetuity. Jamie himself met an untimely death when stationed at Poona; he was accidentally drowned whilst on a fishing expedition.

One more episode of Regimental interest occurred just before the Battalion departed from Jerusalem. It concerned one of the most respected and loved senior officers, known to all the troops as 'Potty' Baily. Potty was a major who had served in the Regiment from early in World War I. He was a bachelor who loved his drink. After Officers' Guest Nights at the Mess he was always prominent and would invariably be seen sauntering round the band as it played outside the Mess. On occasions he was even known to relieve the Bandmaster of his baton and take over the conducting himself.

It will cause no surprise, therefore, to learn that on Christmas Day Potty was celebrating in his own inimitable way and by lunchtime had obviously had quite a skinful. It was apparent too that he had no love for 'the Swine', who was Second-in-Command. So great was Potty's aversion to that officer that when he saw the Swine's dress cap hanging on a peg in the hall of the Mess he essayed to desecrate it by filling it with camel dung before replacing it on the peg. As can well be imagined, the venerable 2 i/c's stutter was even more pronounced when he went to cover his bald pate only to find his cap full of malodorous camel dung. It was a gesture which he furiously resented. Although details of the episode were not fully known by the rank and file of the Battalion, the fact that Potty had been placed under arrest and that a summary of evidence had been taken soon became common knowledge. However, the outcome was far less serious than had been anticipated, and instead of facing a Court Martial Potty was despatched to 'Blighty' to replace his khaki hat with a bowler.

Chapter 9

The Holy Land through a Christian Soldier's eyes

Jim's arrival in the Holy Land was memorable in the highest degree. As the Handing Over procedures were being carried out, a lance-corporal of the Northamptonshires introduced himself to him and told him that he had heard about Jim's talk with the Army Scripture Reader. Despite the fact that within a few minutes he would be departing with his Regiment, he asked Jim to visit the small Soldiers' Christian Association Hut a short distance away as soon as he had settled in. As Jim was thinking over this unexpected welcome, a text from the bible came to his mind: 'When He putteth forth His own sheep, He goeth before them'.

To arrive in Jerusalem, the cradle of Christianity, was an experience that filled Jim with awe. From the moment that he stepped out of the train he was conscious that every step he took was indeed on holy ground. Each time he looked out of his barrack room window he could see the city of Jerusalem with the golden dome of the Mosque of Omar surrounded by minarets and shining in the sunlight above its sand-coloured walls and gates. The Mount of Olives, its lower slopes dotted with green olive trees, made the same impression upon him, as also did the little village of Bethany snuggled under the hillside a few kilometres away on the Jericho Road. Everywhere Jim went he took with him the small Brownie camera which his sister had given him when he left home, so as to record each place of interest. On the first page of his photograph album he wrote those well known lines:–

> Words fail me when I think about the Holy Land,
> I only know that where my Saviour stood, I stand;
> And thus the hills He did behold, mine eyes have seen,
> Where once hath trod the Son of God, I too have been.

The first night in Jerusalem was, perhaps, the most memorable in his whole life. Shortly after tea he walked the short distance across the square to the little wooden hut known as the S.A.C.A. Hut, to be welcomed by Major and Mrs. Lee Spratt, who were the wardens. Over a cup of tea and a piece of home-made cake the Major related the story of his own conversion. He had been in the Royal Artillery – a Gunner. One Sunday night shortly after the turn of the century he had wandered by 'chance' into a chapel at Sandgate in Kent. Here he had heard a Gospel message and had fallen under a deep conviction of its truth. As a result, he had returned to his barrack room at Shorncliffe Camp to kneel beside his bed in prayer for the first time. It transpired that that very barrack room overlooked Jim's own home. The Major went on to say that before the Royal Warwickshires left England both he and his wife had prayed that God would raise up a 'witness' before they reached Jerusalem. Some six years later Jim also learned that on the day he left England his aunt and a few friends had also prayed specially for him. In consequence he has often since testified that it was no 'chance' that had caused him to have that conversation with the Scripture Reader at Southampton. If ever a conversation was 'God-directed', he would say, it was that one.

When he returned to the barrack room that first wonderful night, the moon was shining brightly and as he looked across the valley the vista of the Holy City was indescribable. The air was so still that he seemed to hear a still small voice saying to him: 'Let your light so shine before men . . .' There and then he lifted up his eyes and prayed, asking God to give him grace and courage to enable him to kneel beside his bed as a witness to Christ. As he entered the hut and prepared to get into bed, it appeared that every man in the room was looking at him. Hardly had he dropped to his knees when a chorus of 'Say a little prayer for me' rang out round the room.

For some time afterwards he was subjected to much ridicule and jibing from the other men. On one occasion, on seeing Jim reading his bible, one particular 'barrack room lawyer', known to all as 'Harry', commented: 'I've never known a man read the Bible without going off his head'. Undaunted by all this, however, Jim persisted in his chosen path and some weeks later had managed to read the Bible from cover to cover. At that point he approached Harry and said: 'Harry, I've just finished reading the 'Old Book' from cover to cover and I don't think I'm barmy yet'. Harry's reply was: 'Well, Jim, it seems to have had a profound influence upon your life; I only wish that I could do it also'. From that moment Harry, like many of the rest of the men in the barrack room, ceased to ridicule Jim as a Christian. In fact they would often go to Jim when they were in trouble. At such times he would say: 'Now why have you come to me? In fact you have come to Christ, because He alone has changed my life and it is He that lives in me.'

It was not long before quite a number of Christian soldiers from the Battalion were meeting regularly in the S.A.C.A. Hut, where they were encouraged by several local Christian friends who lived in the vicinity. One of Jim's friends who also worked in the Orderly Room with him was an habitual drinker. Each night he spent all his money as well as his time in the 'wet canteen'. Jim began to pray for 'Reg', entering his name in a small green book which he kept underneath his pillow. It became apparent that some of Reg's drinking pals had peeped into the 'little green book' and were amused to see his name on Jim's 'prayer list', a fact which they communicated to Reg. It was obvious that this had also had an effect on him, and although he went across to the S.A.C.A. Hut, he still continued to drink. From time to time he would curtail his drinking and would follow some of the Christians, but whenever he was invited into the 'holy of holies' (the name which the wags gave to the room where the Christians met for fellowship), he would quietly disappear. On one occasion Reg won a first prize in a football sweep and on the strength of his winnings he drifted back into heavy drinking habits. On Good Friday afternoon, just after the 'wet canteen' had turned out, he returned to the barrack room the worse for drink. In his drunken stupor he walked across and dropped a 50 piastre note (the equivalent of ten shillings) onto Jim's bed saying, 'Jim, I'm not going to drink any more. Take that and buy yourself a bible'. He then went back to his own bed and went to sleep for the rest of the day. Later in the evening, however, he accompanied Jim back to the S.A.C.A. Hut and did indeed enter the 'holy of holies'. When he returned to the barrack room that night he knelt beside his bed. Reg's 'conversion' was the talking point of the Battalion afterwards.

After a short while in Jerusalem Monty appointed Jim as his official guide, so that whenever parties from other Services came up for a few days' leave the C.O. would ring for him and say: 'Off you go, Pickerwing . . . Take them around the places of interest and I will pay any of the expenses incurred. On most Wednesdays Monty himself organised special tours which he personally conducted. On one such tour Jim was with a party which visited Bethlehem. En route they stopped to see Rachel's Tomb, which is a short distance outside the city of Bethlehem on the main Jerusalem-to-Bethlehem Road. Before leaving the tomb, Monty purchased small replicas of the tomb carved out of the local white stone and made a present of them to everyone in the party.

As the Christmas season approached Jim was determined that his Christmas in the Holy Land should be in keeping with his professed faith as a Christian. On Christmas day itself, therefore, he rose early and walked the mile and a half to Jerusalem to attend the 7 o'clock Communion Service at Christ Church, which is just inside the Jaffa Gate of the Old City. As it turned out, the only other soldier at the service was Monty himself. After it had ended Monty approached Jim saying: 'Jump into my car, Pickerwing, I'll give you a lift'. They made their way to the King David Hotel where Monty was staying and as he got out he told Jim that his car, together with his chauffeur, was at his disposal for the rest of the day. What a wonderful Christian gesture!

After returning to Camp for breakfast, Jim was joined by a small party of friends who all went to the Dead Sea for a swim. Then in the afternoon they went to Bethlehem to witness the traditional Christmas Day pilgrimage at the Church of the Nativity, where thousands of pilgrims from all over the world had assembled. The evening was spent with many Christian friends at the S.A.C.A. Hut. It was indeed a fitting climax to one of the most eventful and thrilling years of Jim's life, a year which had a profound effect upon him for good. It was brimful of never-to-be-forgotten experiences such as money could never buy and which, throughout the years to come, were a source of inspiration to him.

During August, a Dr. Orr-Ewing who was a friend of Jim's organised a tour of the Holy Land for him, his brother and two friends. Together they journeyed north by car, stopping en route at Nablus, where they visited the well at Samaria where Jesus had that never-to-be-forgotten meeting with the woman of Samaria of John 4. From there they went on to Nazareth to spend a night at the Scottish Mission before proceeding to Tiberias on the shores of the Sea of Galilee. Here they bathed and enjoyed a traditional meal of fresh fish caught from the Sea. After visiting many of the places of biblical interest, they went down to the southernmost point of the Sea, where it flows into the River Jordan. Thence they travelled westwards to stay with some German missionaries on Mount Carmel. The journey back to Jerusalem was by train via Tel Aviv. Such a journey today would cost a considerable sum, but then, thanks to the generosity of his many friends and hosts, it cost Jim and his friend under one pound.

It will be understood that many visitors came to the Holy Land, a number of them well known. Almost every week a special visitor would speak to the Christian soldiers attending the various meetings in the S.A.C.A. Hut. Among the regular speakers was Dr. Shelley who, with his brother-in-law Dr. Campion, had arrived at Jerusalem as Medical Officers with the Australian Light Horse at the time when the city was captured. At the end of hostilities the whole Shelley family settled in Jerusalem to engage in Christian medical work. The Doctor was a great student of prophecy.

Another regular visitor was Colonel Dobbie, who in later years became General Dobbie and led the heroic stand against the Germans in Malta. But one visitor in particular Jim always remembers with affection. It was Bishop Taylor Smith, who had recently been Bishop of the Sudan and before that Chaplain-General to the Forces during World War I. He was perhaps the most loved Padre of all time, a Christian of a most practical type yet one whose whole life radiated his faith. On one occasion when 'testifying' he told the following story:

When he left England as a padre on a troopship bound for India, he was given the services of a young soldier who was to act as his batman. When the soldier heard that his 'boss' was the Padre, he was petrified. However, on entering the Padre's cabin on the first morning at sea, the latter had just finished shaving and was on the point of absent-mindedly squeezing the sponge on which he had put the razor blade. Just in time he noticed the razor blade on it and was able to prevent what might have been a very serious accident. Turning to the soldier he said: 'You see how I was preserved. That comes of committing myself to the Lord at the beginning of the day'. These timely words had a profound effect upon the batman who, seeing the Padre's practical Christianity, was induced to become a Christian himself.

The story is also told that during World War I, when he was Chaplain-General, the Bishop met an old lady who appeared somewhat angry. 'Shouldn't you be out at the Front?' she asked him. With a characteristically jovial smile he quickly replied: 'Madam, look at me at the side and you'll see that I am out at the front . . . quite corpulent'. He had a pronounced 'tummy'. The old lady was quite taken with the Bishop's manner and was made to realise that he was already doing his duty where he was. Almost every conversation he had and every word he spoke reflected the image of his Saviour. Only twice did Jim hear him preach and the messages and texts quoted over sixty years ago are still fresh in his mind. The first was in the 'holy of holies' at Jerusalem, when he spoke on I Samuel 17, verse 50, 'So David prevailed . . .' He preached again during the Keswick Convention of 1936, when he chose as his text: 'Is not this the carpenter's son?', Matthew 13, verse 55. He was never so much at home as when he was speaking to the men of the Forces about his Saviour's love for them. In his eighties the Bishop was still very active and regularly went for a swim, competing with those many years his junior both in the water and on the diving board. The Bishop slipped quietly out of this life just after saying grace at the breakfast table on board a ship bound for the Antipodes. It was as he would have wished.

Chapter 10

Transfer to Egypt

Mustapha Pasha Barracks, Alexandria, where the Battalion was to spend the next two years, was most pleasantly situated only a couple of hundred yards from the sea and three miles from the ancient city of Alexandria, as well as being only a very short distance from the fashionable and exclusive residential area of Stanley Bay.

In common with most places in Egypt, the barracks at 'Mustapha' were plagued with the familiar 'bed bugs', as they were commonly known. In consequence, it was necessary at least once a week for all beds and barrack room furniture to be 'de-bugged'.

As well as bed-bugs, Egypt appeared to be the home of myriads of frogs; no doubt they were the descendants of those which plagued the country at the time of the Pharaohs. They were certainly deep-throated and every night loud croaking could be heard coming from the many ornamental garden ponds of the palatial residences of Stanley Bay. Apart from large numbers of quail, which appeared during migratory periods, few birds were to be seen other than those familiar scavengers of the East, the kites, and also the large white Egyptian Vultures.

From the beginning of May until the end of September most of the troops, as well as their families, spent a considerable amount of time bathing in the sea. For the families beach chalets were provided. Monty took full advantage of the opportunities available by endeavouring to get most of his troops to qualify for the standard Army Swimming Proficiency Test.

At the time of the Battalion's departure from Jerusalem, Jim, as a member of the 'Rear Party', had been among the last to leave. Naturally he had spent his last Sunday evening with friends in the S.A.C.A. Hut. Here he had met two English ladies who from time to time played draughts and other games with the soldiers and who had been helping at a Mission School in Jerusalem. The spiritual influence of these two ladies can never be measured. They were the daughters of a retired Colonel of the Indian Engineers and were direct descendants of Sir Francis Drake. Until their respective deaths at over eighty years of age, they maintained an active spiritual interest in men of the Forces, being 'prayer partners' to young officers who were members of The Officers' Christian Union.

It now transpired that they too were going down to Alexandria to relieve some missionaries at a Missionary Rest Home for a period of six months. They gave Jim an invitation to visit them once he had settled down. The friendship commenced that night with Miss Marjorie and Miss Nancy Sydenham-Clarke was to last the rest of the latter's lifetime, covering a period of almost fifty years. When Jim's wife went into Warwick Hospital for the birth of Naomi Nancy, Miss Nancy Sydenham-Clarke came up from Lymington to look after Jim. She became godmother to both Jim's children, a duty she undertook with a dedicated interest until her death.

During the time these ladies were in Alex. they became deeply burdened. They realized that there was a dire need to set up a place where soldiers could meet for Christian fellowship near Mustapha Pasha Barracks. In consequence, after they had returned to England in the summer of 1932, they wrote to Jim asking him to look for a house which could be rented. Once one was found, they returned to Alexandria at their own expense, rented the house and suitably equipped it, calling it 'The Welcome Club'.

To return to less inspiring matters, it was apparent that the old biblical reference to the 'flesh pots of Egypt' was still apt. The brothels of the nefarious 'Sisters Street' were the mecca of those so disposed. However, as venereal disease was so rampant, the authorities considered that the only way to minimise the scourge among the troops was to establish their own controlled regimental brothels, where selected women under the control of the M.O. were provided. Soldiers availing themselves of this 'service' did not lose privileges if they contracted V.D. there, provided proof was established by an official chit which was lodged in an appropriate box.

Every effort was made to reduce and prevent V.D. by the establishment of Early Treatment Centres at the rear of every Guard Room where troops were billeted. Despite all these precautions, however, the Special Wing of the Citadel Military Hospital at Cairo, where all such cases were treated, was invariably full to capacity. Understandably, it was laid down that if a soldier contracted the disease he lost all privileges as well as proficiency pay for a year, because it was considered a self-inflicted disorder which prevented him from being an efficient soldier during the period of treatment.

In those days this often covered a period of many months.

A few weeks after arriving in Alexandria, the Battalion proceeded to Mena Camp, under the shadow of the famous Pyramids of Cheops, to undertake Brigade Training. Naturally it was the ambition of every soldier to climb the main Pyramid at least once during his sojourn there. Monty, however, considered the occasion of far greater importance; it was an opportunity to give his troops training in the noble art of warfare and at the same time to demonstrate his own prowess as a commander on the field of battle. I am sure that not one member of the Battalion at that time realised that this was to be the now famous Monty's baptism in the art of desert warfare, an art in which, in years to come, he was to have few if any equals. Among the armies which fought in North Africa during the War he was to acquire the reputation of being second to none. Of course he had had experience of warfare of a different kind when, as a much younger officer, he had fought with distinction on the battlefields of Flanders. Here he had been decorated with the D.S.O. for bravery after having been severely wounded in action.

Monty's first skirmish in the desert near Mena was a portent of many more famous battles to come, in which he was one of the chief, and undoubtedly the most successful, protagonists during that never-to-be-forgotten campaign with the victorious 8th Army during the Second World War. Now, in the course of these manoeuvres in the early thirties, the final exercise set by the Brigade Commander was intended to be a test between the 1st. Battalion, The Royal Warwickshire Regiment, under the command of Lieut.-Colonel B. L. Montgomery, D.S.O., and one of the other regiments of the Canal Brigade. The Brigade Commander of the time was Brigadier Pile, who also made a name for himself during the last War. The Battalion was to be engaged in an 'advance to contact' role against its enemy, which was to be employed in a defensive capacity.

Immediately the narrative was published, the wily Monty, in typical fashion, 'appreciated the situation' and 'after considering all the factors', made his plan. Although no mention had been made of aircraft taking part in the exercise, Monty considered that in war all is fair. In conformity with this view he sought the help of an R.A.F. friend to do a little unofficial spotting. The opposition was completely oblivious to the fact that the solitary Lysander aircraft they had seen overhead was in fact a 'Monty' spy plane on reconnaissance. The information he obtained enabled the 'Warwicks' to use that most essential and coveted element of surprise as a trump card. Having located the enemy position, Monty's Battalion made a forced march under cover of darkness and just as dawn was breaking they well and truly caught the enemy with their trousers down. These latter, situated in a nullah, were all lining up for breakfast with mess-tins in hand instead of rifles when, to their utter astonishment, the 'attacking force' appeared over the brow. The confusion was unbelievable and before they had a chance to take up any of their pre-arranged positions they were all – to use the military term – 'put in the bag'. Thus ended Monty's first desert battle in the same manner as he was so gloriously to finish the last one many years later. The Brigadier, of course, was far less pleased. Whether he later learned of Monty's secret ploy was not known.

On its return to Alex., the Battalion settled down to the normal routine of peacetime soldiering abroad. Periodically Monty aspired to 'show the flag' to the local inhabitants by organising a route march through Alexandria. During one such march the eagle eye of the C.O. espied some soldiers who were not wearing the regulation 'underwear' below their khaki drill shirts and trousers, and here too he did not shrink from using the element of surprise. It was customary, at the end of a march, for him to give the initial command: 'Fall out, the officers!', followed by a further order directing the troops to be marched to their respective company areas to be dismissed. On this occasion, however, to the consternation of all ranks, Monty gave the command: 'Ground arms!'. This was followed by an order for the troops to remove their khaki shirts. Instead of rows of torsos being revealed all clad in the same regulation white vests, the picture resembled a gathering of summer trippers on Brighton beach. The garments being worn beneath those uniform shirts were manifold in colour and shape alike, ranging from coloured scarves to pyjama tops – anything which, to the mind of the individual soldier concerned, was conducive to greater comfort and more effective absorption of perspiration in such tropical conditions. Of course the 'offenders' were too numerous for individual disciplinary action, so Monty ordered the whole Battalion to do another route march the following day, this time to be preceded by an inspection to ensure that all ranks were 'properly dressed'.

One of Monty's characteristic traits during his four years of command was his tendency to introduce innovations which were 'against the run of the mill'. Rarely did he allow convention to hold sway. One instance of this was the occasion on which he introduced what he labelled 'voluntary-compulsory church parades'. It sounds double-Dutch but in practice it meant precisely that. Once every month the normal Church Parade was to be held as usual, but on the remaining Sundays, though it was still compulsory for the troops to attend church, they were permitted to go to any service they wished and to be dressed as they wished. The only condition laid down was that they had to notify the Duty N.C.O. as to which service they had chosen to attend. As most of the troops found the normal service of Mattins rather long, including, as it did, a sermon, most of them, logically enough, chose to go to the eight o'clock Communion service so that they could have the rest of the day to themselves. The Padre, however, was less happy, as most of the soldiers went to Communion and, to make matters worse, he had not bargained for such numbers and in consequence ran out of bread and wine. Accordingly, in true military fashion, he held forth on the solemnity of the 'breaking of bread' and emphasised how wholly wrong it was to attend this service merely to comply with the order. Monty too, I am afraid, regarded the matter somewhat unfavourably, especially in view of the fact that only a handful attended the other services throughout the day. It was also significant that as a result of this innovation the takings in the Sergeants' Mess Bar showed a disastrous drop because hitherto, when there had been a ceremonial Church Parade every week, most of the sergeants' wives and their friends had resorted to the Mess for drinks after the parade had ended.

Another of Monty's innovations was to permit all soldiers to take their leave in barracks. During this time they could remain in bed until 9 o'clock; their breakfast time was extended until 9.30 a.m. They were also excused from the task of making up their beds for inspection. Even then some were not satisfied; they said jokingly that Monty was a spoil-sport because he would not permit them to take their 'bints' to bed with them.

At that time one of Jim's duties in the Orderly Room was to check the Army Forms B.256 (Sick Reports) before putting them in the C.O.'s in-tray for his perusal. Whenever the M.O. had diagnosed V.D., Jim had to underline the entry in red ink so as to bring it to the C.O.'s notice. At the end of one particular month the scourge had increased dramatically, with no less than thirty new cases reported. Suddenly the C.O.'s bell rang three times, signifying that he wished to speak to Jim. As Jim entered his office he observed an unusually stern expression on Monty's face. Without lifting his head, and with his eyes still grimly fixed on the sick reports, he said: 'Pickerwing, tell the R.S.M. to parade the whole battalion immediately on the sunken football pitch as I wish to address all ranks. I want every soldier to be present except the duty cooks. Off you go!'

Within a few minutes the bugle had sounded 'Fall in "A", Fall in "B", Fall in every Company!' The whole Battalion was duly assembled and while they awaited the arrival of the C.O. there was much speculation as to what it was all about. Then Monty arrived brandishing the horse-tail fly swat he always carried. Standing on the bank surrounding the football pitch he looked down on the assembly and commenced to speak. 'What I am going to talk to you about this morning is venereal disease'. Holding the month's sick reports up in front of him, he continued: 'This past month there have been thirty cases . . . I cannot tolerate this any longer . . . I am determined to stop it . . . Stop it I will . . . But firstly I will find out where it is coming from . . . In order to do this, every man in the Battalion will, from this moment, only proceed out of camp dressed in uniform. . . We can then see where you go'. With this he walked slowly away. Very shortly after this it was discovered by Monty's 'eyes' that a couple of local 'bints' had taken up residence in one of the beach chalets just outside the Camp and were there carrying on that most ancient of trades at the cost of a few 'ackers' (piastres) a time. These were the ones who were principally leaving their insidious trade mark on their unfortunate clients.

Shortly after this inglorious episode in the Battalion's history, Jim noticed in Battalion Orders that a soldier who had been made lance-corporal only a short time before and who had not, in fact, passed the C.O.'s promotion exam., was now promoted corporal. Having remembered what the C.O. had said in his inaugural address on board ship some eighteen months previously, Jim contended that the C.O. had not kept his word and that it ought to be brought to his notice. Plucking up courage, he went to see the R.S.M., who told him that if he had a grievance he could apply, through his Company Commander, for an interview with the C.O. This he did and was granted a formal interview with Monty.

When he was marched into the C.O.'s Office there was quite a few seconds' silence, as was customary with Monty. Then the C.O. lifted his head, holding it a little to one side, and with his sparkling blue eyes appearing more penetrating than ever said in a quiet but pointed manner: 'Well, Pickerwing, what's all this about . . . what?' Summoning all the courage he could muster, Jim responded by reminding the mighty Monty of his talk to all the N.C.O.s on board the ship on the subject of promotion qualifications, and in particular of his promise that only N.C.O.s who had passed his own set of promotion examinations would be considered for promotion. Jim then went on to say that a particular lance-corporal who had not passed the set promotion exam. and who had, in fact, been a lance-corporal for only a very short time, had been promoted corporal over a considerable number of more senior N.C.O.s.

There is little doubt that Monty had been put on the spot, but all those who knew him intimately will realise that in this matter as in all others he had a mind and will of his own. Right or wrong, he would not be deterred from doing what he thought fit. Jim's veiled attack was followed by another of those characteristic pauses as Monty 'appreciated the situation' before launching his own counter-attack. He then pointed out that he considered the N.C.O. in question 'his ideal N.C.O., worthy of promotion'. He then said: 'How old are you, Pickerwing?' 'Nineteen years, Sir,' replied Jim. There was another pause before Monty completed his coup de grace. 'There's plenty of time yet for you, Pickerwing, you're only a youngster! . . . March him out, Sergeant-Major'.

It was obvious that Monty had smarted a little and had taken a poor view of such a whipper-snapper as Jim telling him that he had not kept to his word. The cheek of it was something which he remembered for some time, as was apparent from subsequent events. However, within a few days Jim was given cause to consider that he had had the last laugh. As he was reading over the Sick Reports preparatory to putting them on the C.O.'s table, he observed that Monty's 'ideal N.C.O.' was a confirmed case of V.D. That day Jim underlined the name with a more pronounced stroke of red ink. So, for at least once in his life, Monty's judgement had failed him.

As was the general custom throughout the Army, each day a Guard was mounted for twenty-four hours, undertaking duty at the Guard Room which covered the entrance to the Barracks. The Guard consisted of a Guard Commander of the rank of sergeant, an N.C.O. i/c Reliefs who was a lance-corporal, and a squad of private soldiers, the number of whom depended on the number of sentry posts to be manned. One extra private soldier was added to this number. On normal working days the Adjutant mounted the Guard or, in his absence, the Orderly Officer performed the duties. After the officer's inspection the soldier adjudged to be the best turned-out man was detailed to perform the duties of the C.O.'s 'Stick Orderly' for the day. He was then relieved of sentry duties and had to report to the C.O.'s Office to accompany the C.O. wherever he went throughout the day. For this duty his rifle was dispensed with and replaced with a walking-out cane – hence the name 'Stick Orderly'. He also wore a white belt and satchel over his shoulder. At the end of each week Monty selected the best Stick Orderly to accompany him on Sunday's Church Parade. In church a chair was placed in the aisle at the end of the C.O.'s pew and here the Stick Orderly sat. As an incentive, Monty used to give his Stick Orderly one hundred piastres (equivalent to a pound in English money) out of his own pocket.

Each night the Quarter Guard was supplemented by 'prowlers'. These were detailed as a mobile foot guard to prevent 'loose wallahs' from raiding the barracks. However, even with such precautions, successful raids did occasionally take place. On one such occasion the Drums were due to carry out an early morning ceremonial parade for which they had prepared their uniforms the previous night. Before retiring to bed they had hung their red ceremonial jackets on the mosquito net wires above their beds. When they awoke they found that all their uniforms had disappeared. At first it was thought that someone had been playing a practical joke, but the reality proved quite different. Ultimately all the uniforms were traced to a nearby bazaar and the culprits were dealt with by the local police.

At the beginning of 1934 the Battalion was due to proceed to Aboukir, an R.A.F. base on the Nile Delta where it was to carry out field training. The distance was only about thirty miles and it was planned that the march should be completed in two stages. True to form, however, just as the march was about to commence Monty made an announcement. He had decided that the trip should be completed in one 'hop'. 'If you march well,' he said, 'I'll give every soldier three days' extra leave'. Such incentives had become quite common. Shortly after the Battalion's arrival in camp Monty ordered that to break the monotony every company should produce a concert. The company which in his opinion produced the best, he declared, would be given an extra three days' leave on returning to Alex.

The opening concert, by 'A' company, was entitled 'Desert Song' and few who saw it will forget it. One of the items was a one-man show by Private (later Corporal) 'Ginger' Aston, a forerunner, in aspiration at least, of Mike Yarwood in the present day. He had the tenacity and brazenness to impersonate the C.O. with a classic dialogue on the subject of 'Venerweal Disease'. Certainly he succeeded in bringing the house down. The following morning, to his fear and trepidation, Ginger found himself summoned by the R.S.M. to appear on C.O.'s Orders. It was obvious, he believed, that he was in for a 'rocket'. Such, however, was far from being the case. When he was marched in front of Monty he said: 'Aston, any man who can take me off as you did last night is worthy of promotion. You will be made a lance-corporal forthwith'. At the same time, Ginger had his leg pulled with a vengeance as to the manner in which he had been promoted. He was one of those whose cheerful natures invariably prevail, and whenever spirits began to flag, especially towards the end of a long march, Ginger could always be heard leading the singing of 'Happy is the day when the Warwicks get their pay . . . rolling, rolling, rolling home'. The last time Jim saw Ginger was just before he went to France in 1940. It was later learned that he had been killed in action. As a soldier, he was certainly one of the 'salt of the earth'.

After returning from Aboukir, Jim developed sinus trouble, which was very prevalent in Egypt at that time. In consequence he had to go to the

British Military Hospital at Cairo. Even this, however, had its compensations, for while he was convalescing he was able to visit the world-famous Cairo Museum with all its Tutankhamen treasures. It had previously been his fortune to hear Howard Carter, the last survivor of the Tutankhamen Expedition, when he gave a slide talk on the whole unforgettable operation, culminating in the discovery of the tomb itself and its magnificent treasures. In recent years people in Britain have had an opportunity of seeing some of these treasures in London at the exhibition at the British Museum.

Whilst Jim was in the Citadel Hospital in Cairo another 'military incident' occurred which is worth recording, although its ending was particularly sad. Today such an episode would be given wide coverage in the British press, but at that time, when soldiering was tough and the rights of individuals far less respected, it passed almost unrecorded at home. The individual involved was a trooper in the 12th. Royal Lancers, a cavalry regiment stationed at Abassia, the British military garrison a short distance from Cairo. It transpired that this soldier was incensed by what he considered the bullying behaviour of a particular sergeant to such an extent that his mind had become affected. Evidently it was the practice of the sergeant to rush into the barrack room immediately after Reveille and, without warning, tip all the soldiers out of their beds. So infuriated did the lad become by this treatment that he vowed he would shoot the sergeant if he did it again and to this end placed a revolver under his pillow the night before. The following morning when the sergeant tipped him as usual out of his bed, the soldier drew the revolver and shot him dead. For this he was sentenced by Court Martial 'to be shot by firing squad'. The execution by a firing squad of his own regiment took place in the Citadel Detention Barracks. An eye-witness who was subsequently in hospital with Jim described the execution to him. It is believed that this was the last peacetime instance in the British Army of a soldier being executed by firing squad.

The Citadel, which had been transformed into a Military Hospital, had at one time been the Sultan's Palace. It occupied a commanding site on one of the highest spots and overlooked the magnificent panorama of the city of Cairo with its innumerable mosques and minarets. It also overlooked the River Nile, which flows from north to south towards the Nile Delta. The picturesque vista of the great river always included numbers of fallukas laden with grain and cotton, which could be seen with their spectacularly tall sails swaying in the breeze as they plied up and down. The Pyramids some distance away to the west and the fertile plain stretching to the desert beyond formed a backdrop to this scene.

Inside the Citadel itself the chapel had been adapted from a building which had once been the bathing place of the Sultan's harem. Its beautifully tiled bath was still surviving, though now covered by a temporary boarded floor. The wards of the hospital had once been the palace reception rooms. These too were decorated with beautiful painted panels and other murals in the classic Egyptian style. In the lovely gardens, where up-patients were able to walk, Hoopoes and many other tropical birds with exotic plumages could be seen.

Even in the Military Hospital, however, the soldier never really escaped from regimentation. Each day, in addition to the routine visit from the doctor, the patients were subjected to a special inspection by the Matron. This bemedalled senior member of the Queen Alexandra's Military Nursing Service was ranked as a Lieut.-Colonel. In appearance and manner, however, she might well have been a female R.S.M. She carried out a most critical inspection, for which the wards had to be absolutely spotless. Every piece of brassware had to be highly polished by the up-patients. Beds had to be in line and all sheets folded to a uniform width, namely that of the temperature board. At night, when she occasionally visited the wards, she expected all clothes taken off for the night to be folded as if they were on display on a shop counter. It was said that even bed-patients had to sit to attention when the Matron visited the wards. However, the care of the doctors and nurses was of the highest standard and showed that devotion to duty always associated, in peace and war alike, with the Royal Army Medical Corps and Queen Alexandra's Imperial Military Nursing Service.

Back in Alex. Monty had decided that the Battalion needed a second football pitch, which, he decreed, should be excavated by the troops. In the course of this task an ancient Roman villa was unearthed. Although it was only about six hundred yards from the sea, some of the mosaics and painted frescoes on the walls of the building were in an exceptional state of preservation. At quite an early stage in the excavations the Egyptian Antiquities Department took control. Nevertheless, before they did so some of the troops had already possessed themselves of souvenirs in the form of early Roman coins. Jamie Wright (he who had made Bobby the antelope's gravestone) found in the vicinity a rare gold coin which he later sold to the British Museum.

While serving abroad, most soldiers managed to pick up at least a few words of the local language. Thus in Egypt it was never 'hurry' but 'igaree'. 'How much?' was 'cum felos?'; 'Come here' was 'talaheena' Most of the inhabitants spoke several languages. It was not uncommon for children to speak Arabic, English, French, Italian and Greek, some speaking other languages as well. One soldier in the Regimental Band learned sufficient French, Arabic and Urdu to pass the Army Special Certificate (equivalent to the present 'A' Level exam). In the case of the two last-named languages he had to learn the script as well.

For three mils (about three farthings of English money) a soldier could travel any distance on the network of tramways in Alexandria. Soldiers were paid in Egyptian currency, but so many counterfeit twenty-piastre pieces were in circulation (they were about the size and weight of a half-crown) that at Pay Parade the paying officer always had to have a piece of marble on the table. With this he would sound each coin in front of the soldier receiving payment to ensure that it was not a 'dud'.

During the Battalion's stay in Alex. Monty continued his fitness campaign, but as the terrain and climate of Egypt were not conducive to cross-country running, he introduced a series of 'standard tests' which every soldier had to pass in order to qualify for proficiency pay. One of these tests was a mile road-run carried out over a course inside the Camp perimeter. The run started outside the C.O.'s Office, continued to the Abercrombie Memorial at the Camp's entrance, and returned to the starting-point. As it was not possible to keep the whole course under surveillance, the supervising officers were at a distinct disadvantage. On the day that Jim, together with most of H.Q. Company, took part in the run, a number of 'fly boys' (including the astute Cockney George) waited until they had gone out of sight of the course judges and then surreptitiously slipped into a latrine block which lay en route. There they waited until the main pack of runners were passing on the return journey, when they again slipped out and joined in the run. At this point Jim was astonished to find the dwarf Cockney suddenly sprinting past him fresh as a daisy – a feat of which, in normal circumstances, he was quite incapable.

Another incident which became a talking point in Alex. will be remembered by every soldier who served there. Just after arriving in Alex. Monty had an Armstrong-Siddley car, specially designed for the tropics, sent out from Coventry. Most car enthusiasts will remember the model, which had the famous Sphynx emblem on the front of its bonnet. In preparation for taking charge of the car, Monty's chauffeur had attended a maintenance course at the Coventry works. As with most staff cars carrying senior officers today, the Regimental pennant was flown on the car's bonnet whenever the C.O. was being driven in it. One Friday evening the alert sentry on duty outside the Guard Room of the main gate to the Camp noticed the C.O.'s car approaching with pennant flying and, as trained, summoned one of the other soldiers on guard to open the gate. As the car sped past they presented arms in the appropriate manner. The following morning was a Saturday and Monty decided to go out for a drive by himself. When he opened the garage door, however, he found that the bird had flown; his car had disappeared. Immediately a general hue and cry was raised and what later became known as 'the great car hunt' began in earnest. Several hours later the car was found abandoned on the Aboukir Road some distance away. From certain 'articles' discovered inside and around it, it was abundantly clear that it had been defiled and had been used for an 'unauthorised purpose'. Fortunately for them, neither the soldiers who had misappropriated the car nor the 'bints' they had entertained in it were ever traced. Later, rumour had it that the C.O.'s chauffeur himself was the culprit but that was never substantiated as a fact. Monty, however, was determined that such unlawful desecration of his automobile should never occur again. Thereafter, to prevent any such recurrence, after use the car was driven up onto the verandah of the Guard Room behind the sentry. One wag later drew a cartoon depicting it chained to the sentry's leg.

The soldiers' families appeared thoroughly to enjoy the life of leisure which they were able to lead at Alex. – in particular the superb bathing facilities afforded them. Each family had the use of a bathing hut on the special part of the beach allotted to them. In the midst of all this there occurred one of those 'married quarter episodes' which were all too prone to arise from time to time. A young lance-corporal became friendly with the wife of one of the sergeants, she being highly attractive and obviously seductive in her ways. As so often happens, they were waiting for an opportunity to be alone together when, to their joy, Bill, the sergeant in question, was sent on a course out of station. Molly was quick to invite her boy friend to her quarter one Friday evening. Unfortunately for them both, their short-lived enjoyment was rudely interrupted by the unexpected return of Bill, who had accepted a lift home for the weekend. He was an habitual heavy drinker and on the way home had imbibed a real skinful. On entering his quarter in the small hours of the morning, he was enraged to find Molly ensconced with the young lance-corporal. Without any fuss, he seized the unfortunate interloper and threw him over the balcony, but not before giving him a pretty savage roughing up. The commotion aroused several N.C.O.s and W.O.s living in nearby quarters and the upshot was that the following morning both Bill and the badly battered N.C.O. were arraigned before the C.O. The lance-corporal was deprived of his stripe while Bill received yet another Severe Reprimand to add to the many others already on his conduct sheet. At the same time Molly was despatched back to 'Blighty' on the first available boat.

As is now known, Monty's wife Betty, to whom he was extremely devoted, died very suddenly some years later at Portsmouth, where he was serving as a Brigadier. Jim remembers well seeing her on many occasions at Alex. where their only son David had just been born. A large pram had been brought out from England and as she took David out for walks in it she used to radiate happiness. It has often been said that losing his wife had a profound effect upon Monty's life. However, it may well be that such a loss had its advantages later on, when the famous soldier was able to carry out the formidable task laid upon him without ties which would undoubtedly have added some weight to his mind and possibly detracted from the task in hand.

One of Jim's friends was 'Leslie', who, like himself, had the reputation of being a 'bible puncher'. Unfortunately he got himself into some minor trouble and was awarded a few days C.B. Then again, whilst he was still a 'defaulter' and confined to barracks, he stupidly ventured out of Camp to attend a late evening 'meeting'. Alas, his sin found him out and as a result he was awarded 96 hours detention. The cells were situated in a separate block on the opposite side of the road to the Guard Room. It was the custom for prisoners to be permitted, after six p.m., to read a book of their choice. Leslie asked the Guard Commander for a bible but had his request refused. This rebuff seemed to have a most unsalutary effect upon him. He decided that if he was not given a bible to read, then he would get out of his cell and procure one for himself. Later that evening the prisoner in the next cell asked to be taken to the toilet, which was in a different building. An N.C.O. of the Guard unlocked the cell door of the soldier concerned but left the keys in it. Whilst the two were out, Leslie put his arm through the grill of his own cell door, took the keys and unlocked his own cell, replacing them once more in the cell door from which he had taken them. After a while he quietly walked out and proceeded to get a bible. When he returned, he naturally supposed that his departure would have been discovered so he walked into the Guard Room to surrender himself formally to the Guard Commander. Strangely enough, he had never been missed at all and the Commander could hardly believe his eyes when Leslie walked in with a large bible under his arm. Realising that he might himself get into serious trouble for permitting a prisoner to escape, the sergeant decided to call it a day and, without further fuss, took Leslie back to his cell to read the 'Old Book' in peace and without further recriminations.

Before leaving Egypt, Jim went to Cairo for the last time to undergo a further operation for recurring sinus trouble. The surgeon who had operated on the previous occasion had just returned from England after obtaining his Master of Surgery degree. Although the troops had given him the nickname of 'Dracula', his skill was beyond question and Jim has to thank him for the fact that for sixty subsequent years he has not had a single day's recurrence of sinus trouble. Before his retirement from the Army, General Harsant (as he became) was Surgeon-General during the War and also became Honorary Surgeon to the late King George VI.

During the time Jim spent in hospital he experienced his first earthquake. He was already an 'up-patient' when one morning he arose from his bed, as was his custom, whilst most of the other patients were still sleeping. Suddenly, while he was on his knees, the whole building began to shake violently. Immediately, just as if they were so many puppets on a string, the patients sat up in bed in unison, wondering what was happening. The tremor lasted for two or three minutes and although considerable damage was done to the flimsy buildings in the poorer districts of the city, there was no visible damage to the Citadel, which was substantially built.

A soldier's normal stint of service in the tropics lasted six years and during this time there must, I suppose, have been very few who were not, at some time or other, accosted by a prostitute hawking her wares. Twice in his stint Jim remembers that had he been a weak character he might well have fallen, as so many soldiers did. On the first occasion he was waiting for a tram at one of the more isolated stations. It was a particularly hot day and he noticed a young Egyptian girl of about twelve years of age approaching him. As she walked past she whispered: 'You want bint, Sir? . . . You give me five piastres'. This poor little creature was prepared to trade her body for a sum equivalent to about one shilling of English money, which indicated the extent of her depravity. Jim merely replied quite sternly: 'Yallah . . . imshi . . .', telling her to go away. She hurried off, obviously impelled by the fear that she might be arrested. The second occasion was at Poona. He was returning to barracks one Saturday evening on a particularly dark night. As he was walking along the road under the shadow of an avenue of banyan trees, he heard the patter of feet behind him. The next minute he heard a woman's voice say: 'You want bibby (woman), Sahib?' At once he remembered that a considerable number of troops had contracted V.D. from an Indian prostitute around the Camp. Jim took no notice, despite the fact that the woman continued to follow him to within a few yards of the Guard Room. Then, without warning, he turned quickly round, seized the wretch by force, and bore her screaming to the Guard Room. She was subsequently handed over to the civil police so as to prevent further soldiers from being scarred for life by the pernicious disease.

There can be little doubt that most soldiers enjoyed their sojourn in Alexandria. Almost all had taken the opportunity of visiting the historical places of interest and in consequence had increased their knowledge of the country's history. Of course one of the 'wonders of the world' which they were not able to see was the lighthouse of Alexandria, which had disappeared hundreds of years before. The existing modern lighthouse is situated at the end of the narrow peninsula at the entrance to the large present-day harbour known as Ras-el-Tin. It was adjacent to the then King's Summer Palace, part of which was later converted into a military hospital. Here, during the North African Campaign, many of the casualties were to be hospitalised.

Each of the regiments which had preceded The Royal Warwickshires at Alex. had moved on to the Far East, and hopes ran high that the Regiment would follow the same pattern. Hence it was a major disappointment to learn that it was to go to India, where it had already served for long periods in the past. Only six soldiers serving in the Regiment had ever had the fortune to serve in China. That was during the Boxer Rebellion of 1900. They were included in a large number of stretcher bearers who had been gathered from each regiment serving in India at the time. Jim met one of these old campaigners in 1936 while walking round Southampton in the course of a furlough. He noticed that the old soldier was wearing a number of medal ribbons on his waistcoat, including the treasured Boxer Rebellion ribbon. It was when Jim spoke to him that he discovered that the 'old sweat' had been one of the privileged six of the 'Saucy Sixth' who had served as stretcher bearers in China during the Rebellion.

Chapter 11

Soldiering in Poona under 'Monty'

The Battalion's stay in Egypt came to an end on 24th December 1933. On that date it entrained for embarkation at Suez on the H.T. *Nevassa*, a sister ship of the *Neuralia* on which the Battalion had left England three years earlier. It was late on Christmas Eve as the ship weighed anchor, and when dawn broke she was sailing through the glassy waters of the Gulf of Suez, moving towards the Red Sea. Christmas Day or no Christmas Day, however, Monty was determined that his troops should first acquit themselves as Christian soldiers and second conform to the normal ship's routine before relaxing for the rest of the day. He therefore ordered that all troops were to attend a Drumhead Service, and immediately afterwards lay their kits out for inspection so as to ensure that they had complied with orders by carrying the statutory items in their 'small seakit bags'. If anyone on board had imagined that a true festive board, including turkey and the like, would be set before the troops, he must have been speedily disillusioned. The Christmas dinner consisted of tinned rabbit, this being followed by a 'sweet' which, while it resembled pudding in appearance, tasted of anything but. It was covered with a yellow custard-like substance which contained no sugar and was starchy to the taste. However, those who liked English beer did find some consolation. For the first time for a considerable period each soldier was given a tin of canned Ansells' Aston Ale. What memories that must have brought back – perhaps of a noggin imbibed before going into Villa Park on a Saturday afternoon to watch their famous team in the claret and blue soccer strip!

The rest of the voyage passed without any incident of note. It took them through the Red Sea and Straits of Babel Mendeb and so on through the Indian Ocean. The early morning of 5th January, 1934, however, brought great excitement for by this time the ship was approaching Bombay, that great city of the Orient, with the long vista of the Western Ghats in the background. To the north side of the Colaba Peninsula could be seen the highly attractive sea front of Back Bay, with its modern blocks of flats glistening in the sun. Away to the south, along the Malabar Coast as far as the eye could see, rose an unending line of palm trees growing almost down to the water's edge. In the foreground, standing like a giant out of the beautiful bay, loomed the historical Elephanta Island with its ancient temple and magnificently carved caves. As the ship slipped along the Colaba Peninsula, the old and experienced 'India Wallahs' pointed out Colaba Barracks, the Afghan Church and the Married Families' Hospital where 23 years before Jim had been born. A few minutes more and the ship had passed the famous 'Gateway of India' which had been opened by King George V in 1911, the year he visited India for his momentous Durbar. At the time the Regiment had provided the Guard of Honour. A building of equal interest to the officers, no doubt, was the no less famous Bombay Yacht Club next to the Taj Mahal Hotel. In Monty's case, I am sure that he must have remembered that in that same Yacht Club he, together with other subalterns, had been accused of ungentlemanly conduct in December 1912 prior to leaving Bombay. They had caused annoyance by shouting and drumming on the brass tables, behaviour which was considered unbecoming for members of the Club.

As the troopship drew alongside the quay at Ballard Pier, the Band of the Durham Light Infantry (68th Foot) gave the Regiment a musical welcome. The Durhams had always had a reputation for their fighting qualities in battle. They had fought with distinction at Salamanca and in the main battles of the Crimean War in the mid-nineteenth century, and since then, in the late twenties, had been engaged in several 'battles' on the soccer field against The Royal Warwickshire Regiment, when the two regiments were rivals in the Army Cup. They were now waiting, it was rumoured, to get their revenge, since in their last encounter they had succumbed to the 'Warwicks' in extra time. Now, however, they bore the reputation of having one of the best teams in India.

Shortly after the gang plank had been lowered, the diminutive figure of Monty, immaculately dressed in khaki drill and topee, walked slowly onto the quay, to be welcomed by a large crowd of well-wishers. One of the first to greet him in true Indian style, by placing a large garland of flowers round his neck, was a gentleman clad in immaculate white and with a gold coloured turban. It was Mohammed Ali, whose father had said goodbye to the Regiment on that same quayside on the 12th December, 1912, and who had 'presented gifts of gold, frankincense and myrrh' on visiting the C.O. as soon as he had heard that the Battalion was proceeding abroad again. 'Mo', as he was affectionately known to all ranks, was the Regimental Contractor, an appointment which his whole family had jealously guarded for many years. Within a few minutes Monty found himself almost weighed down by the weight of so many garlands placed around his neck by other well-wishers. Parked a short distance away was a brand-new Chevrolet limousine which Mo had brought to put at Monty's disposal. Later, however, it became known that Monty had declined the generous offer, obviously believing that the acceptance of such a gift would place him under some obligation to Mo. Nevertheless, such practices were considered quite normal in those days. Not to be denied, however, Mo placed the car at the disposal of the P.R.I. to be used generally by all officers of the Battalion.

The P.R.I. at that time was 'Pip' Hicks, then a major. He was yet another officer of the Regiment to acquit himself with distinction during the 1939/45 War. Later he became a Brigadier in the Parachute Regiment. His first big operation was with the Allied landings on the Island of Sicily. Unfortunately, while parachuting from an American plane, he was ditched in the sea some distance from land. He still managed to get ashore, however, and in the subsequent fighting distinguished himself in action, for which he was later awarded the D.S.O. He was again to distinguish himself during the memorable airborne operation at Arnhem, where his Brigade was severely mauled. During the night he was successful in leading a party of survivors across the river to safety, for which he was awarded a bar to his D.S.O.

As so often happens in India, the train journey from Bombay to Poona was to commence at about 23.00 hours. This was a disappointment to the troops, who had hoped to have an opportunity of seeing the magnificent scenery of the Western Ghats. The line between Bombay and Poona is an outstanding feat of British engineering, being fully electrified with the overhead system. The powerful locomotives were all made by Metropolitan Vickers. Its most famous train was called the 'Deccan Queen'. It ran in both directions each day, covering the distance of about 110 miles and negotiating about thirty tunnels and many viaducts in a time of about two-and-a-half hours. The highest point in the journey was about 3,000 feet above sea level.

Whilst spending the day on the quayside at Bombay, the troops had their first glimpse of the many and varied activities of the country, with its broad and diverse range of customs and creeds. It was not long before they witnessed a troup of wandering acrobats, complete with bear and monkey, performing their many tricks. In particular a small boy, who performed his repertoire of acrobatic manoeuvres with marvellous dexterity, would not have disgraced many circuses at home. The operations of the caste system soon became apparent. Beggars were active with their customary begging bowls. They also saw for the first time women labourers working as dock hands accompanied by small children. Some of these were slung on their backs and toddlers were running beside them as they went about their arduous work. A further novel sight was the uniform of the Bombay policemen: sandals, blue knickerbocker trousers, blue overall jackets and bright yellow beret-like headgear, not forgetting the umbrella sunshade which each policeman carried stuck in his leather belt. In this way his hands were left free to control the traffic whilst at the same time he carried in his teeth a whistle as an added means of controlling vehicles and pedestrians alike.

As for the wildlife of Bombay, Kite-hawks, those proverbial scavengers of the East were swooping to and fro. The troops soon learned to call them 'shite hawks'. Before long quite a number of them, all unsuspecting, had lost sandwiches and other food which they were carrying, as the astute birds swooped down from behind and snatched such provender agilely from their hands in their talons. Always having an eye open for bird life, Jim watched the graceful Brahminy Kite or Fish Eagle, with its chocolate coloured plumage and white collar, as it glided above the water of the harbour, suddenly plunging down to take an unsuspecting fish in the manner of an osprey. He also noticed a crow, round the neck of which some cruel person had placed a metal collar. Later he learned that the uncivilised natives did this to crows that had been trapped after stealing food as a means of punishment.

Soon after arriving in Bombay each soldier was given, according to custom, a packet of 'Cissors' cigarettes, a two-bar pack of 'Lux' soap and other complimentary gifts of various kinds from well-known manufacturers.

Whilst waiting on the quay, Jim wondered whether his old ayah Luxshembai was still alive. It seemed unlikely since few women in the India of those days lived to any great age. Theirs was no life of ease. In the main it was dominated by child-bearing and hard work. Many women were, by custom, married shortly after birth and it was not uncommon for them to have children at the age of twelve years. Thousands became widowed in early childhood and – again by custom – were not permitted to marry again. The status of the low-caste Indian women was such that they were expected to carry on working almost up to the time when they gave birth. On a later occasion Jim saw a gang of women working on a building site in Poona, where they were acting as hod carriers. At a certain point one of them, without any fuss, gave birth to a baby, which was then placed in a basket. Only a very short time afterwards the mother continued with her work of carrying heavy loads on her head. It was obvious that this poor Indian woman, like so many others of her kind, simply could not afford to stop working for fear of starving, a fate which would have overtaken both herself and the baby she had so recently born.

It was said that at that time the average peasant family lived on four annas a week, which in English money was equivalent to fourpence.

Before the troop train left Bombay it was nearly midnight. As always, the officers and their ladies had first-class compartments, the W.O.s and their families travelled second-class, whilst the troops were accommodated in what was termed third-class, in which they had only wooden slats to sit and sleep on. In point of fact, on a standard railway in India there was an additional class, halfway between second and third, which was termed the 'intermediate' class. Normally only the low-caste people travelled in third-class carriages. Neither third nor 'inter' had toilet seats – only holes over which to squat. When the train was in motion the operation which this entailed was far from easy. All in all, it can be imagined that when travelling by train it was difficult for a soldier to get much sleep.

The train arrived at Ghorpuri Military Siding, Poona Cantonment, at about 6.30 a.m. Here once more Jim felt that he was receiving help from God. He was given a most unexpected welcome by one 'Clive' Eynott, a sergeant in the Indian Army Corps of Clerks, who had been seconded from the 2nd. Battalion when stationed in Bombay some four years previously. He was a Christian and a fellow member of the Soldiers' Christian Association. Jim saw this as yet another fulfilment of the promise of John 10, verse 4: '. . . and when He putteth forth His own sheep, He goeth before them'. Clive and his family, with whom Jim became great friends, lived in Ghorpuri Barracks, about a mile from Wonowrie Barracks where the 1st. Battalion was to spend the next four years.

Before Jim had been able to find out where he was to 'bed down', he was detailed by the R.S.M. as N.C.O. i/c a picquet posted to guard some tents which had been erected close to the sports field. Soon after nightfall he and his fellow 'prowlers' became acutely aware of the many local sounds of the night. Having heard many stories about India from the old 'Indian wallahs', they imagined that almost at any moment they might be confronted by a marauding tiger or the like.

Having had no previous experience of soldiering in India, they had left some food in the containers at the entrance to one of the tents. Suddenly they were awakened by a sound of scuffling and the lid of one of these containers started to move, lifted apparently by some four-legged creature. As several members of the picquet started up, an animal resembling a large cat ran off. One or two thought that it looked like a small leopard and afterwards, as they related the incident, it grew in size – if not in reality, then certainly in imagination. It later transpired that it had been a civet cat, a wild animal frequently to be found scavenging around residential buildings at night. If cornered, civet cats could be extremely vicious. Periodically, when they became a nuisance, the local natives would organise a civet-cat hunt, for which they would use all the dogs they could muster. On one occasion Jim saw a civet cat which had been knocked off a double-storied building in the course of a hunt and had had its leg injured. Despite its injury it was defending itself ferociously against a large pack of dogs, several of which it badly scarred. In the end, however, it was overcome by sheer weight of numbers.

At that time the Poona Garrison consisted of a British Brigade of two infantry battalions together with ancillary units, an Indian Infantry Brigade, and a battalion of Indian cavalry. The second of the two British battalions was the 1st. Battalion, The Green Howards (19th. Foot), which had formerly been known as 'The Princess of Wales' Own Yorkshire Regiment'. It had fought in the Crimean War and later at the Relief of Kimberley during the Boer War. True to tradition, the Green Howards had an outstandingly good cricket team. Colonel Ramsden, their C.O., had at one time played in one of the Yorkshire County elevens.

Throughout India most barracks appear to have been of standard construction, with large double-storied barrack blocks, well spaced and with latrines and other ablution buildings some little distance away. They had no windows as such but rather 'window spaces'. These were provided with shutters to keep out the heat during the day and the rain during the monsooon. No modern sanitation had been provided and the lavatories were of the type known to the troops as 'thunder boxes'. These were emptied twice daily into a cylindrical bullock-drawn vehicle which went by the name of the 'Bombay Mail'.

One morning, shortly after arriving at Wonowrie Barracks, one of Jim's friends was sitting on one of the thunder boxes when he suddenly became aware that he had a companion in the form of a live cobra. No sooner did Frank move than the large snake lifted its head in readiness to strike. Frank for his part did not wait for this to happen. He dashed headlong out pulling up his shorts as he ran. Thereafter most of the troops would take a stick with them when they visited the 'bogs'.

Among other creatures which scavenged at night were the large rat-like animals called bandicoots. Some time later, Jim was living on the third floor of an officers' hostel in Bombay, where it was forcibly brought home to him that bandicoots would penetrate even that far into a building. In the course of one particular night he was awakened two or three times by the sound of something moving on the bedside table. Soon afterwards he heard it again and it seemed to be eating the soap which he had placed there. He took a swipe at the creature and as he did so the large bandicoot (for that was what it was) ran straight across his face and out of the window.

There were many other nocturnal creatures, including hordes of 'flying foxes' (fruit bats). They could be heard screeching as they ravaged the fruit of the banyan trees which abounded around most camps. These bird-like creatures were often killed by flying into telegraph wires and their corpses could be seen lying beneath the poles.

Even in the cantonments an abundance of bird life was to be found. Mynahs were as common as sparrows in England and the staccato piping of the Coppersmith Bird or Crimson-breasted Barbet persisted monotonously throughout the day. Large flocks of Rose-ringed Parakeets would occasionally wheel past at great speed before settling chattering in a nearby tree. Of course the proverbial Kite-hawk was always around, lurking unobtrusively round the buildings ready to swoop down on anyone who ventured outside with food in his hand. From time to time Kite-hawks could be seen attempting to catch a quick-running tree rat as it scavenged for food round a tree trunk, but Jim never saw a kite actually succeed in catching one of these nimble, squirrel-like creatures.

Poona was one of those pleasant stations in India situated almost on the western edge of the Deccan Plateau and sheltered under the lee of the Western Ghats. Even the nights were never really cold and although in the hot weather day-time temperatures sometimes reached 110 degrees fahrenheit, it was not nearly so hot as stations in the United Provinces, where for long periods during May and June temperatures were rarely lower than 110 to 115 degrees. In comparison with most places in India, the rainfall too was quite low, an advantage it owed to the shelter afforded by the Western Ghats. During an average monsoon the rainfall would amount to about 25 to 30 inches as compared with 300 inches of rain recorded at Mahbaleshwar, only 40 miles away in the Western Ghats.

On the field of sport officers and other ranks alike could always enjoy plenty of activity in the traditional games. Apart from these, clubs were available for all, where they could take part in pleasant social activities. The Poona racecourse, situated just outside Wonowrie, provided an excellent racing calendar.

As the Battalion arrived in Poona, about five months of hot weather lay ahead. During this period the daily routine commenced with Reveille at 5.30

a.m., followed by one period of work or training before breakfast. This was followed by a further two hours of work until 11 a.m. The mid-day meal was at 12 noon, after which everyone rested until about 4 p.m. In the evening after tea almost everyone took part in some sporting activity. So far as Jim was concerned, he actually got up about five a.m. to go for a run and perform physical exercises.

It was during this half hour before Reveille that the 'Nappi' (Indian barber) would commence his rounds, carrying a small charcoal brazier for hot water, an open razor, and a lather brush. He would lift up a soldier's mosquito net, lather his face, and then shave him, all this being done while the subject himself was still comatose. This daily service cost the individual one anna per day. Every soldier had the services of a bearer (servant), one being shared among several soldiers at a cost of eight annas a week. N.C.O.s usually had one bearer between three, whilst those living in married quarters had a bearer to themselves as well as a 'bawarchi' (cook), at a cost of about one rupee eight annas a week plus any food that was left over. Dirty washing was collected each evening by the dhobi and returned the following day. Most items of underwear would cost an anna each, and the cost of laundering a complete khaki drill suit was four annas. The dhobi had an incredible system of marking. He marked each soldier's clothes with an invisible 'dhobi mark', which consisted of a series of hieroglyphic lines and dots. Jim's particular mark happened to be relatively simple: three perpendicular lines.

In those days the basic rate of pay of a private soldier was a mere two shillings a day while that of a sergeant was six shillings. However, providing he obtained the necessary qualifications, a soldier could add substantially to this by earning proficiency pay. Despite these extremely low rates of pay, the cost of living in India at that time was so amazingly low that any soldier, provided he was reasonably thrifty, could make quite substantial savings. To give one illustration: wherereas the actual rate of exchange was thirteen rupees eight annas to the pound, the official rate at which soldiers were paid was fifteen rupees to the pound. Hence it was possible to spend a pound in Indian currency and still have one rupee and eight annas left, equivalent to about two shillings in English money.

Because of the extreme poverty among the majority of Indians, stealing by 'loose wallahs' was always a major problem and the soldier always had to take every precaution against it. All weapons had to be made secure at all times. Rifles were placed in a large rack which had a bar or chain running through the trigger guards, attached at either end to a large lock. At night a pilot-light was kept burning over each rifle-rack, and in addition four soldiers would place their beds round it as protection. Nevertheless, despite all these stringent precautions, cases were known of loose wallahs penetrating the defences and stealing rifles. For any soldier to lose a rifle or bayonet was a very serious crime indeed. Any instance of this usually resulted in the negligent soldier being tried by Courts Martial.

Innumerable hawkers used to hover constantly round barracks and married quarters, endeavouring to make a little money. At meal times a number of them would wait on dining room verandahs to sell their wares. Thus there would be the 'fruit wallah', the 'dhud wallah' selling milk , and even a man who sold eggs and bacon heated on a small charcoal fire so as to provide a supplement to breakfast for those who wished.

In the evenings, when the soldiers were not playing games, they would sit on the barrack room steps, where they were often visited by the 'corn wallah'. For a few annas he would perform the duties of a chiropodist, though with very primitive tools. He had an old cut throat razor which he used to trim down hard skin, while to extricate corns he used a minute horn with which he used to suck them out. A fortune teller also used to ply his trade. His patter invariably commenced with: 'Sahib, me tell you good fortune... You go soon on a long voyage. You then marry dark lady and have many children'. When he was pressed to say when the journey would take place he would always reply: 'Very, very soon, Sahib'.

While serving in India many of the soldiers, especially those who did not participate in the sporting activities, found themselves with much time on their hands. This they used to apply to the cultivation of various hobbies. One of the most popular was the crocheting of large bedspreads which they made out of the wool of old army socks supplemented by wool of more variegated colours. Some soldiers developed more elaborate skills, equipping themselves with wooden frames on which they made table cloths.

Shortly after the Battalion arrived in Poona, General Sir George Jefferies, the G.O.C. of Southern Command, carried out his inaugural inspection. The Battalion was formed up in Ceremonial Review Order on the Poona race course. General Sir George's reputation had preceded him. He was known to be brusque in manner and to expect an extremely high standard of turnout 'à la Guards'. On the morning he arrived for the inspection, following the correct procedure, Monty gave the order, 'General salute, present arms!' the moment he stepped out of his chauffeur-driven car. A moment later Sir George walked up to the subalterns carrying the Colours and gave a demonstration of the correct way of carrying them. He certainly gave the impression that in his Command there was only one boss. In retrospect, indeed, this was, perhaps, one of the few occasions when Monty looked rather sheepish as he trailed a step or two behind that commanding figure. Sir George then went on to inspect the Band and Drums and was highly critical of the way in which the various accoutrements had been blancoed. As he sauntered, still talking to Monty, along the rear rank of the drummers, he noticed out of the corner of his eye that one of them did not have his heels together in the prescribed military fashion and, with a single deft kick, he quickly rectified the soldier's slovenliness.

After the inspection had been completed, everyone expected that the Battalion would march back to barracks. Here again, however, Sir George, true to form, proved that he had other ideas. He ordered Monty to march away all companies with the exception of 'A' Company, which, he said, he would like to see carrying out certain drill movements. The Company Commander of 'A' happened to be 'Pam', who had never really aspired to be a soldier and was, perhaps the least qualified of all the Company Commanders in the noble art of 'square bashing'. Sir George, on the other hand, Guardsman that he was, knew the Drill Manual from A to Z. He indicated what movements he wanted performed and then left Pam to issue the relevant orders. There is no doubt that Pam would have felt himself far more at home had he been questioned on the liturgy of the Church of England. It was painfully obvious that his knowledge of the Drill Manual left much to be desired. Orders he gave, for all that, though not the ones therein prescribed. Even so, the C.S.M. and senior N.C.O.s of the Company, determined not to let him down, quietly relayed to the troops what to do, thereby managing to ensure some uniformity of movement.

After it was over it was all too obvious that Sir George had not been fooled, and he later communicated his displeasure to Monty. Although no one, apart from Monty himself, really knew what the General had said, the outcome was that Pam was made a scapegoat and almost immediately returned to England to retire. He later became a parson, which was certainly more up his street. Afterwards, when those who had taken part in those memorable manoeuvres were talking them over, they concluded that on that particular day 'A' Company had been like a flock of sheep without a shepherd. Knowing Monty, however, one can hardly doubt that once Sir George had departed he would have lost little or no sleep in worrying over such trivialities.

Keen horseman that he was, Monty could be seen on most evenings riding his charger. Even in this sphere, however, he managed to break with tradition. Whereas other officers would wear a white silk shirt for such activities, Monty sported one of a distinctive open-necked type of dark blue.

Absence from home for such long periods, coupled with the strain of serving for several years in the heat, often told on the health of certain soldiers. Sometimes a letter bringing bad news from home would add to the depression. The upshot would not uncommonly be that such soldiers, if they had no real 'anchor' in life, would crack under the strain of their private miseries and take their own lives. Strangely enough, this frequently happened while most of the other men were out of barracks on Church Parades on Sundays. At this time the troubled soldier concerned might be acting as Room Orderly for the day and therefore have access to the rifles and ammunition box.

It was the custom in India for a soldier who died in the morning to be buried by military funeral at sundown, while one who died in the evening would be buried the following morning. A couple of coffins were always held in readiness in the Pioneers' Shop. Those were the days before antibiotics were available and death often struck quite suddenly. It was also a period when malaria was quite prevalent. Although Poona itself was almost free of the disease, at Kirkee, only five miles away, it was rampant. Companies of the two battalions stationed at Poona used to take it in turns to do duty at the Arsenal and Ammunition Factory at Kirkee. On one occasion when Jim's Company was doing a stint at the Factory at Kirkee, almost every soldier went down with malaria – and this despite all the precautions which soldiers had to take! Jim, for some reason or other, was evidently immune to it. One possible explanation is that at the time of his birth his mother was suffering from the disease, which may have given him a built-in immunity.

By the end of their first May in India all troops were eagerly awaiting the monsoon. It could be counted upon to provide a much needed respite from the long period of hot weather. By the time it arrived, throughout the entire countryside not a blade of grass was to be found and even the poor sacred cows that wandered about the cantonment could be seen eating every piece of litter they could find. Oh for a few sacred cows round the streets of England! Within a few days of the rains coming, the whole countryside would be transformed, with vegetation and new life springing up everywhere as reptiles and other creatures emerged. It was during this period that the birds made their nests and hatched their eggs, for it was then that ready sources of food became available for the young ones which they had to rear.

Although other stations suffered from a superabundance of monkeys, Poona was comparatively free of this scourge. However, the soldiers were able to buy them as pets from natives who came in from other parts.

One soldier in 'A' Company acquired a small brown monkey as a pet and it became a 'monkey' indeed – in more senses than one. So much was this the case that the soldier concerned became tired of its antics and offered it free to any prospective handler. A certain 'Tich', an animal lover from the Transport Platoon, took the little animal under his care. The first day he had it he left it tethered to his bed in the barrack room, but the monkey slipped its lead and on his return he found a trail of carnage. When he finally captured it, it had covered itself in ink, so he decided to give it a bath. Taking it to the ablution room he chained it to a tap, but the moment he began pouring water on it the creature went completely berserk. No one could come near it without being attacked. In attempting to calm the frightened animal Tich received a very nasty bite. So sharp were the monkey's teeth that it actually bit a lump of flesh out of Tich's chest; it looked just as though it had been done with two razor blades. Of course Tich had to get his chest stitched immediately but this was not all; he also had to undergo an extremely painful course of injections against rabies and in the end the monkey had to be destroyed.

Mention of anti-rabies treatment brings to mind another incident which befel a lance-corporal in Jim's barrack room. One of the inmates was a soldier named Luke. He was one of those characters who have no sense of humour and are often the subject of leg-pulling on the part of his comrades. The episode of the monkey had evoked a general awareness of the need for anti-rabies precautions. Now Luke had a pet dog and one day, when he returned to the barrack room, he was told that there was a scare about rabies; all dog owners were advised to report to the M.I. Room for treatment as a precaution. Taking this as gospel, Luke went immediately to the M.I. Room and volunteered to have the anti-rabies injections. In physique he happened to be one of the 'lean kine' with little superfluous flesh, but so uncharacteristically large was the swelling resulting from the first injection that he looked almost as if he were pregnant. The same procedure had to be repeated every day for a fortnight and the discomfort which poor Luke had to endure can well be imagined. It was only after the full course of treatment had been completed that Luke learned of the horrible joke which had been played upon him.

During the hot weather many of the troops used to go to bathe at a lake about twelve miles from the barracks called Karakvasla Lake. Even this, however, had its repercussions. A party of men from Jim's barrack room, ignoring all the advice they had been given about the importance of treating the sun's rays with respect, lay in the sun after bathing and as a result were so severely burnt that their backs were simply raw and they had to go to hospital for treatment.

A frequent visitor to Karakvasla was 'Taffy' Evans, the Sergeant of the Signal Platoon, who was an incredible character. At times he could memorise as though his brain were a computer, yet on other occasions he could appear unusually forgetful. Often he would cycle to the lake, but sometimes he would walk the entire distance there and back. One day he was seen to cycle off with his bathing kit underneath his arm. It was late evening before he returned to barracks and he declared that while he had been away someone had stolen his bicycle. 'But Taffy,' one of his comrades protested, 'I saw you going off on it this morning.' 'Did you?' he rejoined in surprise and then, looking as though a flash of light had struck him, he suddenly turned away. He had just remembered that he had cycled to Karakvasla that morning! In the end he walked the entire distance back to the lake before retrieving his cycle and returning on it. Despite all this, the following morning when Taffy called the roll of the Signal Platoon he was certainly thoroughly alert. As was his habit, he called the roll of the whole Platoon of some thirty soldiers entirely from memory, without once having to consult a book.

Another incident occurring about the same time might have had far more serious consequences. A small party of soldiers from the Battalion went exploring in the vicinity of the foothills of the Western Ghats. On their return journey they were passing a small native village where, as in so many Indian villages, the young boys and girls were completely naked. Being very thirsty the soldiers said to the children: 'Pine ka pani kahan se letcho?', which means: 'Where do you get drinking water?' While they were still talking, they were suddenly attacked by some men from the village with large 'lahtis' in their hands. It was obvious that the villagers thought that the soldiers were trying to molest the young girls. However, the troops lost no time in beating a hasty retreat before other men from the village arrived.

Some misunderstandings did arise in India from time to time, invariably caused by the lack of communication. A few incidents had more serious consequences and one such occurred at Jubbalpur, a military station in the Central Provinces. The regiment involved in this instance was The King's (Liverpool) Regiment (8th. Foot). It always had the reputation of being a tough regiment, a fair proportion of their soldiers being Liverpool Irish. It transpired that after a member of the regiment had been beaten to death by some local Indians in their village, some of his pals went back there bent on revenge. An extremely bloody battle followed, culminating in more than one native being killed. Naturally the incident, being detrimental to the British Army, received wide coverage in most Indian newspapers. As a direct result, all the soldiers who had been involved were tried by Courts Martial, some of them receiving very heavy sentences. In addition, the 'King's' were immediately transferred to Mooltan, a station in the Punjab which had the reputation of being a 'punishment station'. Strangely enough, the Commanding Officer of the King's at that time was a Lieut. Colonel King, who was known as 'King of The King's'.

At an earlier stage in the Battalion's history mention has been made of Norman Boyer, who won the King's Medal at Bisley in 1930. Norman already aspired, whenever an opportunity should arise, to become a shikari. Soon after arriving at Poona, he joined a party of local shikaris on a panther shoot. This was his first 'tiger hunt' and of course, being a proud shot, he would not lower his dignity by resorting to the use of a machan built in a tree for safety. Instead he used the cover of a 'ground machan'. When all the other arrangements had been completed, he tethered a small kid to a tree stump with the object, of course, of attracting a panther by means of the kid's cries during the stillness of the night. The first two nights which Norman and his friends spent in their ground machan were devoid of success, though they did give them a chance to accustom themselves to all the other weird calls of the night and the general sounds of the jungle. They heard a panther calling to its mate some distance away, but it did not come anywhere near them. It was decided to spend just one more night of vigil in the ground machan in the hope of a kill. Just as they were beginning to lose hope, Norman suddenly observed the silhouette of a large animal approaching the kid. As it came closer he realised that his chance had come at last. Before its final approach to the kid the panther paused in an obvious listening attitude and looked all round it prior to going in for its meal. All this time Norman was keeping absolutely motionless, imagining that even his breathing would attract the leopard's attention. By this time he had raised his rifle in readiness. Though the animal was perfectly visible in his sights, he had decided to wait until it was preoccupied with its intended victim before pressing the trigger. At that point he noticed that the large 'cat' was behaving as any other cat would have done when confronted with prey. It pawed it with its rapier-like claws, knocking it to the ground. Then, just as it paused before seizing it in its mouth, Norman slowly squeezed the trigger. With a savage growl the large animal rolled straight over on its side. This was followed by a somewhat ominous silence. Norman's first thoughts were for safety, for he knew that once wounded, a 'tiger' becomes far more cunning and dangerous. He therefore decided to wait a few moments longer. Then, carefully approaching the animal with his finger still on the trigger, he stood a few feet away where he could ensure that it was indeed dead. What a thrill it was to realise that at long last, after becoming a successful target shot, he had achieved one of his lifelong ambitions and had become a successful shikari too! Soon afterwards the rest of the party arrived and the panther was lashed to a pole in the customary manner, to be carried triumphantly back to the 'dak' bungalow. Finally the party returned to display the trophy for all to see before handing it over to the local taxidermists to preserve the skin.

This tale brings to mind another shikari episode with which Jim was concerned while stationed at Poona. A friend of his, one Robin Heathcote, was an Assistant Surgeon in the Indian Medical Service. He shared Norman's love of big-game hunting and he and another doctor friend used to pay the natives from several villages in well known panther country for information of animal sightings. The amount they paid, though in itself quite small, was naturally greatly increased when the information supplied resulted in a kill. One day they received a telegram saying: 'Three tigers in our village. Come at once'. They lost no time in setting off in Robin's old open Chevrolet Tourer. On arriving at the village they found the inhabitants waiting for them in a state of tremendous excitement. Almost every native had equipped himself with a stick in readiness to act as a beater. They learned that one adult panther and two small cubs had been surrounded by the villagers in a small thicket. As the animals were not immediately visible, the head beater gave the order to close the cordon in. The scantily clad natives, brandishing their lathis and beating cans, slowly advanced into the bush. Such was the noise they were making that by this time the very demons in hell must surely have begun to take fright. As the cordon closed, the animals were spotted from time to time until finally they were completely isolated in a small clump of bamboo, only about twenty yards in diameter. Suddenly, almost without warning, there was a general stampede. The adult panther, realising that they were being trapped, had made a dash for freedom followed by her cubs. As they did so, all three broke through the cordon, scattering the natives in all directions. As they shot past they actually bowled some of them over like ninepins. In the course of this animal charge the smaller panthers became separated from their parent, whereupon they ran into a small thicket and froze. Meanwhile the larger animal, more experienced in eluding the wiles of mankind, had last been seen disappearing into thicker jungle some distance away. The young – almost full grown as it turned out – were soon killed and were then lashed to the two front wings of the car to be taken back to Poona. At the same time the jubilant villagers were paid off, returning to recount every joyful detail of the successful day's work. There can be no doubt that such episodes as these were red-letter days in their otherwise drab and uninteresting existence. Today, of course, such wanton sacrilege as panther-hunting is completely taboo.

Not every 'tiger' hunt was as successful as the ones just described. Another episode, reported by *The Times of India*, had very serious consequences. It took place near a village named Yesvantapur, some few miles distant from Bangalore in South India. Here a careless shikari committed one of the cardinal sins by failing to follow up a tiger which he had wounded. As a result the animal became a man-eater. Jim Corbett, that great shikari of the Kumaon Himalayas, has said that a tiger usually becomes a man-eater either because it is too old to catch its normal prey or because it has been wounded. In the latter case, he explains, it will become much more dangerous as well as extremely cunning, often seeking to seize unsuspecting humans, normally young children or peasants working in the fields close to the animal's cover. The 'Tiger of Yesvantapur' killed no less than six people before it was ultimately despatched by an organised shoot of experienced shikaris. During the first decade of the century two man-eaters between them killed over eight hundred human beings in the Kumaon Hills of Northern India.

Monty's last nine months in command of the Battalion were quite uneventful except for two unfortunate incidents. During that period another officer was ordered to curtail his tour and take early retirement because of his habits of excessive drinking, while another was given an ultimatum for having failed to pass the entrance examination prior to attending a course of instruction. Monty always made it abundantly clear that he would not tolerate any officer failing to maintain a high standard both in efficiency and behaviour.

In the autumn of 1934 it was learned that Monty had been appointed Chief Instructor at the Staff College, Quetta and was to be promoted Colonel. On the day of his departure from Poona in November of that year, he maintained his reputation for originality to the last, for he decided that he would shake hands with every soldier in the Battalion. In the cool of the evening, clad in his customary blue shirt and shorts, he stood on the verandah outside his office whilst every man filed past to shake his hand. Significantly, when it came to Jim's turn he paused, obviously remembering the confrontation they had had in the C.O.'s Office at Alexandria. 'Well, Pickerwing,' he said, 'I'm going. You'll get on well now!' At that time Jim was still only a lance-corporal even though he had qualified for promotion nearly four years before.

Chapter 12

A Change of Command

The officer who succeeded Monty as Commander of the Battalion was Lieut.-Colonel J. P. Duke. He introduced himself to all the W.O.s and N.C.O.s by means of a 'pep talk' with the slogan, 'Smartness on all occasions'. He made it clear that his aim was to maintain an unvaryingly high standard of turnout.

It seemed no coincidence that no sooner had Monty departed than Mollie (she who had caught an early boat from Alexandria after her affair with the young lance-corporal) returned to the Battalion for another tour of duty or, as later transpired, to pastures new in her love life. Somehow she seemed to have a passion for good-looking young lance-corporals and in little or no time her endearing ways had won the heart of yet another young chap with one stripe on his arm and an inability to resist her seductions. At what seemed an opportune moment he acceded to an invitation to visit her in the 'boudoir' of her married quarter, naturally at a time when her husband Bill was out of station and naturally under cover of darkness. Her house happened to be in the centre of a block of terraced married quarters near the football field, very conveniently situated and easily accessible. In order to enable the air to circulate during the hot weather it was normal for the doors of married quarters to be kept open, protected only by curtains of bead or bamboo. At a time they had previously arranged, the 'lover', clad in a pair of light shoes (known to the troops as 'brothel creepers'), surreptitiously approached the quarter. Quietly and unobtrusively he entered the doorway, his heart, no doubt, beginning to throb with anticipation. 'Mollie', he called softly, 'it's all right, it's only me'. Somewhat to his surprise there was no Mollie waiting suitably attired and with arms outstretched to receive him. Thinking that she must be in the room through the middle door, he called a fraction louder. Suddenly, to his utter astonishment and confusion, who should he find confronting him but 'Big Sid', the C.S.M. of

'C' Company. He too was somewhat taken aback by the intrusion, although later it became apparent that he had been well aware of the blossoming friendship between the young N.C.O. and his next-door neighbour. He soon realised, however, that the unexpected visitor had mistaken his married quarter for the one next door. By this time the lance-corporal was thoroughly frightened but Sid, without asking any further questions, seized him by the collar and pants and ejected him, depositing him with considerable force on the football pitch outside. The upshot of this second nefarious episode was that Mollie once more departed prematurely for the U.K.

Mention has previously been made of the Regimental Contractor who was present when the Battalion arrived at Bombay. Every Regiment of the British Army in India had its own Contractor, who was a leading figure in the system which then prevailed. His responsibility was to provide a comprehensive service covering tailoring, shoe repairing, laundering, hair-cutting, canteens, families' shop and numerous other small amenities. In consequence he employed a fairly large Indian staff, many of whom were Mohammedans. The shops and canteen were usually situated in the centre of barracks. Although many of the services were provided on a cash system, those of tailoring, shoe repairing, laundering and hair-cutting were operated on a system of 'chits'. This meant that the soldier signed the appropriate 'chit' and the relevant sum was ultimately deducted direct from his pay. C.Q.M.S.s were responsible for controlling and collecting cash at the end of each month. As companies were normally about one hundred and fifty strong, the amount of money involved was quite considerable.

Although no official signed agreement existed on the matter, it was common knowledge and universally accepted that the C.Q.M.S. received about ten per cent of the cash he collected on behalf of the Contractor. Naturally, therefore, the C.Q.M.S. was in an enviable position and it is understandable that many were reluctant to accept promotion because of the financial advantage which they enjoyed.

Some families used the Contractor's services when it suited them, whilst others, particularly when it came to tailoring, would go to the local bazaar, purchase the necessary materials, and then employ a private 'dursi' to carry out the work on their own verandah. In an emergency a dursi would measure, make up, fit and finish an article of clothing in twenty-four hours at a very small cost – perhaps as little as from five to ten rupees.

Troops were always encouraged to have pets, the most common being dogs. However, a strict registration procedure was in force and all animals were periodically inspected by an official vet. Occasionally a mongoose was kept and a few men had parrots. The origin of the Army phrase, 'Pick up your parrots and monkeys', emanated from India, where in times past most troop movements were carried out on foot. Prior to moving off after a halt, the Sergeant-Major would give the preliminary order: 'Pick up your parrots and monkeys'.

Some years later, Jim was staying with friends in Bombay who had a Himalayan green parrot called Popeye. In the quietness of the afternoon when most of the household were resting, Popeye could be heard reciting his own pet piece as follows: 'Pretty Polly, Pretty dear, all the way from Kashmir. Did he walk it? No fear! Too far for Pretty Polly, dear'. The phrase 'TOO FAR FOR PRETTY POLLY DEAR' would be repeated loudly and again and again.

A month after the arrival of the new C.O. the Battalion proceeded by train to a camp in the vicinity of Sholapur, some 180 miles by train from Poona, to carry out its annual training. Although it had been intended that the return journey too should be by train, the C.O. decided that despite having only just completed a march of 42 miles during its last training exercise, the Battalion would also march the whole distance back to Poona, making a grand total of 220 miles of marching. The irony of it was that at that time reports in British newspapers had indicated that in order to save money one of the Battalions of His Majesty's Guards was going to march from London to Purbright, a paltry thirty miles or so! During the long march it was decided that in order to avoid the heat of the day, the march would be carried out in stints of approximately 20 miles each night. For even the fittest of soldiers, to complete such a march was no small feat. Nevertheless, it was announced before it began that any soldier who failed to complete it through sore feet would lose his proficiency pay for the following year.

Marching by night was at best thoroughly tedious, but over and above this, the dusty roads on which the Battalion was travelling were grooved by the tracks of bullock carts, rendering the going extremely difficult. At the beginning of the march the men were singing the familiar tune, 'Happy is the day when the Warwicks get their pay, marching, marching, marching all night long'. As the march progressed, however, and stragglers began to fall by the wayside, the words were changed to 'Shocking is the day when the Warwicks lose their pay, falling, falling, falling on the way'. On the whole, the Battalion marched extremely well, although this march could never be compared with the legendary one from Kabul to Kandahar during the previous century. However, as they approached the great city of Poona, the troops, for all their weariness, braced themselves with pride as they entered

Wonowrie Barracks to the strains of 'The Saucy Sixth' and 'Warwickshire Lads and Lasses' played by the Band and Drums.

Many of the soldiers, though taxed to the very limits with exhaustion and sore feet, had refused to give in, some even carrying their badly worn ammunition boots on their shoulders for the last few miles rather than fall by the wayside and lose their proficiency pay.

It was Christmas Eve when the Battalion arrived back, and on the following day, Christmas Day, 1934, over a hundred men had to attend sick parade to obtain treatment for their blisters. The few soldiers of the 'Rear Party' who had not gone to Sholapur did their utmost to give the Battalion a cheery welcome back by decorating all the dining rooms in a thoroughly festive manner. Each Company had worked hard to produce the best decorated hall, for which a prize was awarded out of P.R.I. funds. Some of the wall decorations were highly ingenious. Army brown blankets had been decorated with cotton wool to resemble Christmas cards. Nevertheless, many of the troops were so exhausted that they chose to remain in bed all Christmas Day and Boxing Day in order to recover.

Early in January, 1935, Jim had to make a journey of about two hundred miles south to Belgaum in order to attend a course of instruction at the Army School of Education. The journey from Poona to Belgaum was made on the narrow gauge railway known as the Maharatta and Madras South Indian Railway. On this particular journey he experienced a convenience seldom provided on any other railway in the world. During one of the stops the train guard visited each carriage to take orders for the evening meal. At the appropriate station all the passengers who had ordered a meal were ushered to the restaurant to find it waiting for them. Moreover there was no hurry; the guard told them that the train would wait until all diners had completed their meal and were ready to depart.

Nine years later, in 1946, Jim happened to be travelling with his wife and two children from Bombay to Bangalore when they came to this same station and had an experience which they would never forget. On this occasion, because of the presence of young children, the bearer brought the food to the carriage. It comprised curry for the adults and other dishes for the children, together with fresh bananas. To the consternation of everyone, however, no sooner had the bearer put the fruit on the table than a large monkey shot through the open window, snatched up all the fruit, at the same time knocking the tray of curry and rice onto the floor, and finally disappeared by the way he had entered.

So far as the two children were concerned, the incident had a profound effect. Ever afterwards, whenever they saw an animal approaching they were petrified. Subsequently it became apparent that the local hordes of monkeys swarmed towards the station whenever they heard a train approaching, and although seasoned travellers were aware of the menace, those who were new to the journey, as in the case of Jim's family, often lost a good part of their food.

It will be remembered that Belgaum was the station where the Battalion had been stationed about thirty years before in 1906, and that it was here that the three soldiers had cut cards to decide who would shoot the Adjutant. Belgaum was also the Depot of The Maharatta Light Infantry, one of India's famous regiments. It is situated on a plateau under the lee of the Western Ghats. It lies almost directly inland from the ancient Portuguese Port of Goa, and also a short distance from that most beautiful of all South Indian cities, Bangalore, which has often been called 'The Pensioners' Paradise'.

In the Course-joining Instructions it was laid down that on arrival students would be met by a 'dumni' or trotting bullock cart. It was a 'covered waggon' type of vehicle with no seats, so that when and if the bullock did begin to trot, the poor occupant crouching in the back had a most uncomfortable ride. The normal conveyance in most parts of India was a 'tonga', a two-seated horse-drawn cart which was both comfortable and cheap. A few of the larger cities also provided coolie-drawn rickshaws and a few horse carriages of Victorian type could sometimes be found.

Shortly after arriving at Belgaum, Jim was sitting studying under a Banyan tree one afternoon when an English-looking gentleman approached him. He was highly surprised to find that it was indeed himself that the man was looking for. He was, it transpired, a Mr. Atkinson, an Australian missionary who lived with his family in a village called Khanpur, some twelve miles down the railway line, and he now invited Jim to spend a weekend with them. The Atkinsons were one of only two English-speaking families living in a small Hindu village on the banks of a minor river. Mr. Atkinson's missionary work was carried out on foot. He visited the many small hamlets within a radius of about thirty miles, as well as working among a very large 'criminal tribe' in a Government-controlled settlement nearby. Early on the Sunday morning which he spent with the Atkinsons, Jim went for a walk through the village down to the river, where he saw the Hindu women washing the family's clothes by beating them on large smooth rocks at the water's edge. As he passed through the village, he saw for the first time an original 'juggernaut'. It was not what we in England now know as a juggernaut, namely a larger-than-large motor vehicle.

Rather it was an immense Hindu idol made of wood and on wooden wheels. Evidently it was taken out on Hindu festivals to form the spearhead of the celebratory processions.

After breakfast the whole family took part in an open-air Sunday School meeting, which was attended by well over a hundred children of all ages from the nearby criminal tribe. They sang many of the familiar C.S.S.M. choruses in their own language of Tamil. Later they had an opportunity to quote verses of scripture which they had learnt by heart, and for which they were rewarded by being given pieces of bread. After this a special picnic was held at which the families were joined by a young Scottish woman missionary in her early twenties, together with her 'family' of some twenty or more orphan children. These she had taken under her care at a small village some distance away in the jungle. Whilst all the children and some of the grown-ups were enjoying a pre-lunch swim in the small river, Miss Robertson and Mrs. Atkinson prepared the dinner of curried chicken and rice. The whole company sat down in a large circle around the edge of a very large 'durri' (Indian carpet). In front of each person a banana leaf had been laid to serve as a plate. On these helpings of hot food were placed. Of course there were no eating utensils other than the fingers of either hand. Coconut milk was drunk from the shell, after which the children were given a real treat in the form of delicious mangoes as the fruit course. When the party ended the grown-ups returned to the Atkinsons' bungalow for yet another small party, at which the guest of honour was a small Hindu girl named Shanta. It was her seventh birthday.

Later Jim heard the story of this child's remarkable deliverance from the insidious slavery of pagan worship. Shanta's home had been a Hindu temple, where she had been subjected to treatment of a pagan ritualistic sort. Then suddenly she had been taken very ill and had not been expected to live. At that point the priests had sought the help of the local missionaries. These had agreed to provide medicine and care, provided that she was permitted to be looked after by them. The outcome was remarkable. After the child had been restored to good health, Miss Robertson was able to take her into her own 'family'. Although only seven years of age, Shanta repeatedly expressed a wish to be trained as a 'Bible Woman' so that she could go back and tell other Hindu children about the Lord Jesus who had 'saved' her. The child's face simply radiated happiness – so different from those of many of the Hindu children brought up in pagan homes, surrounded by superstition and lacking in love.

It was through the Atkinsons that Jim received another invitation to spend a weekend with a Mr. de Carteret and his family, who were working among lepers at a nearby leper colony some five miles from Belgaum. The route to the leper colony took him past the notorious Belgaum Jail. The gallows, a permanent fixture at the jail, could easily be seen as he passed by. In the grounds prisoners could be seen working in the fields and tending the crops. They also worked in teams to draw water from a large well. All their legs were in chains and those working by themselves had their legs attached to a heavy iron ball so that whenever they wanted to move they had either to drag the ball or else lift and carry it. Close to the jail Jim saw a colony of flying foxes (fruit bats). Their roosting place was a large tree devoid of any leaves and the creatures were hanging like coconuts, swaying in the breeze and keeping up a ceaseless jostling and screeching. At dusk the colony must have looked like a large armada as it sallied forth to maraud and pillage fruit trees in the vicinity.

On the Sunday morning of his stay with the de Carterets Jim joined the family at the service of the Breaking of Bread in the colony chapel. It was attended by a considerable number of Christian lepers, though of course they had their own chalice and loaf of bread. Many of them were seriously scarred and maimed by the dreaded disease, some with 'stumps' where limbs had once been and others with gaping eye sockets minus the eyes. Nevertheless, all appeared to have acquired a peace and dignity which Jim had not seen among the other lepers who could be found grovelling in the cities and towns of India. That evening Jim had the rare opportunity, as well as the privilege, of being invited to give the 'message' at the evening service in the chapel. As he spoke, Mr. de Carteret translated what he was saying into the native tongue of the congregation. It was a truly awe-inspiring experience of real missionary work.

One afternoon Jim decided that it would be interesting to look around the Military Cemetery at Belgaum. Unfortunately it was not particularly well kept. It was not long before he came across the graves of those – a considerable number – who had died during the time when the Battalion had been stationed there about 1906. Two graves in particular interested him. The first was that of a subaltern who had 'died of gunshot wounds', while the other was that of a private soldier who had died about six weeks later. The latter bore the bald inscription, 'Died', together with the date. No cause of death was assigned, and in this respect it was at variance with all other soldiers' graves. These, therefore, could well have been the graves of the Adjutant murdered on parade and of the soldier who shot him.

It was also apparent that a number of soldiers, as well as wives and children, had died as a result of a cholera epidemic. Among these was the wife and infant child of Colour-Sergeant Girling. This particular family had served the Regiment well. In 1925, when Jim joined, one of Colour-Sergeant Girling's brothers was still serving; he too was a Colour-Sergeant. Many years later, in the late fifties, some time after he had retired, Jim found himself sitting opposite a gentleman and his wife in a cafe at Uckfield. In the course of conversation Jim remarked that his face appeared very familiar and asked whether he had ever been a soldier and whether he lived in the vicinity. The man replied that he and his wife lived in Bristol and were merely passing through the town. Then to Jim's utter amazement he discovered that this man was in fact the brother of that C.Q.M.S. Girling whom Jim had known in the Regiment forty years before. He also confirmed that he was the brother of the C.Q.M.S. Girling whose wife had been buried in Belgaum.

When he had first been selected to attend the Education Course at the Military School of Education at Belgaum, Jim, who had left school at fourteen, had felt himself wholly inadequate. One slight saving grace was that he had had a few months' experience in the Regimental School, helping with the teaching of 2nd. Class Certificate candidates. Nevertheless he now made a determined effort to do well, and on returning to the Battalion after completing the Course he was informed that he had obtained a 'Qualified Class I' Certificate with 'Distinction' in the subject of 'Army and Empire' (Imperial Geography). He was summoned to appear before the C.O., who congratulated him on his achievement, and at the same time he was immediately promoted corporal. He later learned from the R.S.M. that the new C.O. had enquired why Jim had not been promoted by Monty; the R.S.M. had informed him that it was because Jim had informed the former C.O. that he did not keep to his word.

Early in the year 1936 Jim received news that his mother was ill. In consequence the C.O. applied to the War Office for him to be repatriated to the U.K. prematurely, for he still had one year of the statutory six to serve abroad. The War Office replied that Jim could have an 'indulgence passage' and proceed to England for six months' furlough, but that he would have to pay the sum of £50. This he accepted. A few days before he was due to sail to the U.K. Jim happened to be the Guard Commander when the C.O. came to inspect the Guard. After his inspection Colonel Duke drew Jim aside and asked him how he had managed to save £50. He had been told by the Adjutant how Jim had been supporting his mother. The C.O. then told him that he was to report to his office the following Monday morning. He then informed him that he was making him a grant of £25 from the C.O.'s discretionary fund.

It was in the early 1980s that Jim read the announcement of Colonel J. P.

Duke's death at the age of ninety-three. As he was to be cremated at Tunbridge Wells, a short distance from where Jim was then living, he attended the service to show his respect for this fine officer and gentleman, under whom he had served so many years before in India.

Shortly after arriving in England, Jim was notified that he had been promoted lance-sergeant. Thus he had regained the seniority he had lost as a result of his outspokenness to Monty. Despite this good news, however, Jim's joy was soon turned to sadness. The sheer excitement of her son's return caused his mother to break down completely; she was never really to recover her full faculties again.

Early in September Jim was due to return to India. Due to trouble in Palestine, however, every troopship was transferred from normal trooping duties to conveying troops to the Middle East on internal security duties. It was then that he received a communication the like of which few soldiers have ever received. He was asked whether he wished to remain on leave for an indefinite period or to report for temporary duties at the Regimental Depot. Realising that the extended leave would not be lasting very long, he chose the former alternative.

It will be remembered that King Edward VIII had succeeded his father, King George V, to the throne but had not yet been crowned. As the young King was to open Parliament, Jim took the opportunity to go to London to see the State Opening. It was actually while he was watching the procession that a fanatic in the crowd produced a revolver, thereby posing a possible threat to the King's life. Fortunately a vigilant policeman disarmed and arrested the man. The incident took place only a few yards from where Jim was standing.

In the July of that year, during his leave in England, it was Jim's privilege to be a guest of the Soldiers' and Airmen's Christian Association at the House Party for the annual Keswick Convention. This was an unforgettable experience. He was able to meet Bishop Taylor Smith again, for he was a member of the same House Party. One memorable event was an open-air Gospel Meeting in the market square of Keswick. Among those who spoke was another sergeant on leave from India. 'Wally' Wagg was a sergeant in The Royal Signals. Certainly his approach was original and arresting. He commenced his message by informing his listeners that he had come from India. 'India', he said, was a 'bad' place. There was Allahabad, Fyzabad and many other 'bad' cities. He went on to say that India was a very 'poor' country. 'There's Jubblepur, Sholapur, Cawnpore, and many other "poor" cities'. Thus he wove his message round the words 'bad' and 'poor', holding his audience spellbound by the originality and directness of his message. In his Regiment Wally had the reputation of being a fearless witness for Christ. Jim renewed acquaintance with him only a few months later in India, where they met at the annual S.A.C.A. Convention at Agra. There is little doubt that the Forces provide a wonderful training ground for Christian character. The opportunity of witnessing as a Christian provides wide scope, as Jim found. Those who make a profession but fail to live up to it are always ridiculed and often persecuted. Those who maintain their witness, on the other hand, are always respected.

Whilst on leave, Jim completed the arrangements for his younger brother Len to join the Regiment as a Band Boy, thus making a trio of brothers all serving in the same regiment. He returned to India in November and Len was to follow shortly afterwards, when, it was hoped, all three brothers would be serving in the 1st. Battalion together. However, this was not to be for 'Nank', the second brother, left Poona for the U.K. whilst Len was still on the high seas. Although they were unaware of it at the time, they actually passed one another in the Red Sea. It was nearly six years since they had met, and as misfortune would have it, it was to be yet another seven before they would see each other again. Such are the disappointments of Service life!

Boys Pickering and Brown leading 'Billy' Antelope in front of Band and Drums 1st Battalion, Schoncliffe, 1925.

Lt. General Sir Archibald Nye G.C.S.I., G.C.M.G., G.C.I.E., K.C.E., K.B.E., M.C.

*Monty with 'Nicky Yates', Mark and Naomi Pickering,
Budbrooke Barracks, Warwick, 1951.*

L/Cpl. Bill Price.

Sgt. Howard Pickering with Bride, Christmas Day, 1906 (Bride's Birthday).

Monty as Staff Officer, France 1916.

Bruce Bairnsfather in his militia uniform 1908.

The most famous cartoon ever published (by Bruce Barinsfather) 'Well if you know a better 'ole, go to it'. With courtesy of Tonie and Valmai Holt.

Frances and Baby 'Jim'
with Luckshambai
(Ayah, Bombay 1911).

Lt. General Sir Jeremy Reilly, KCB, DSO, Present Colonel of the Regiment.

Chapter 13

Return to Poona

When Jim arrived at Poona station on his return from furlough he learned of a great tragedy which had occurred in the Battalion some little time before. It involved two soldiers, both of whom he had known very well. As pals they had been inseparable until one day a tiff had developed between them. Thereupon the younger of the two had broken off their friendship and made friends with a lance-corporal. This had created feelings of deep jealousy in the mind of his former pal. The latter soldier was well known to everyone in the Battalion. Always a quiet, affable sort, he was the R.S.M.'s batman as well as being one of the best cross-country runners in the Regiment.

After the rift which had occurred, however, his jealousy was such that one evening he told his former pal's new friend that he should go out and enjoy himself for it would be his last night and he would never have another opportunity. Quite naturally, the soldier paid little attention to the veiled threat behind this exhortation. Nevertheless the following morning certain sinister developments might have been discerned. The jealous soldier sought out the Room Orderly of the day and told him that as he did not want any breakfast, he would be happy to take over the duty himself. This was readily agreed to, but in retrospect it was realised that the jealous man was merely using it as an excuse to put his plan into execution. He availed himself of the opportunity he had contrived to take a rifle from the rifle rack and a round of ammunition from its security box. Then, as soon the unfortunate lance-corporal returned to the barrack room after breakfast and was bending down to replace his eating utensils, he stood a few feet from him, lifted the rifle, and shot him dead. As soon as the deed had been done he ran straight down to the Guard Room and said to the Guard Commander: 'Please put me inside – I've just shot a bloke.'

Because of the laws then prevailing in India, he was tried not by Courts

Martial but by the Indian Civil Court, which duly sentenced him to death. At the Regiment's request, however, he was kept in the cells of the Regimental Guard Room up to the time of his execution. A few nights before his death Jim was the Guard Commander. A young sentry had been posted immediately outside the condemned soldier's cell but when Jim went to relieve him he said: 'Sarge, please don't put me outside D...'s cell again.' It transpired that a short time before, the sentry had said to the condemned man: 'Isn't it cold?' 'Not as cold as I will be soon...' the latter had replied. Poor lad! Before his final journey to the scaffold he became quite demented. Strangely enough he is buried in Poona Cemetery only a few yards from his victim.

There can be little doubt that today such an incident would receive widespread coverage in the National Press. At that time, however, only the briefest mention was made of it in the daily papers in England. What made the whole story so peculiarly poignant was that throughout the several years that Jim had known this soldier and shared a barrack room with him, he had never once known him lose his temper or become involved in an argument with anyone else. The whole tragic episode appeared completely foreign to his normal excellent behaviour. In those tough days of soldiering for long periods in the tropics, however tragic the circumstances might be, mitigation played no part in the fulfilment of the law.

That Christmas Jim received an invitation to go to Agra for a Christmas Convention for Service personnel. It was an opportunity too good to be missed. In order to economise, however, he made the entire journey of some eight hundred miles travelling by rail third class. This was his first trip northwards to the United Provinces and at the same time his first really long train journey in India. Although the scenery was quite unremarkable, to the eyes of one seeing it for the first time it was more than a little fascinating, and throughout the journey Jim found much to interest him.

To begin with, there were his fellow travellers. They were of every class and creed. Whenever the train stopped, Indian vendors would come to the carriage window with the familiar cries of: 'Beedi . . . beedi (cigarette) . . . pan, Musilman pan,' 'Duhd . . . duhd . . . garam duhd,' or the more familiar 'Chae . . . chae . . . garam chae (hot tea)'. At Jansi, one of the large railway junctions of Central India, native women came to the carriages selling picturesque painted clay models of Indians of every type. Coolies could be seen in their red shirts and turbans carrying the travellers' trunks and bedding rolls on their heads. For those who decided to employ a coolie, however, one precaution was absolutely imperative: to take note of the particular coolie's number from the brass arm-band which they all wore.

Otherwise he would simply disappear with one's baggage, never to be seen again.

It was not unusual for a railway inspector to invite a traveller to accompany him to the luggage room for his baggage to be weighed and checked for excess weight. Of course, as so often happened in India, the slipping of a rupee or two into the palm of the inspector would be sufficient to enable the traveller to proceed on his way without further delay or hindrance.

During the Indian Mutiny it had been at Jansi that a fanatical Indian woman soldier, the 'Rani of Jansi', led her Indian troops in their heroic and stubborn defence of the Fort against the British. Only after achieving considerable success on the field of battle was she killed in action. Those who love history should read the account of this woman's remarkable talents of leadership and courage as a soldier in one of the many books on the subject. The accounts of the numerous battles fought during the period of the Indian Mutiny give one an insight into the conditions of both soldiers and their families serving in India during that memorable period. They paint a vivid picture of the appalling rate of mortality, when whole regions were smitten by epidemics of cholera, plague and dysentery as well as by numerous other tropical diseases. It was not uncommon for whole families to be wiped out and serious inroads to be made into the strengths of British units. Such were the sacrifices it took to preserve the British Empire in India. No railways existed by which to convey soldiers and their families. The roads were extremely poor and dusty, and in the hot and rainy seasons the climate was all but unbearable. The only mode of travel for families was in the dire discomfort of bullock carts, and where the going was too rough even for these, the families were carried by the natives in 'doolies'. At that time soldiers still wore the uncomfortable heavy serge uniforms designed for the cold climates of Europe, and it was not until fairly late on in the century that the lighter cotton drill uniforms were introduced.

To Jim his stay at Agra was quite unforgettable. He was able to visit and photograph the many wonders of the ancient city of Fatepur Sikri, with its famous Elephant Tower, as well as that supreme 'wonder of the world', the superb Taj Mahal. Visitors from all over the world will still pay large sums to visit this unique masterpiece. It was constructed of white marble by the Mogul Emperor Shah Jehan in 1650 in memory of his favourite wife, Mumtaz Mahal. Viewed by the light of a full moon it is utterly breathtaking.

The uninitiated might imagine that Central India is always hot. This is certainly true of the months of March, April and May when, during daytime hours, temperatures are well in excess of 110 degrees fahrenheit. During the 'cool' months, December and January, however, the daytime temperatures are no more than a pleasant 70–75 degrees, while by night the thermometer may fall by as much as 40 degrees, making the hours of darkness seem extremely cold.

Jim well remembers one of his fellow travellers on the journey between Kalyan Junction and Agra. When he entered the carriage, there was but one seat vacant in the crowded compartment. This was next to a fearsome looking bearded Sikh with a large square jaw and enormous black eyes. When Jim climbed onto the top berth to sleep at night, the eyes of the Sikh appeared to be staring at him incessantly and the look on his face suggested that at a single erring word he would draw a huge knife and decapitate him. It later transpired, however, that that was far from being his fellow traveller's attitude or nature. When the train stopped on the following morning for breakfast, the Indian gentleman immediately invited Jim to accompany him for 'chota hazri' (breakfast). It was only then that he learned that his travelling companion was a Punjab farmer with a university degree. Somehow or other, the subject of conversation turned to religion and the gentleman became deeply interested as Jim related his own Christian experience. He even asked Jim to correspond with him so that he could learn more about Christianity.

On returning to Poona, Jim learned that each Company was to spend a fortnight at a special holiday camp just outside a small fishing village on the Malabar Coast, some twenty miles north of Bombay. It was the Brigade Commander's idea of giving all the troops a break during the period of hot weather. The tented camp was situated among palm trees at the edge of the long sandy beach. In fact very little else could be seen except palm trees and sand along the sea shore. Whilst most of the troops spent their time reading, swimming and sleeping, they could also, on occasion, watch the women from the nearby Hindu village as they landed catches of fish from small boats early each morning and again just before sundown in the evening. With their shining jet-black hair heavily coated in coconut oil and with the bun at the back surrounded by a coronet of plaited flowers, these women were strikingly picturesque. Once the fish had been sorted, they put the large baskets laden with the catch upon their heads to carry it back to the village, first ensuring, of course, that the fish were covered up. If they had not done this the sharp-eyed Brahminy Kites or Fish Eagles would very quickly have divested them of the contents of their baskets.

One evening, just as the sun was setting, the troops heard sounds of chanting and wailing from outside the camp. Their interest was immediately aroused and they soon realised that a Hindu funeral procession was moving down a small track towards the beach. The body of the dead Hindu was being carried on a bier constructed of two bamboo poles laced together with sisal. The corpse was not covered and the mourners, all men, took turns in bearer duties as they slowly advanced, chanting, wailing and swaying their bodies. Every now and then the corpse was lowered to the ground and the mourners 'fed' it with small lumps of rice soaked in coconut milk. The burial place was a small cove on the beach where the funeral pyre had already been prepared. Two iron stakes had been driven into the ground a couple of feet apart, and between them pieces of palm wood had been stacked to a height of about three feet. When the procession arrived, the body was laid on top of the wood and then covered with thin pieces of bark, leaving the head and feet protruding at either end. Then after a ceremony entailing curious rituals, palm oil was poured over the whole of the pyre and ignited. A small quantity of kerosene was added to assist the process and ensure that the corpse was fully cremated. The mourners then returned to the village but the Hindu priest remained. When the fire had died down he scraped the ashes together and then placed a brass bowl containing rice, together with a small cruse of coconut milk, beside the pile he had gathered. We were later told that these were to provide the spirit of the dead man with sustenance for his journey. In the course of the following night it became evident that the contents of the bowls had been surreptitiously emptied so as to convey to any relatives who might visit the site the following morning that the spirit had indeed availed itself of the food and drink. This was only one of many ways in which Indians disposed of their dead. Only a short distance from Wonowrie Barracks was a typical Parsi 'tower of silence'. Here members of that particular sect placed the corpses of their dead on an iron grating at the summit of the tower, where they would be devoured by the ever-expectant vultures. These could always be seen patiently waiting for their next meal.

The year 1937 saw two more changes in officer appointments in the Battalion, both of them fairly dramatic in their effects. One day when Jim was taking his customary rest during the heat of the afternoon, the head of a gentleman with a prominent black moustache appeared round the door to ask the whereabouts of the Company Commander' office. To any long-serving soldier in India the act of disturbing a soldier during his afternoon siesta was almost a sin. However, when the stranger informed Jim that he was the new Company Commander, his instinct immediately prompted him to show the new officer round.

At that time little was known about the new Company Commander except that he had been given accelerated promotion from the rank of lieutenant to that of captain, something which in peacetime happened only to officers of exceptional merit. Indeed, so slow was promotion at that time that it was not uncommon for an officer to remain a subaltern for anything up to fifteen years. Whenever an officer was given accelerated promotion, he was invariably transferred from his own regiment to another. Presumably this was to avoid causing any embarrassment to other officers of the regiment concerned. 'Jimmy' Carter had come from the Dorsetshire Regiment, 39th. and 54th. Foot, whose great boast it was that they were 'Primus in Indus', the first regiment in India, with Plassey as their first Battle Honour.

In next to no time 'A' Company's new Commander was the talk of the whole Battalion. Normally in peace time a change in command of a Company passed without much fuss. On this occasion, however, the new Commander made his presence known and felt by ordering a full kit inspection of the entire company, during which all ranks became aware of his insistence upon turnout of the highest standard. As he inspected each man's kit, he used his cane to thrust aside any article that was not up to his standard of cleanliness, and it was obvious from the outset that he had an eye for spotting the most minute speck of brasso (metal polish) which had evaded the polishing cloth. His stock phrases became well known: 'Look at it – there's a tin of brasso in the corner of your mess tin . . . in the stud of your belt' etc. Among all ranks he acquired forthwith the nickname of 'Brasso'.

Not long afterwards 'Brasso' was appointed Adjutant of the Battalion, a post which gave him tremendous influence in setting extremely high standards of turnout and drill. Jim has a vivid memory of the first time Brasso was due to play cricket for the Company. Until that day punctuality in such events had rarely been practised. This occasion was no exception. At the time appointed for the match to start only a few players had arrived. By contrast, punctual to the minute, the figure of Brasso, stern of countenance and immaculately attired, stood holding his wrist watch to his face and, as each player sauntered along, he shook him out of his lethargy by informing him that on future occasions he would arrive properly dressed and at least ten minutes before the game was due to commence. It soon became apparent that their new Commander was a first-class player at most ball games. During his first season in Poona he had a batting average of over a hundred runs, and during the annual officers-versus-sergeants cricket match he scored a hundred in each innings. That particular match remains in Jim's memory for another reason. Following Jimmy Carter's first innings of over a hundred, not out, Jim was determined to show his new Commander that he too could play the game of cricket, and by the lunch interval he was 46, not out. The two teams then resorted to the Officers' Mess, where it was always customary for the sergeants to be given a good spread. That particular day the sweet course happened to be an extraordinarily enticing trifle. What Jim had not bargained for was the fact that it had been well and truly laced with brandy. It was highly significant that on resuming his innings after lunch he was out first ball. He later declared that he saw three balls coming towards him but struck out at the wrong one. There was some compensation in the fact that at the end of the match Jimmy Carter commented to Jim that but for his agile fielding he would have scored two hundred runs per innings.

Another incident which remains vivid in Jim's memory took place when he was to be Guard Commander on a particular 'Old Soldier's Day'. On such occasions its was customary for the Adjutant to relinquish the daily duty of Mounting the Guard which normally fell to him and to delegate it to the Orderly Officer of the day. It was a gesture which most of the troops appreciated, and perhaps the knowledge that 'Brasso' would not be inspecting them made them less conscientious in their preparations. In this particular instance, the Wednesday evening before 'Old Soldier's Day' was the occasion of a Company Dance. Several members of the Guard for the following day stood by the bar drinking, completely oblivious of the fact that 'Brasso' was cocking his ear in their direction. He actually heard one of them say: 'It's all right, chaps – Brasso won't be mounting the Guard tomorrow morning, so there's no need for so much bull!' The following morning at the appointed time, as the Guard stood waiting on the parade ground in anticipation of the Orderly Officer arriving, they received a considerable shock. In place of the Orderly Officer they had been expecting, the Adjutant's car drew up and in a moment the immaculate Brasso, complete with sword, approached and stood facing them. 'Yes, Gentlemen,' he said, 'No doubt you're all a little surprised to see me today, aren't you? Perhaps another time when you're at the bar, you'll be a little more discreet in your conversations with one another!' Thereafter, as he sauntered round on his inspection, his beady eyes magnified many times over the minute particles of brasso he observed on the studs of each soldier's accoutrements. Here again, therefore, it was he who had the last laugh.

Shortly after this incident, Jim was Battalion Orderly Sergeant for the day. One of his duties was to parade and inspect the soldiers who had been given the minor punishment of attending Retreat Parade. On questioning one particular soldier who had arrived from England only a few days before, he enquired who had given him his punishment and why. The soldier's reply was: 'Sarge, I don't know the officer's name but all the blokes call him 'Brasso'. He said that I had a tin of brasso in one of the studs of my leather belt on Adjutant's Parade last week. With a subdued smile, Jim passed along the rank of erring soldiers to learn that most of them had received similar punishment for the same military offence.

A further change in officer appointments created tremendous interest, not only among all ranks in the Battalion but throughout the personnel of the entire Garrison. It was learned that Colonel J. P. Duke, M.C. was to hand over his command to one of the most highly decorated officers serving in the British Army at the time, namely Major (Temporary Lieut.-Colonel, Brevet-Colonel) 'Frank' Roberts, V.C., D.S.O., O.B.E., M.C. Not only had he won high distinction on the field of battle, but had proved himself a fine Staff Officer as well. However, at the outset it should be stated that the 'mad major' (as he was called in the Regiment) had been awarded the Victoria Cross whilst serving in the Worcestershire Regiment during the First World War. This regiment (29th. Foot) was a county neighbour of The Royal Warwickshire Regiment. Its Battle Honours were many and distinguished, and no less than thirteen of them had been won in battles of the Peninsular War. Nevertheless, with the 'Warwicks' the 'Worcesters' had acquired a less salubrious reputation and they were known among them as 'The Posi Wallahs'. 'Posi' is the Hindustani word for jam, that staple food of the soldier during the 20th. century. Rumour had it that on one occasion, at a time when both regiments were serving in India, the 'Worcesters' stole the 'Warwicks' jam ration. Hence the nickname, 'Posi Wallahs'!

To return to the new C.O.'s arrival. A number of soldiers had served with the 2nd. Battalion of the Regiment in Bombay in 1928–29, when he was Second-in-Command. They remembered his exploits well. According to them it was at this time that he acquired his nickname of 'The Mad Major'. Evidently, during the communal riots the natives were running amok, shooting, looting, setting fire to buildings and generally causing havoc far and wide. In the midst of all this 'The Mad Major' could be seen riding on the running board of an armoured car brandishing his revolver. He was over six feet in height, and when he wore full-dress uniform on ceremonial parades, complete with chestful of medals, he presented a truly striking figure. When not engaged in such formal activities, however, Colonel Frank Roberts was a quiet, unassuming gentleman, beloved by all who served under him. During the early part of World War II he became the youngest Major-General in the British Army. His period of command with the 1st. Battalion, The Royal Warwickshire Regiment was very short. Only six months after his arrival at Poona he was promoted Brigadier with an ante-date of seniority.

The Battalion's last big parade at Poona at the end of its stay there was to be a Trooping of the Colours before the Viceroy of India, who at that time was the Earl of Linlithgow. As can be imagined, this entailed prolonged and careful preparations. Every single soldier taking part was fitted with new khaki drill uniform and new topee. Unfortunately, as it turned out, the tense political situation in Europe demanded the Viceroy's constant presence at Delhi. Hence the Trooping was carried out before the Governor-General of the Bombay Presidency, Sir Roger Lumley. It was one of those occasions on which it was not only the soldiers who wore new uniforms. As soon as they received their invitation, every wife and girl friend, as well as any other female guests who intended being present, hurriedly resorted to the local bazaar, or even made a special journey to Bombay, to purchase dress material. Then they would summon their own 'dursi' to have the outfit of their choice made up. Jim's girl friend, who was a teacher at a local Mission School, was one of the girls who dressed up specially for the event. As was usual on such auspicious occasions, a Sergeants' Ball was held on the evening after the ceremony, to which the officers and their ladies were invited. Although these latter dispersed at a reasonable hour, the sergeants, their wives and friends continued their revelry until dawn, after which, still attired in their evening dresses, the wives took themselves off to the kitchen and prepared a breakfast of bacon and eggs. Then they went home to sleep for the rest of the day, which was a holiday.

The Governor of the Bombay Presidency before Sir Roger Lumley was Lord Brabourne. On two occasions Jim had the pleasure of playing cricket for the Battalion against the Governor's eleven at the Governor's Summer Residency at Ganeshkind. It was situated in a delightful setting in the foothills of the Western Ghats, not very far from Poona. This was always a most enjoyable outing. In those days of the 'Raj' it was well known that the Governor had a staff of several hundred. Lavish living and pageantry were the order of the day.

Chapter 14

Fyzabad and Chaubattia

In November, 1937 the Battalion moved to Fyzabad in the United Provinces. It was a military garrison situated on the River Gogra, a tributary of the mighty Ganges. One Company was to be stationed at Benares, the sacred city of the Hindus. The journey of about eleven hundred miles took three days by troop train; in fact there were two trains, one for the troops and the other for the married families.

Fyzabad was completely different from Poona. Although to the thousands of Hindu pilgrims who went to visit the temples along the river it was a most holy place, the surrounding countryside was flat and relatively uninteresting. The barrack blocks were of single-story construction, and far more primitive than the accomodation at Poona. Instead of bladed electric fans, the air in each barrack room was cooled by punkahs. Invariably the 'punkah wallah' would doze off to sleep, to be rudely awakened by a kick in the pants from one of the occupants of the barrack room concerned. Sometimes, where punkahs did not exist, the air was kept cool by hanging a 'tatti' (woven mat) over the doorway. The servant then spent all day splashing water over it, which had the effect of cooling the air passing through.

Fyzabad was noted for the abundance of its monkeys. They appeared to live in a paradise of their own, with their homes in and around the Monkey Temples on the banks of the River Gogra. Here they were treated with the utmost reverence by the Sadhus and pilgrims, who regarded them as mystic beings. To the inhabitants of the Cantonment, on the other hand, they were nothing but a nuisance. When cycling down the road one had to run the gauntlet of them and, as Jim discovered to his cost, they appeared to resent human beings attempting to ride through their pack. One afternoon as he was cycling to the Post Office, a particularly aggressive animal seemed to think that he was trying to run him down. Straightway he began to chase

Jim in a highly belligerent manner. Assuredly Jim did not take the same route on his return journey. He knew that monkeys have good memories and also remembered what had happened at Poona when a monkey bit one of the soldiers. Their teeth are razor sharp.

As monkeys reigned by day, the night belonged to the hordes of jackals and hyenas which marauded and scavenged around the Contonment in search of food. No sooner had the sun set than packs of jackals could be heard howling throughout the surrounding countryside. In consequence there was a high prevalence of rabies, carried by the infected animals. Very often the disease was transmitted to the troops' pet dogs. On arriving at Fyzabad, the 'Warwicks' learned that several fatalities to the scourge had occurred among soldiers of the regiment previously stationed there. In an attempt to reduce this jackal population, shoots were arranged from time to time. As they appeared to be unafraid of human beings, culling them presented no difficulty. Often when one was out walking at night a jackal would pass at a distance of no more than a few feet, as though it were a pet dog. To attract them to the guns food would be placed a few feet away from the verandah, where the executioners would be waiting ready in the shadows. When the silhouette of a jackal was seen approaching the bait, one of the hunters would shine a torch straight at it. Invariably it would stand and stare at the light, thereby presenting a sitting target. One evening Jim was accompanying another sergeant named 'Mac' when a dozen jackals were killed in a surprisingly short time. However, the shoot did not pass without a moment or two of amusement. Several times, just as a jackal approached, the dhobi's donkey (normally used for carrying large bundles of washing) suddenly appeared in the line of fire; it too was scavenging for food. After several such interventions Mac exclaimed: 'The next time that bloody donkey appears I'll put a burst of shot in its backside!' Fortunately for the donkey, it disappeared. Obviously it was endowed with second sight!

Apart from the noise made by the jackals, the night air was filled with the screeching of myriads of Little Owls. These had their homes in the many banyan trees surrounding the Cantonment and they too obviously thrived on the large quantities of vermin that infested it.

To a nature lover it was not only the range and variety of nocturnal sounds that were of interest. In the daytime too he could listen to the calls of many different species of bird. During the heat of the day the monotonous 'tk... tk... tuk' of the Crimson-Breasted Barbet or (as some call it) the Coppersmith would predominate. The latter name was highly appropriate for the incessantly repeated call sounded as though someone were tapping on a sheet of metal at the top of a high tree. Occasionally a flock of fast-flying Rose-Ringed Parakeets would swing chattering past, reminding one of a flight of swifts in an English summer. Occasionally the beautifully coloured Golden Oriel could be seen. Because of this particular bird's extreme shyness, however, more often than not the only indication of its presence would be the rich mellow whistle it emitted, sounding something like: 'pe-ole... pe-ole'. Once Jim had the good fortune to see one of them sitting on its hammock-like nest, slung from a high branch like a cup. Among other birds which could be spotted was the gorgeously coloured Roller or Blue Jay. The troops used to call these the 'R.A.E.C. birds' because their plumage was light and dark blue and these were the colours of the Royal Army Education Corps. Mynahs, of course, were as profuse as starlings in England. While the troops were resting during the afternoon, they could be heard chattering in their favourite haunts under the eaves of the barrack rooms, where they enjoyed the coolness and shade.

When the River Gogra was not in flood, crocodiles could be seen sunning themselves on the mud banks. Local shikaris often went shooting 'mugger' (young crocodiles), the skins of which were cured and used to make shoes, ladies' handbags and belts. A pair of made-to-measure mens' crocodile shoes used to cost about ten rupees (under one pound in English money), while a pair of ladies' shoes would cost about twenty rupees.

Although the Gogra was only a tributary of the Jumna, it was so wide that when in flood during the monsoon it was difficult to make out one bank from the other.

During the hot weather period, between March and early June, the heat in Fyzabad, as in most places in Central India, rose to about 115 degrees fahrenheit and sometimes even higher. At night, in order to get some sleep, most of the troops would take their 'charpoys' (beds) outside, well away from the buildings, where the air could circulate as much as possible.

In March all the families moved up into the hill station for a period of nearly six months. The soldiers joined them for half of the time. The Warwicks' hill station was Chaubattia, which was situated in the beautiful Kumaon Himalayas, the foothills of the main Himalayan Range, at an altitude of 7,500 feet above sea level. It was about 1,500 feet above the highly popular hill station of Ranikhet.

The journey was made in two stages, the first being by rail via Lucknow, Bareilly Junction, and so on to the terminus of Kathkodam. The travellers would then continue by bus up a winding road leading through thick pine forests, where packs of Langar or long-tailed monkeys with white faces abounded. Chaubattia was a 'picture paradise', with the barrack bungalows scattered among the pine trees and with a background panorama second to none in the world. The magnificent vista of the main Himalayan Range, with its snow-capped peaks, extended from east to west as far as the eye could reach. The nearest peak was Trisul (21,000 feet), about 75 miles away, while Nanda Devi (26,500 feet) was about 105 miles distant. This last was the highest peak in the British Empire. The air was so clear that the magnificent snows appeared to be only a few miles away. They never failed to draw the eye like a magnet and their beauty was quite irresistible. Even at night when the moon was shining, the snow-capped peaks of the Great Range appeared as a back-cloth of fairyland enchantment. It is unfortunate that at the time colour photography was in its infancy, so that photographers, however keen, had to be content with black-and-white pictures.

From time to time the sturdy hill men and women would pass through carrying heavy loads on their backs suspended from their foreheads by means of cloth bands. They would be on their way to Nepal, many miles distant.

Even by comparison with the easy pace associated with peacetime soldiering on the plains of India, the soldier's life at Chaubattia was leisurely indeed. In fact it was only on three mornings a week that any organised programme of training was carried out. Monday morning was devoted to a little weapon training, Tuesday to education training and map reading, whilst on Wednesday every soldier took part in what was known as a 'dog-and-stick walk'. It involved sauntering along the mountain paths with either a dog or a thumbstick. The only drawback to these walks was the inevitable leeches which attached themselves to one's legs. Unless the bloodthirsty creatures were removed immediately, the process of detaching them was a painful one. From after Pay Parade on Thursday morning to the following Monday morning a soldier was free to do as he pleased. A wide variety of pursuits was open to him. Most soldiers took the opportunities afforded them to explore the beauty of the hills either on foot or, for those inclined, on one of the 'tats' or ponies that could be hired for the pleasure of journeying on horseback along the many well-constructed rides. Even this was extremely cheap. Some would organise a more ambitious trek to the foothills of the main Himalayan Range. This, of course, took some time, but leave for such expeditions was readily given since they were considered good military training. On trips of this sort experienced guides would be hired.

From that part of India it was both cheap and highly convenient to reach Kashmir, where superb boating holidays were to be had. The cost would be about one hundred rupees (equivalent to £7. 10s of English money) for a two-week holiday on a houseboat – this to include the use of servants and food. Jim and his wife had planned to take one of these lovely holidays after the War, but unfortunately the British withdrawal from India prevented this from materialising.

Most people, no doubt, have heard stories of 'good times' being had by wives in the hills while their husbands were still on the plains. These were not entirely without foundation. The old adage, 'When the cat's away . . .' applied here too. Jim certainly knew of one 'mouse' which used to return to its 'hole' just before daylight, and beyond any possible doubt the activities in which it had been engaging on its sorties down to Ranikhet and back each night were far from those of any bona fide 'war game'.

Although here, as on the plains, most soldiers kept pets of various kinds, at Chaubattia it was necessary for them to keep their dogs inside the bungalows when they were not out with their masters, because even by daylight it was not uncommon for a panther to steal up and take a dog which had been tied up and left on the verandah.

It was about this time that the famous shikari Jim Corbett was conducting his now legendary hunts of man-eating tigers in the same Himalayan territory. Those who had the great privilege of soldiering in those parts before the departure of the British Raj from India naturally found his thrilling descriptions of those hunts all the more enjoyable in virtue of having known the region in which they took place.

One of Jim's particular memories concerns a visit he made to Ranikhet. It was his custom to go with another pal, Jesse Boulton, down through the wooded 'kudhs' to visit the Sandes Soldiers' Home. One particular Sunday Jesse happened to be delayed on some duty and told Jim that he would follow later. During daylight hours the three-mile walk down through the pine woods caused Jim no particular anxiety, even though wild animals were known to frequent the area. However, when Jesse failed to turn up at Ranikhet, he found himself faced with the prospect of returning by the same route alone in the dark – a far more formidable undertaking. Miss Symes, the Superintendent of the Soldiers' Home, gave him some encouragement by pointing out that most wild animals will not normally attack human beings unless they are provoked or have been injured.

To show that he was not a funk, therefore, Jim set out to walk back alone. The moon was shining brilliantly, which made the journey a little less frightening. Yet even the crackling of twigs underfoot appeared like thunder, broadcasting his presence to every animal in the vicinity. Occasionally he could hear the night call of a panther, which in turn disturbed the roosting birds. Such noises spurred Jim on to walk even faster and as he did so he was sure that any animal lurking nearby could hear his very heart beating louder and louder. Afterwards he was sure that that night he had covered the journey from Ranikhet to Chaubattia in record time. The following day he was informed that a panther was actually killed by a shikari close to the track he had traversed the preceding evening. Strangely enough, because of the unpredictability of the large cats if met face to face while hunting food during the hours of darkness, the fearless Jim Corbett always resorted to the safety of a tree at night.

Even by Indian standards, the birds to be seen in those lovely wooded hills were exotic to a degree. The brilliantly coloured Scarlett Minivets danced around the branches at the tops of pine trees and occasionally the beautiful Paradise Flycatcher could be spotted. One morning when Jim was out early for his customary jog, he saw a bird of a striking blue colour dart into a hole in the bank beside the road. Upon investigation he discovered that he had added a Verditer Flycatcher to the list of Indian birds he had spotted.

Abounding in wild life as they do, the Kumaon Hills cannot fail to impress anyone interested in animals, whether he be naturalist, shikari or angler, as a veritable paradise with an unique power to captivate and enchant all who are privileged to visit them.

In addition to tiger, panther or leopard and (in the lower foothills and nearby plains) elephant, antelope of many species are to be found in abundance, the most numerous being, perhaps, ghoral, chital and sambur. By the warning sounds they make they invariably betray the presence of their enemies, tiger and leopard.

Most people will have heard of the sport of pig-sticking, which in those days was avidly pursued by many Europeans in India. Some of the wild pig in this part of Kumaon are not only large but can be exceptionally dangerous too, especially if cornered. Their large curved tusks have been known to sever the limbs of human beings.

Porcupine also abound and once their miriads of sharp quills have been disposed of, are considered a very tasty meal. The large cats also find them pleasant eating, but unfortunately many instances have occurred of tigers having become severely injured by the large quills becoming embedded in their paws. This sometimes hinders them from catching their natural prey and they resort to the killing of human beings, who are less fleet of foot. Women gathering firewood or crops near their territory are often victims. Some man-eaters have been known to kill several hundred individuals within a relatively small area. Now that I look back, I find it quite frightening to reflect that at a time when man-eaters were in the vicinity, I used to wander through the pine forests bird-watching and generally enjoying the countryside, never realising that a panther or tiger might have been passing nearby.

Among the ground birds which abounded, providing food for the natives as well as sport for shikaris, were several varieties of partridge, pheasant and the beautifully plumaged jungle fowl. Most of the villages and small towns such as Ranikhet, Nani Tal and Almora are situated in commanding positions, with views covering hundreds of miles. It was at the first-named of these that the summer residences were situated, away from the heat of the plains. Nani Tal in particular lies beside a deep and beautiful lake.

For the most part, the hill women of Kumaon remain in and around the home, where they live a most industrious life. As well as doing the housework, they tend and harvest the crops and look after the cattle. However, whenever possible, the latter task is undertaken by capable children or young men. Unlike South India, where women are often to be found working away from their villages, in the Kumaon they rarely make visits outside the bounds of their own village. Many of the men, including the younger ones, work on forest projects as labourers, as well as cutting ringals (bamboo canes) for the making of baskets and fly-fishing rods.

Among the snakes sometimes encountered are python, which can measure up to twenty feet or more in length. Pythons can often be found enjoying the crystal-clear water of a mountain pool, where an unsuspecting bather would soon find himself in desperate trouble if he disturbed one of the aggressive monsters. Wrapped round an animal or human being, the grip of its powerful body would soon prove fatal. Another dangerous reptile, extremely beautiful yet frightening at the same time, is the hamadryad or king cobra, which grows to between twelve and sixteen feet in length. When its head is raised the hood is extended to roughly the size of a kitchen plate. It has a gorgeously coloured throat of golden yellow and a back of olive green banded with ivory-coloured chevrons, whilst its front is of shining black patterned with white chevrons. Should it be disturbed, its speed and aggressiveness are alarming in the extreme. With its neck and head raised to three or more feet from the ground, and with its hood extended and fangs protruding menacingly, the sight of it is enough to cause even the most experienced shikari to retreat to safety with all speed.

A fairly common animal is the Himalayan bear. Normally quite unobtrusive and inclined to avoid confrontation with human beings, when roused it can become decidedly aggressive and bad-tempered. Yet I once read a true story of a Christian missionary who had a most unexpected meeting with one of these creatures while journeying unaccompanied in the

Himalayas. It seems that the missionary, having been almost overcome by the severity of the cold, took shelter in a mountain cave where, though still almost freezing, he soon fell asleep. At some point he became subconsciously aware that he had become extremely warm and he continued to sleep for some time in far greater comfort. When he awoke, to his great surprise and apprehension he discovered that a bear, whose home the cave was, had returned during the night and had actually snuggled down beside its human 'lodger'. Finding the unexpected companion to its liking, it too had fallen fast asleep. When the missionary eventually plucked up courage to try and withdraw cautiously from his temporary abode, the bear merely opened its eyes and gazed, apparently in disappointment, as its new-found companion left the cave. Then it simply turned over and went to sleep again. If ever a human being enjoyed divine protection it was that desperately cold missionary!

Occasionally the keen eye of a bird-watcher could mark down one or other of the larger birds of prey such as Palles' Long-tailed Fish Eagle, which have been known to take fish of up to thirteen pounds in weight on the wing, or perhaps the rarer Crested Serpent Eagle or the Indian Great Horned Owl.

The vegetation and flowers of the hills of Kumaon are exotic beyond description, especially during the month of May when many kinds of orchid grow in profusion. In particular the beautiful Butterfly Orchid carpets the ground, providing a botanist's paradise, while many rarer types of orchid are also to be found.

One of the key sporting events for the troops during their sojourn in the hills was the annual 'khud' race, a gruelling contest if ever there was one. The participants were taken to a rendezvous some distance away and at an altitude of some thousand feet below the finishing line. The difficulty of the the climb lay not merely in its extreme steepness. Over and above this, the course ran through thick jungle strewn with large boulders. The already high altitude was yet a further factor ensuring that most of the competitors would be utterly exhausted at the finish of the race.

The altitude was also the cause of a traumatic experience of quite a different kind which Jim happened to undergo. One of his wisdom teeth was causing him trouble and the Army dentist decided to extract it under a general anaesthetic. To perform this seemingly simple operation he had the M.O. in attendance but unfortunately neither of them had had any previous experience of performing even so minor an operation as this at that altitude. Soon after the anaesthetic had been administered Jim's heart collapsed, causing some panic. The M.O. immediately commenced artificial respiration whilst at the same time an orderly was hastily despatched to the Married Families' Hospital nearby to obtain a heart stimulant. All this Jim learned afterwards, but unfortunately for him the general furore had caused the extraction itself to be abandoned. Nevertheless, as often happens in the East, the tom-toms had been beating and the news soon spread that Jim was 'murda' – in other words that he had died. When his bearer, Alopi Ram, heard the sad news he at once ran to the nearby Hindu temple to pray. When he returned, apparently having spent the entire night in prayer, Jim's fellow sergeants started pulling his leg. However they were speedily rebuffed. 'Pickering Sahib nay murda,' said Alopi, 'Alopi pray all night for him – him soon get better'. Such was the faith of this simple and very loyal Hindu servant.

Jim's Company was due to return to Fyzabad just before the monsoon broke late in May; this was heralded by the most vivid and spectacular electric storms, which seemed to envelop the hill station completely. Forked lightning appeared to dance round every peak in the Himalayas, exceeding in beauty any imaginable firework display.

On their return to Fyzabad the troops found the heat most oppressive, with midday temperatures reaching about 115 degrees fahrenheit. One day just before the rains came, Jim was standing outside the entrance to the Sergeants' Mess when he saw a mongoose watching him with intense alertness from the other side of the road. It turned out that the little creature had its home right beneath the culvert on which he happened to be standing. At that moment he witnessed a remarkable piece of fieldcraft, far superior to that achieved by any soldier. 'Appreciating the situation' and 'taking into consideration all the factors', the little animal quickly 'made its plan'. As it crept stealthily and unobtrusively away, Jim watched it with close interest. It made its way along the nullah on the far side of the road until (as Jim felt) it considered that he was no longer able to see it. Then, like greased lightning, it shot across the road and disappeared almost in a flash to safety under Jim's feet.

When Jim returned to India after the War, he experienced the antics of another mongoose. This one had made its home underneath the floor of the Officers' Mess dining room. It soon became attracted by the pungent smell of eggs and bacon at breakfast time. As is well known, mongooses are extremely partial to eggs. This particular Rikki Tikki Tavi proved quite incapable of resisting the smell of the eggs provided for the officers' breakfasts. At first his approach would seem as friendly and harmless as could be. As soon as the bearer carried in a plate of eggs and bacon, he would appear under the table and from there, exactly like a friendly cat, he would find his way onto the officer's lap. Then, before the officer had so much as become aware of his presence – much less his true intentions – he would make his next move quickly as only a mongoose can. Placing his two front paws on the edge of the table, he would seize an egg in his mouth and be off in a flash. Several of the officers hoped to catch him and make a pet of him, but somehow he always sensed their intentions, and on the morning when the Battalion was moving from that camp at Avadi, the mongoose failed to appear for his customary breakfast.

The same night that Jim saw the first mongoose, because of the extremely sultry conditions, he went to sleep on the verandah. While he was still asleep he became subconsciously aware that the first rains of the monsoon had broken in earnest; now they were coming down in torrents. On awakening he found the building completely surrounded by a sea of flood-water several feet deep. His first thought was for the poor little mongoose and its family. What had become of them? That morning all the troops had to wade through water to get to breakfast. During the monsoon the rainfall at Fyzabad was comparable to that of Bombay, usually amounting to between fifty and sixty inches over a period of three months or less. Jim well remembers nine inches of rain falling in three hours in Bombay. Even this, however, pales into insignificance compared with the rainfall at Cherapunji at the eastern extremity of the mighty Himalayan Range, where a record quantity of over six hundred inches has fallen in a single year. It must be remembered that it was possible for this amount to be precipitated in the rainy season alone, which certainly lasts less than half a year.

During this time the River Gogra came into spate, conveying millions of tons of water downstream to swell the Ganges. Any abnormal rainfall resulted in these rivers flooding vast areas and washing away whole villages. They caused widespread havoc to the surrounding countryside, in which many poor people would be drowned and thousands would lose their homes and cattle. It was common to witness carcases of animals and human beings alike being carried past on the flood water.

As was the case in every station in India, the soldier always had to be alert and on guard against the prowling 'loose wallah'. Fyzabad was no exception. Jim used to share a double sergeants' room with another sergeant nicknamed 'Tommy'. One night when Jim was Guard Commander, Tommy heard someone trying the latch of the door. He supposed that it was Jim, or perhaps the bearer bringing the customary morning cup of 'chae'.Still more than half asleep, he opened the door and then got back into bed, immediately falling into a deep sleep. Later when he got up and went to breakfast, he learned that almost every other sergeant's bunk had been visited by a 'loose wallah' and that the other unfortunates had lost many of their possessions. The mode of entry, they found, had been the same in every case. The astute native had climbed onto the roof, forced the small fanlight window, and then lowered himself into the room. Then, after collecting what he wanted, he had quietly opened the door from the inside and vanished. Only after hearing this news did Tommy realise that it had not been Jim whom he had heard at the door but the loose wallah! It made him chuckle to realise that in his semi-comatose state he had actually opened the door to the thief. That, however, had been sufficient to make the intruder aware that he was awake, with the result that his belongings and Jim's had remained untouched.

Once the monsoon began to subside, life soon returned to normal, with the evenings being given over to sport of every kind. Whenever Jim played hockey, Alopi Ram, his native servant, would stand on the verandah waiting for the final whistle, and by the time Jim had walked the couple of hundred yards back to his bunk, Alopi would already have filled the bath-tub with hot water and have laid out a clean change of clothes neatly on the bed. He would not even permit Jim to take off his own shoes and socks. Such was his faithfulness that even when Jim had to catch a train at two a.m. in the morning, Alopi would arrive an hour before time with a cup of 'chae', having already packed Jim's case ready for the journey. When Jim returned, there would be Alopi waiting on the platform to greet him and carry his case back to camp.

One day Jim asked Alopi how many children he had. With a very sad face he shrugged his shoulders and replied that his wife had had twenty-one but that they had all died. Such was the staggering rate of infant mortality in India at that time. Even when they lived, it was not uncommon for whole families to be born blind. Often a women stricken with leprosy and with her legs withered away to mere stumps, could be seen dragging herself along with a baby on her lap. On one particular train journey, as the train stopped at the station and the usual horde of beggars came crying to the window of the carriage, Jim was appalled to see a leper whose mangled face had only sockets where his eyes had once been. The nose was non-existent and the teeth protruded without any lips to cover them. Even at that time, in twentieth-century India, stories were told of Indian women who, prompted by superstition, disposed of a newly born baby because it was a girl; not to have a boy as the first-born was considered a bad omen.

That was in 1938 and in the October of that year tension was mounting, with talk of the possibility of a Second World War. All regiments in India were placed on a war footing and informed that they must be prepared for overseas service at short notice. In consequence Jim and his fiancée decided that it would be prudent to bring forward their impending marriage. It was therefore arranged that Jim would travel to Poona, where Lynette was still teaching, and that from there they would proceed together to her parents' home at Bangalore where the wedding was to take place. This necessitated an overall journey of some fifteen hundred miles, which by fast train took two days. The first part, as far as Poona, was by the Great Indian Peninsular Railway (G.I.P. for short), while from Poona to Bangalore they travelled via Belgaum on the narrow-gauge Madras and South Maharatta Railway.

By this time Jim was becoming well accustomed to long-distance travel in India. He had already visited Bangalore for a few days the previous Christmas and now, after years of barrack room life, he welcomed the comfort of a real home once again. Here he sampled many of the traditional dishes of South India. Early each morning the 'egg wallah' would come to the door with his basket of 'chicken fruit' but here in India the sale of eggs was not as in England, where the eggs could always be relied upon to be fresh. Here it was necessary for each egg to be tested and proved. For this purpose the egg-seller used to carry a pan of water in which he would place the selected eggs. Any of them showing signs of buoyancy would be rejected by the Memsahib; only those which sank to the bottom would be deemed fresh. Next came the 'dudh wallah' with his cow trailing after him; no lack of freshness in the milk he had for sale! Even he, however, would undergo a test. He carried a pail and before he began to milk the cow he would hold it upside down to prove that there was no water in the bottom.

In Bangalore the traditional breakfast dish was not cornflakes but a plate of 'idi opper' served with fresh coconut milk. This was usually followed by papaya freshly cut from a tree in the garden. It goes without saying that the main meal of the day was the traditional South Indian hot curry and rice, together with locally produced hot mango pickle and popadums. It was quite different from the Army curry, which consisted merely of curry powder mixed in with stew. In the evening after dinner an Indian fruit seller would come round shouting 'Art nungoo'. This particular fruit was brought up by the mail train from the Malabar Coast; it came from a palm-like tree and in substance was like firm jelly. Served ice-cold it was simply delicious. This would be followed by black coffee.

After his wedding, Jim was to return to Fyzabad via Poona, where his wife was to complete her term's teaching. Unfortunately, however, after sleeping in an extremely drafty carriage, Jim developed Bell's Palsy (facial paralysis), which necessitated his spending a period in hospital and afterwards staying on there for further treatment, there being no facilities at Fyzabad. In fact it was not until January of the following year that he and his wife returned to take possession of their first married quarter, an initiation which Lynette often talks about to this day. Having first taken over the quarter, the next step was to go down to the local bazaar to hire furniture as none was provided in India. Then, having got the furniture home, it was vitally necessary to 'de-bug' it. It was mostly of 'rattan' (cane) construction, which needed constant disinfecting to get rid of the common bed bugs.

The Pickerings' new home was in the middle of a long terrace-like block with a verandah at both the front and back of the quarter. There were just two rooms, one being used as a lounge-cum-dining room and the other for sleeping. The latter had just enough room for two single beds placed together, though they left no room to walk around. At first Lynette was somewhat distressed, but after a while she brought her talents to bear to such good effect that the lounge at least achieved some semblance of comfort.

Within a very short time she had settled down to the life of a soldier's wife. She learned all the bugle calls and so knew when the appropriate call indicated that the R.S.M. was summoning 'A' Company's Orderly Sergeant to his office. Forty years afterwards Lynette still talks of those unforgettable days. She especially remembers the neighbours who occupied the two quarters on either side. There was very little privacy, so that they often heard the family squabbles that used to erupt. On one particular day they were having 'tiffin' (lunch) together when they were disturbed by the sound of a violent row between husband and wife from a nearby quarter. Almost immediately their meal was interrupted by the entrance of a very frightened cook, who said that the Memsahib next door was 'mar kharoing' (striking) the husband with a stick. Not wishing to get involved, Jim watched from afar and was horrified to see the sergeant's wife violently ejecting her husband down the steps of the verandah with such force that he had to go to hospital for treatment. It was discovered that he had suffered a broken arm. The following day Jim was quietly amused when the battle-scarred sergeant appeared on pay parade with his arm in a sling. When the Company Commander offered sympathy, the sergeant explained that he had fallen down the steps accidentally. Said Jim to himself: 'If he only knew what I know!'

As in most parts of India, travelling hawkers used to visit married quarters with their wares, often fruit, sometimes carpets. On occasions soldiers' wives would be favoured with a visit from the 'Chinese Johnnies', as they were known. They would appear with several large bundles stacked on the back of their cycles. When one of these Chinamen called, it was customary to invite him into the lounge, where he would open his bundles and display his wares. The materials and garments he laid out would be varied and strikingly beautiful, and by English standards extremely cheap. On one occasion Lynette was interested in silk dress material for herself and cream Shantung silk to make shirts for Jim. Several times in the course of bartering, the 'Johnny' would refuse her offer and pack up his bundles. Then, as he reached the door and found Lynette still adamant about his asking price, he would come back and open up his wares again. This procedure was repeated again and again and each time he would reduce his asking price a little. On one occasion Lynette told him that her offer was six annas a yard and no more. Ultimately, with a shrug of his shoulders, he asked her how many yards she wanted. 'Missie,' he said as he cut the material, 'you take food from me.' Nevertheless at the time he went off apparently satisfied. The following day, however, he returned saying that his boss was very angry. Lynette did give him a few more annas whereupon he again went off quite happy. The silk shirts which Lynette made for Jim lasted many, many years, while some of the gorgeous Kashmiri garments bought at the same time have lasted for nearly fifty years and even today still retain their colour and beauty.

Chapter 15

Return to England and the Outbreak of the War

A frequent visitor to Jim's home was his brother Len; after barrack room life he found it most enjoyable. However, they had hardly settled down when the C.O. informed Jim that he was sending him back to the U.K. for a period of recuperation and that he would do a tour of two years' duty at the Regimental Depot at Warwick.

It was a sad day indeed for all concerned, including Alopi Ram, when both Lynette and Jim left the Battalion en route for the U.K. As he said farewell to his Sahib and Memsahib poor Alopi broke down in tears. As for Jim's brother, it was to be five years before they met again and by that time it would be during the War.

For the journey Jim and his wife found that a fairly mammoth task had been laid upon them. Before leaving Fyzabad they were informed that they were to 'look after' another young wife who was returning to England with no less than *five* young children, and with only twenty-three months' difference in age between all five! The eldest were twins and less than a year after their arrival another baby had been born. Then the mother gave birth to a second set of twins, all within less than two years.

During the train journey of three days' duration it can be imagined how busy Jim was kept, running backwards and forwards to fetch hot water from the restaurant for mixing with powdered milk for the babies' feeds, as well as assisting generally with coping with the children. What made it even more strenuous was the fact that the weather was exceptionally hot. As if all this were not enough, when they arrived in Bombay they were given another charge, namely to look after an eight year-old girl whose mother was an invalid returning to the U.K. on medical grounds. Once on board ship, however, despite having so large a 'family' to care for, they received valuable help from the ship's company so that all in all their journey passed very successfully.

On arriving at Southampton, Jim and Lynette discovered that out of the many families disembarking they were the only ones to be allotted a married quarter, the others having to find their own accommodation with relatives. They were instructed to proceed to the Regimental Depot at Budbrooke Barracks, Warwick prior to taking a month's disembarkation leave.

It was in the small married quarter above the Officers' Mess at Budbrooke that Jim's elder sister Cissy had been born. It was from there, in 1910, that his parents had embarked for India. Compared to a soldier's married quarter today, the one assigned to Jim and Lynette was far from salubrious. It was the centre quarter of a block, with other blocks on either side. Thus it afforded no outlook whatever. It consisted of just four small rooms. The lounge had 'army brown' linoleum on the floor, an open fireplace, a coal scuttle and iron fire implements, one 'chair, arm, wooden, sergeants, for the use of', and three windsor chairs. The kitchen was equipped with a sink and a wooden draining board, a bath, over which a wooden lid was placed when it was not in use, a small wooden dining table and two more wooden chairs. The bedroom furniture consisted of a double bed together with blankets, pillows and sheets. That was the complete schedule of 'accommodation stores' supplied, and even it was considered an improvement on those provided in India. Nevertheless, for all its drawbacks, Jim and Lynette felt extremely grateful to have this quarter. The frugality of it all was to some extent mitigated by the provision of a small ration allowance which, if desired, could be taken in kind in the form of a piece of beef. In those days it was often despised; today, of course, it would be like gold. Jim's pay as a sergeant at that time was 42 shillings a week, plus ten shillings and sixpence marriage allowance. Small though this wage might seem, it must be remembered that the cost of living was very low, so that it was possible to live reasonably well and still save a little money each week.

Almost immediately after his leave, Jim was sent to attend a course at the Small Arms School at Hythe. Here he was initiated into the use of the bren gun, which was to become the Army's standard automatic small arms weapon, as well as the 'Boys' anti-tank gun. At Hythe he was treading on familiar ground indeed, for it was there, on the rifle range, that he had accepted the King's Shilling on enlistment fourteen years before.

During his stay at Hythe he took the opportunity to visit old friends of the Regiment. The first of these with whom he had hoped to renew acquaintance was Fred Savory, that old soldier who had lost his L.S. and

G.C. Medal by playing Crown and Anchor on board the troopship. Alas for his hopes! When he knocked on the door where Fred used to live he was met by Mrs. Savory, who conveyed the sad news that Fred had passed away. During his visit Fred's widow handed Jim a small parcel which her husband had wished him to have. It contained Fred's medals as well as the bible given to him on enlistment. Although the medals constituted one of the finest rows held by a private soldier in the Regiment at that time, he felt that it was fitting that they should be given to the Regimental Museum where they could be preserved for posterity. It was doubly sad to find that when he called on Mrs. Savory again during the War, it was only to find that she had been evacuated and that her address was not known. So ended one of those cherished links between families in a regiment which lasted over many years and gave so much happiness to those concerned.

Jim returned to the Depot to take his place as an instructor of recruits and for a few short weeks he settled down to his work, as well as playing some cricket for the Depot team. Visits were made to the Depots of neighbouring regiments such as the Worcesters and the Leicesters. All this time, however, the clouds of war were rapidly building up over Europe.

It was in July of that year that Hore-Belisha, the then Secretary of State for War in Neville Chamberlain's government, introduced 'National Service' in the Forces for the first time. All youths of 18 years of age were called to the Colours for a period of military service, with the result that fortnightly intakes of recruits had to be received by every Regimental Depot throughout the United Kingdom. Although this measure appeared to come too late, nevertheless, two months later when war did break out, many thousands of the country's youth had received a basic training as soldiers and were soon ready to join battalions for active service. It also meant that a good framework had been constructed for rapid expansion to meet the Army's needs once war had been declared.

It had been planned that in order to distinguish National Servicemen from Regulars, the former were to be issued with a regulation mufti outfit of clothes for walking out. This consisted of grey flannel trousers and a navy blue blazer with gold buttons.

By the beginning of August, every Regimental Depot throughout the land was the scene of tremendous activity. Vulnerable points such as key railway bridges and tunnels were being manned and guarded, as well as vital industrial installations. In conformity with this measure, a platoon of recruits under Jim's command was despatched to guard the perimeter of Allbright and Wilson's Chemical Factory at Wednesbury in the West

Midlands. A spirit of genuine and fervent patriotism was sweeping the country. On the first Friday at Wednesbury, after the workers of the factory had received their pay, Jim was handed a worker's cloth cap filled to capacity with copper and silver coins; it was the outcome of a 'whip round' on the part of all the workers in the factory. Although such remunerations were frowned upon in the Service, the men insisted that the money was to be used to buy drinks for the troops.

On the six o'clock news on Friday, 1st. September, general mobilization of the Forces was declared, and within twenty minutes of this announcement the first Reservist had reported for duty at the Regimental Depot, Warwick. Private Sabin (whom Jim had known in the First Battalion in India) was the first of many thousands to join the Regiment within the next few days. As the Depot was capable of accommodating only 423 soldiers, the Reservists were issued with their clothing, equipment and blankets and told to find a sleeping place wherever they could. By Sunday morning, 3rd. September, over three and a half thousand men had flooded into the barracks, which soon resembled a vast refugee camp. Fortunately the weather was dry and warm and the men slept wherever they could: in the N.A.A.F.I., the gymnasium, the sports pavilion or simply in the open.

Despite their living conditions, their spirits were high. The scene was unforgettable. By 10.30 a.m. on that historic Sunday morning the entire company of troops had been assembled on the barrack square to listen to the Prime Minister addressing the nation. Precisely at eleven o'clock there was a deathly silence as the loudspeakers (usually used to transmit military music for marching recruits) echoed those now familiar words of Neville Chamberlain: 'We are at war with Germany'. This was the signal for one of the most dramatic scenes ever witnessed at the Depot of the Royal Warwickshire Regiment. Spontaneously and almost as one, every soldier gave a tremendous and ecstatic cheer. It must have wafted right over Warwick's famous racecourse to the county town a mile and a half away. There can be no doubt that such graphic scenes were being repeated at that same moment at every Regimental and Corps Depot throughout the length and breadth of the British Isles.

Before the great assemblage of soldiers dispersed, the men were told to form into three ranks and a call was made for some three hundred volunteeers to join the 2nd. Battalion for immediate overseas service. Again a tremendous spirit of loyalty and esprit de corps evinced itself. Almost as one, every soldier on parade stepped a pace forward, signifying that he was ready to join his comrades in the 2nd. Battalion to fight the common enemy. Those first few days of the War saw reunions between hundreds of soldiers who had served together in past years in Palestine, Egypt, the Sudan, or India, and the air seemed full of stories of bygone days as they indulged in reminiscences of the years spent soldiering in those far-off countries.

That same Sunday afternoon about thirty of Jim's Christian pals of 'yesterday' met in his married quarter, as they had done formerly in India. There they chatted over cups of tea prepared by Lynette, and then prayers were said before they finally departed. In the case of some of those friends, that was the last time Jim and Lynette were to see them; they were later to pay the supreme sacrifice in laying down their lives for their King and Country.

From that day onwards the momentum of the country's war effort began to take on a new significance and an ever-increasing urgency. Preparations were intensified to guard against enemy air attack upon civilians as well as upon soldiers. Air-raid wardens were appointed for every street, every building of any consequence, and from every section of the community, no matter what its status. Women too began to join the armed forces in their thousands, and could be seen drilling on the barrack square beside their male counterparts. To increase the production of food, so vitally needed to make the nation self-sufficient, a Women's Land Army was formed.

All this time the British Army was expanding rapidly and in consequence the Territorial Battalions of the Royal Warwickshire Regiment were mobilized. The 5th. and 6th. Battalions mobilized at the Drill Hall, Thorpe Street, Birmingham, the 7th. Battalion at the Drill Hall, Victoria Road, Coventry, and the 8th. Battalion at Whitton, Birmingham; the latter's original home was the Drill Hall, Aston. Once the men joined their battalions, centralised accommodation was obviously needed and hutted camps of 'militia' type were springing up all over the country. In order to facilitate administration, most of them were built adjacent to the permanent Depots. However, so great was the influx into the Army, and so rapid the expansion, that in many cases temporary accommodation was requisitioned. At Warwick (as in other places) the local racecourse was used to house troops.

Among the thousands of young men joining the Regiment at Budbrooke Barracks shortly after mobilization was a young lad whose father had served in the 8th. Battalion during the years 1890 to 1892. The father had become Staff Sergeant Albert Enoch Powell in 'K' Company, which was in fact the Cadet Company of the Saltley Teachers' Training College. Young James Enoch Powell returned from Australia (where the family was living at the outbreak of the War) and immediately went to Australia House in London to volunteer to join his father's old regiment. He arrived at Budbrooke Barracks on the 20th. October to commence his basic training.

It may well be that Jim was his squad instructor. Young Enoch soon commenced to climb the ladder of promotion, for two months after joining the Regiment he was made a lance-corporal. In January, 1941 he proceeded to Aldershot to join 164 Officer Training Unit. Then, only just after being commissioned into the Regiment in September, 1941, he went to Camberley on a Staff Course. By the end of the War he had risen to the rank of Brigadier.

Those endowed with a keen eye will observe that on the numerous occasions on which Enoch Powell, that now familiar politician, appears on television, he invariably wears the Royal Warwickshire Association tie of royal blue embroidered with small gold antelopes.

In October, 1939 Lynette gave birth to a daughter. A few days later Jim, together with two other sergeants, was summoned to the Orderly Room. By this time, with the expansion of the Forces, it had become necessary for many experienced soldiers to be given promotion to officer status. To their astonishment all three sergeants were now marched in to see the General Commanding the local District to be told that as part of the general procedure they had been recommended for training to commissioned rank. Within a few days they were on their way to Bulford Camp in Wiltshire to report to 162 Officers' Training Unit. Jim was commissioned into the North Staffordshire Regiment on 18th. February, 1940, being one of the first 'other ranks' of the Regiment to be given commissioned rank at the beginning of the War.

By this time the 2nd. Battalion was already in France, being a unit in the British Expeditionary Force. It was during the winter of 1939-1940, in the course of the 'probing and patrolling' phase of the War, that the Regiment received its first awards for bravery in action against the Germans. 'Nick', the subaltern who, it will be remembered, had floored the champion in the boxing ring at Woking, was awarded the Military Cross, as was another subaltern, Mark Fisher. It is interesting, however, to record that the first decoration for bravery during World War II was, in fact, won by a corporal of the 1st. Battalion of the Regiment who was serving on the North-west Frontier in India. Corporal Sutton was actually in command of a section of 'D' Company once commanded by Jim. It was stationed in the vicinity of the River Tochi. During the operation his section was trying to help in extricating another section which had become isolated by fire from tribesmen. Then the corporal's own section came under heavy fire and he himself was wounded twice. Nevertheless he continued to operate his section's Lewis gun until the withdrawal had been completed. For his courage and coolness Corporal Sutton was awarded the Distinguished Conduct Medal.

During the fighting which preceded Dunkirk, the 2nd. Battalion lost many of its men, a considerable number being taken prisoner by the Germans. Among them was 'Pat' Burge, who had spent many years with the 1st. Battalion in Palestine, Egypt and India. Such is the irony of War that Pat spent four years in a prison camp, and upon release he returned to find that many who were far his juniors had, through the fortunes of war, become senior to him. Pat had one consolation, for he was awarded the Military Cross for his bravery.

The 7th., 8th. and 2nd. Battalions were engaged in what can truly be called some of the bloodiest hand-to-hand fighting of that desperate retreat towards Dunkirk. During the fighting one of the worst atrocities on the field of battle occurred, and it involved, amongst others, soldiers of the 2nd. Battalion. A batch of between eighty and ninety of all ranks of the Battalion, as well as of the Cheshire Regiment and some Artillerymen, was murdered by the S.S. in a barn on the outskirts of the town of Wormhoudt, about twelve miles south of Dunkirk. The Royal Warwickshires comprised about fifty soldiers of 'D' Company, together with Captain Lynn-Allen, who was the only officer. There were also men from 'A' Company. They were double-marched to a barn, being thrust at with bayonets on the way. Both wounded and unwounded were herded into the barn, but at that point Captain Lynn-Allen strongly protested. He was answered with taunts and several hand grenades were thrown in among the crowded troops, killing and wounding many. Those still surviving were taken outside three at a time and shot. After this had happened twice, those still inside refused to come out, whereupon the Germans fired indiscriminately into the barn until they thought that no one had survived. A few men did survive, thanks to the self-sacrifice of C.S.M.A. Jennings (with whom Jim had served in India) and Sergeant S. Moore. These threw themselves on top of grenades and were killed instantly. Another survivor was Private A. Evans. His arm was shattered by a grenade. In the confusion he was pulled out of the barn by Captain Lynn-Allen, who dodged round the corner of the building and supported him to a pool of water some two hundred yards away. Here they concealed themselves in the water. However, a German appeared, took out his pistol and shot them both. Captain Lynn-Allen died but Private Evans, though again wounded, survived and was later able to tell the whole story of this atrocity and to ensure that those responsible were punished.

Monty, together with the remnants of his Division and a total of 338,000 British troops, was safely evacuated in that memorable operation which all the world now remembers simply as 'Dunkirk'. It was perhaps one of the largest and most successful withdrawals in the annals of warfare, due in no small measure to the outstanding gallantry and resourcefulness of the hundreds of small ships which ferried the survivors across the English Channel.

Some time after Dunkirk, Monty told of an incident which took place during the withdrawal. Among the many troops whom Monty met was one bedraggled soldier who obviously failed to recognise his Divisional Commander. In his dishevelled state he turned to Monty and said, 'Where are the bloody boats?' Observing that the soldier was not carrying a weapon of any kind, the Divisional Commander retorted: 'And where's your bloody rifle?' He obviously assumed that to lighten his load the soldier had discarded his rifle en route to the beaches. Monty did not say what the soldier's reply was; his own reaction was merely to point him in the general direction of the part of the beach where most troops were being evacuated.

Although the gallant British Army had received a severe mauling both on the way to being evacuated and on the beaches themselves, its spirit never flagged and over the next three years it was transformed into a fighting machine second to none in the world in preparation for its return to liberate Europe. During this period it was not only the Army that was in the forefront of the battle. The civilian population of the British Isles was no less so, for it had now to experience the full fury of the Luftwaffe's diabolical and indiscriminate bombing of British towns and cities.

Shortly before leaving Warwick for Devon, where he was to join the 14th. Battalion of the Regiment, Jim and his family spent a night in Birmingham in order to attend his brother's wedding. They found themselves caught for eight hours in an air-raid shelter in Long Street, Sparkbrook during one of the city's heaviest raids. It was the first occasion on which the Luftwaffe used parachute mines, which were designed to do a maximum amount of damage at ground level. Among the targets hit was the Market Hall, next to the Bull Ring. Some days later Jim's aunt, with whom they had stayed, was again in the same shelter, which received a direct hit. Miraculously, however, she survived, and was dragged from the debris without serious injury.

On the Monday of the week in which Coventry was blitzed Jim proceeded to Devon whilst Lynette and Naomi remained with friends just outside Warwick. Here they were forced to be spectators on that horrific night when Godiva's city was razed to the ground. Ted Letts, who was a reporter on the *Coventry Evening Telegraph*, and who later became a subaltern in Jim's Company, cycled to Rugby the following morning to convey to the London Press the news of Coventry's appalling disaster. For this he was highly commended.

Chapter 16

With the Fourteenth Battalion in Devonshire

The 14th. Battalion Headquarters was at the Devonshire town of Sidbury, and on arriving there Jim was greeted by the C.O., 'Ray' Boyd Mansell, who had been his Company Commander in Chaubattia. As there was so much to be done, the C.O. lost no time in getting down to business. Pointing to Colyton, a small village some ten miles away, he told Jim to proceed there, find accommodation, and prepare to receive one hundred and forty soldiers who would be arriving from the Depot on the Friday of that week. This was no mean task, for it necessitated the requisitioning of accommodation for billeting the men, as well as obtaining suitable facilities for cooking and dining.

On arriving at Colyton, the first man he met was a local bakery owner named Will Glover. His knowledge of the village and all its folk was of inestimable value, and in little or no time he had accompanied Jim around the whole village, making his task infinitely easier. The people of Colyton, although slow of speech and perhaps of thought, as people from Devon are reputed to be, turned out to be quite marvellous. They had hearts of gold and went out of their way to play their part in the war effort. Those who were unable to offer accommodation helped by providing bathing facilities for soldiers whose billets were without a bath. Temporary covering was erected, and by this simple means the back yard of The Globe public house was transformed into a cookhouse, with an adjoining building, the Buffaloes Hall, serving as the dining hall. The local Village Hall, known as The Feefees Hall, became Company H.Q., whilst officer accommodation was provided by several of the local hotels. A Mrs. Mills, a friend of the Glovers, offered the flat above her shop for Jim and his family.

The Sunday after the arrival of the troops was Remembrance Day, and all the people of the village turned out to see their first Parade Service, which included detachments of all the local voluntary organisations including the Home Guard. It must have been a long time since that beautiful church, with its lantern tower, had witnessed so memorable a gathering.

Early in the New Year of 1941 it was learned that Monty was to visit the Battalion area. By this time Jim's old C.O. was a Lieut.-General commanding the British 5th. Corps, a Command which stretched from Cornwall to Hampshire. Shortly after their arrival, Company Headquarters had been moved into a lovely Devonshire thatched house known as The White House.

As it happened, on the day of Monty's visit the C.O. did not appear. It was said that he was 'sick', but it was generally accepted that he did not get on with Monty during their time together in the Regiment.

It was also significant that after his visit, true to form, Monty appointed a C.O. of his own choosing. When the Second-in-Command went to introduce Jim to Monty, the General's quick brain reminded him of the days when the two had served together in the 1st. Battalion. 'Let me see, Pickerwing . . . You were a Boy in 1925 and a lance-corporal on my staff when I left . . . What since?' Almost equalling that quickness of mind of his, Jim thought to himself: 'If you had remained in the Battalion I would still be a lance-corporal'. He remembered his audacity in challenging Monty for failing to keep to his word in the matter of promotion. It was perhaps inevitable that in replacing the C.O. Monty should have had a few unkind words to say about the state of the Battalion. However, it was no fault of the C.O.'s that the Battalion was scattered in penny packets about the Devonshire countryside, spending most of its time constructing beach defences and being unable to do any military training whatsoever. About two months later Monty visited the Battalion again. By this time it was under canvas and together for the first time since its resuscitation (for it had already been in existence in World War I).

Two incidents stand out in Jim's memory concerning that camp. The first occurred one Sunday afternoon when he, 'Nick' (who was then Second-in-Command), and another officer were together in one of the tents. Suddenly a low-flying aircraft came buzzing overhead. Almost as one, the three officers went outside to investigate and were soon under no illusion as to the identity of the plane. So low was it flying that the ominous swastika markings on its fuselage could clearly be seen. Almost as they spotted it, they could see that it was preparing for a run over the camp. 'Into that bloody slit trench!' shouted Nick, and as all three ignominiously dived for cover, there were three loud crunches. Jerry was dropping his load of 'presents' and accompanying them with bursts of cannon fire. Although 'muck' seemed to be flying in all directions, miraculously no one was injured, and so well were the tents dispersed that the damage was only superficial.

The second incident concerns the Regimental Padre. This cleric was billeted at Battalion H.Q., some fifteen miles away from Jim's Company, and Jim had become aware that he was having an affair with a young evacuee girl of 16 years of age; the Padre was a married man. One day he approached Jim and requested that he might be permitted to be temporarily attached his Company so that he could give religious instruction to the troops and in addition perform the duties of Welfare Officer. However, conjecturing that there was an ulterior motive, Jim would not agree.

The formation of the camp provided the first opportunity for the whole Battalion to be together, and for the first time in its existence there was to be a Battalion open-air Church Parade Service, commonly known in the Army as a Drum-head Service. 'What a wonderful opportunity for the Padre to address his flock,' thought Jim. Naturally he listened attentively to the sermon, but to his utter disappointment it appeared that little preparation had gone into it. The Padre did not use a text of scripture, but contented himself with reading extracts from 'Rip van Winkle' and hesitatingly attempting to draw spiritual lessons from it. After the service Jim sat next to the Padre at lunch and at the first opportunity he said: 'Padre, if that is the best you can do, it is high time you gave up the Cloth and became a combatant!' The story had a sequel. A few days later Jim's wife met a friend who said that she had the Regimental Padre staying with them for the weekend with his wife 'Ruby'. 'Ruby', however, was the name not of his lawfully married wife, but of his girl friend. It came as no surprise to Jim when some years later he met the same gentleman, who by this time had renounced the Cloth and joined the R.A.F. It must be emphasised that this was a wholly isolated case, for during Jim's thirty-six years' experience of the Army, and of Army Chaplains throughout that period, it was the only case of a real 'round peg in a square hole'. Almost all of the padres he met were dedicated to their calling and were a tremendous influence for good among the troops.

During the summer of that year Monty carried out an exercise involving most of the fighting formations in the Fifth Corps, which was under his Corps Command. The battleground covered a large area of Dorset and Hampshire and the exercise lasted several days. As was always Monty's custom, he ordered that an 'inquest' should be held after its completion.

Every officer of the Corps was to assemble in the Odeon Cinema, Bournemouth. On the screen was a very large map of the battlefield and, as was usual, the senior officers sat in the front rows, then the next senior and so on, graduating to the most junior officers at the rear. It was obvious that of the officers present, apart from those of his own Regiment, very few had met Monty before. In true Montgomery fashion he forbade any smoking, and as he confronted the large gathering of officers he began: 'Gentlemen, you may not cough while I am speaking, but those who wish to cough may do so now for a minute, after which you must wait until the interval both to cough and to smoke.' Then, without looking at a note, he proceeded to give a resume of the whole battle, referring at times to the fighting which had taken place right down to Company level. He gave praise to commanders and troops at all levels, as well as criticising some actions taken by junior as well as senior officers, making points of lessons to be learned.

Some months later Monty was passing through Plymouth and the local Commander thought it prudent to invite the Corps Commander to say a few words to an Officers' Forum which was in progress. Again, the front rows were occupied by Lieut.-Colonels and Majors. Monty commenced in his customary brusque manner: 'Gentlemen, what I am going to say today concerns physical fitness. I am not at all worried about the rank-and-file soldiers and junior officers. It is these corpulent majors sitting in the front row'. At that moment I am sure that they would not have minded if the earth had swallowed them up. Shortly afterwards a directive was issued from Corps Headquarters addressed to every officer, stating that the Commander expected them all to take part in physical exercises as a means of getting fit for the big offensive which was to come in the not-too-distant future.

On the formation of 21st. Army Group, Monty was appointed as its Commander with the rank of General. It was about that time that Churchill was visiting the troops in the South-East of England and the subject of physical fitness again reared its head. In the course of a conversation with the Prime Minister Monty said: 'I neither drink nor smoke and I'm a hundred per cent fit.' To this Churchill retorted, as he puffed his usual large cigar: 'I smoke and I drink and I'm two hundred per cent fit'. Enough was said.

Although for the time being the sound of gunfire had ceased on the mainland of Europe, tremendous preparations were being made by both the British and the Allied Forces for their return to the Continent. Nevertheless, the fortitude of the civilian population was being tested to the utmost by the continual bombing raids of Hitler's Luftwaffe by day and by night. Not a day passed without incidents occurring which brought sadness into the homes of innocent people. One such took place on a cold January day in 1941 when snow had fallen in Devon. Jim was hastily summoned to the small hamlet of Roosden, some two miles east of Seaton. It was there, on the coast just below All Hallows School and close to the beach, that one of Jim's platoons was manning part of the 'thin red line' of England's defences. As it was impossible to have troops dispersed to cover every yard of the coastline, mines had been laid at those points which were considered-vulnerable or isolated. This had been done on this particular stretch of coast, known as 'The Land Slip', which lay between Seaton and Lyme Regis.

Despite the snow cover on the ground, the day was beautifully fine with not a cloud in the sky, and a small party of local teen-agers, together with the mother of one of them, had decided to go to Lyme Regis by bus and then walk back home to Seaton along The Land Slip. The party had started their day's outing from Colyford. For some distance they had enjoyed the winter beauty as they walked westwards, when suddenly they found themselves confronted by a barbed wire obstruction on the pathway and a large notice saying 'DANGER! KEEP OUT!' By this time it was about four o'clock on a January day and there was little daylight left. As they were unwilling to retrace their steps all the way back to Lyme Regis, they sought a way round the obstacle confronting them. The son of the lady of the party believed that he had found a way round, namely a place where the wire was only waist high and could easily be stepped over. Accordingly he got over it and walked across the path to the other side. This gave the rest confidence and another member of the party held the wire down for Mrs. Coon to get over. Having done so, she took one more pace forward. This was followed by a terrific explosion. The boy and a fifteen year-old girl accompanying him were blown off their feet by the force of the explosion and as soon as they picked themselves up they saw the badly mutilated body of the unfortunate mother lying in the minefield. As if the shock and tragedy of all this were not enough, soldiers from a nearby post ran out and, supposing them to be enemy infiltrators, covered them with their loaded rifles. Reports had previously been received that suspected enemy raiders had landed in the vicinity.

During the Spring of that year Jim was cycling towards Colyton when he saw a low-flying Beaufighter with British markings. Suddenly and without apparent warning another fighter plane, also with British markings, swooped down on the first from above firing a burst of cannon fire at it. The plane under attack immediately attempted to make a crash landing in a nearby field to the rear of the railway station of Seaton Junction. At once Jim cycled to the place where the plane had crashed, to find three young Canadian airmen lying around it. Two were already dead and the third seemed to be trying to struggle to his feet but then collapsed. As he did so he exclaimed: 'It comes to something when you're shot down by one of your own planes!' Before any medical help could arrive, he too had died. In the jacket pockets of the young airmen were unopened letters from their loved ones in Canada. Obviously they had been given them just before they set off on their ill-fated mission across the Channel. It later transpired that during the mission they had been attacked by enemy aircraft and had had their radio communication system put out of action. Consequently, when they were challenged by a Polish fighter, they had been unable to respond. The Poles, thinking that they were Germans masquerading as British, had taken offensive action resulting in this terrible tragedy. It was understood that on numerous occasions about this time German planes had been found masquerading as British ones.

Even in seemingly remote parts of the country such as Devon, German planes never seemed far away. One sunny afternoon Jim's wife and baby daughter Naomi went to sit on the beach at Seaton for a short time. Suddenly, without the slightest warning, a low-flying plane with prominent Swastika markings flew along the seafront spraying all and sundry with cannon fire and finally depositing one of its deadly load of bombs onto a house on the front. All the occupants were killed and among them was a young girl who had just gone to visit her friends.

Sometimes, however, the locals did obtain some satisfaction, as on one occasion in Colyton. As an air raid warning had sounded, indicating that enemy aircraft were in the vicinity, the Home Guard and duty fire watchers were out on the streets of the village. The Germans were, in fact, attacking the cathedral city of Exeter. Then the defenders at Colyton learned that a German plane had been hit by flak either from the Exeter defences or from a British night fighter. News soon spread that a parachutist had landed near the village and almost immediately afterwards that one of the German crew had been captured alive. The excitement was terrific as, in true military fashion, the Luftwaffe pilot was marched through the village blindfolded, to be taken to the Company Headquarters of the local troops. There he was to await an escort to take him to a nearby R.A.F. Interrogation Unit. Lynette had been one of the firewatchers on duty that night.

On another occasion Jim witnessed an episode in which a patrolling Polish fighter did get his 'bird'. It was off the Rame Peninsula close to the entrance to Plymouth Sound. A flight of German aircraft had been taking advantage of bad weather conditions to carry out a 'tip-and-run' raid on isolated targets along the Cornish Coast. However, the alert Poles were in readiness and quickly scattered the enemy fighters, shooting one of them into the sea a short distance from the shore. The German airman, an unusually tall man wearing the insignia of a warrant officer, was seen to bale out by parachute into the sea. Despite the fact that he was wearing a 'Mae West' type of lifejacket, he had apparently drowned; only his body was recovered.

At that time there was always considerable activity in the air. Apart from the heavy bombing which our cities had to endure from German raiders, an increasing number of our own planes could constantly be seen flying towards the Continent on bombing missions. Sometimes Allied aircraft could be seen limping back to their bases after having been caught by German anti-aircraft defences or Luftwaffe fighters. One such was a Wellington bomber which had made a desperate attempt to get back home after a severe mauling. When the pilot realised that he was unable to make base, he decided to ditch in the sea at high-water mark, just below the cliffs at Portwrinckle near Downderry in Cornwall. One of Jim's platoons quickly went to the rescue and, with the aid of ropes, secured the plane. Then they went straight to the help of the crew, all of whom had been wounded. The pilot had been severely wounded in both his legs and hands, and had yet succeeded in getting his badly damaged plane back across the Channel.

The Second-in-Command of the 14th. Battalion was a major known to the other ranks as 'Pook', a nickname which, it must be said, was befitting. Tall, angular, with a somewhat prominent nose, he was rarely seen without a monacle. He was one of the officers who had been under Monty's command at Poona in the thirties, but who had fallen short of his C.O.'s requirements by failing to pass the required entrance examination while attending a course at the Indian School of Signals. It became common knowledge at the time that Monty had given him an ultimatum: unless he passed on a second attempt he would be sacked. However, it was said afterwards that through the generosity of a member of the staff at the School of Signals who was in the Regiment, Pook had managed to scrape in.

One particular morning The Divisional Commander had arranged to visit the 14th. Battalion. In consequence it had been arranged that the Second-in-Command should meet him on the sea front at Seaton prior to a later meeting with the C.O. Jim met Pook at the pre-arranged time and the two officers were standing waiting for the General's arrival when a tandem cycle was seen approaching. As it passed the girl in the rear seat tapped her boy friend in front and shouted in a loud voice: 'Alf, did you see D'Arcy standing there like Burlington Bert . . . If the Germans saw him they'd invade straight away'. However, knowing Pook as Jim did, he was sure that he was well accustomed to such disparaging remarks.

Shortly after this, an exercise was being held on Bodmin Moor. Pook was officiating as C.O. for the duration of the exercise. After a fairly hectic day's 'fighting' he ordered the Battalion to 'rest for the night'. Sentries were posted and patrols sent out to locate the enemy. On such occasions it was Pook's invariable custom to take every available opportunity to 'get down to it' in what the troops called his 'flea bag' (valise). Certainly he believed in comfort in all possible circumstances. On this occasion, true to form, he placed his clothing and equipment underneath a groundsheet and was soon in a deep sleep. Suddenly, without the slightest warning, an enemy patrol was detected close by and the alarm was sounded for Battalion Headquarters to 'stand to'. In the hubbub that followed, and by the light of a fairly full moon, the gaunt silhouette of Pook, clad in striped pyjamas, was clearly visible. The troops of his own side (and quite possibly those of the enemy too!) could all see him as he bellowed at the top of his voice: 'Finch (his batman), dress me for battle!' Thereafter, whenever Pook was seen approaching, whatever the occasion, the troops could be heard muttering: 'Finch, dress me for battle'.

A further incident in which the gallant Pook was involved caused Jim and his wife some amusement. One lunchtime he paid a surprise visit to their flat at Colyton. Leading down into the lounge of the flat were two particularly steep steps. Jim and Lynette had just sat down to their lunch when they heard a knock on the door. 'Do come in,' they called, whereupon the door opened and in came Pook. Always a little ungainly in his movements, on this occasion he was even more so than usual. Unaware of the steps, his entry took the form of a sprawling dive which scattered some of the furniture. Meanwhile his monacle flew in one direction and his cap, gloves and cane in another, thrown down like a gauntlet before Jim and his wife. Lynette, who soon realised who it was, found it decidedly difficult to restrain her laughter.

Later that summer the Battalion moved westward and set up a new H.Q. at Crownhill Barracks, Plymouth. Jim's Company was fortunate enough to have its H.Q. at the lovely Cornish resort of Downderry, with two small detachments at Portwrinckle and Cawsands. After only six weeks, however, they moved to the Rame Peninsula overlooking Plymouth Sound. The Company was accomodated in one of the many Napoleonic fortresses built to guard the English coast at the beginning of the nineteenth century. Situated close by were a couple of heavy anti-aircraft batteries of Artillery, a 'Z' Rocket Battery and a contingent of the Pioneer Corps. Immediately an attack on Plymouth commenced, these would light large decoy fires, at the same time operating a convoy of smoke-producing vehicles. Whilst the decoys certainly had the desired effect of drawing off many bombs which would otherwise have dropped on the city, they undoubtedly made things uncomfortably hot for Jim's troops on the Rame Peninsula.

One Sunday evening Jim had arranged a small church service for his troops. Ted Letts (the reporter late of the *Coventry Evening Telegraph*) was by this time a subaltern. He was playing an organ which had been acquired for the service when suddenly all hell was let loose. As the heavy Ack ack guns went into action, supported by several fusilades of rockets from the 'Z' Battery, the heavy iron shutters of the look-out slits of the old fort began to swing and rattle like chains in a dungeon. As Ted and Jim emerged from their fortress home to see how the battle was going, they suddenly heard a tremendous cheering from the neighbouring batteries. Looking up, they saw what was obviously a German plane plummeting to the earth in flames. That was the first of three nights on which the Luftwaffe attempted systematically to destroy Plymouth.

Although Jim's Regiment was Infantry of the Line, almost all of his Company were tradesmen who, prior to being called up, had been employed in the car industry at Coventry. They were perhaps some of the country's most highly skilled technicians. It was discovered that when the Company moved into their fortress, no electricity had been laid on, the mains being about five hundred yards away. A group of men approached Jim saying that if they were given the necessary equipment, they would themselves install the electricity supply. It was not long before this was agreed by higher authority, and in an amazingly short time those boys had given the Company the lighting and power necessary to make their lives far more comfortable. Jim often thinks of those men as being the cream of British youth, many of whom made the supreme sacrifice so as to ensure that we today should be free of Nazi tyranny. Nowadays, when he sees the disruptions in the motor car and other contemporary industries, he wonders what those lads would think.

'B' Company, the neighbour of Jim's Company, was occupying another fort a couple of miles away at Tragantle. As Christmas was approaching, they had been making preparations to the extent of having 'acquired', earlier in the year, several goslings which they had been fattening up for the festive season. Some of Jim's lads had been eying these birds with envy and had planned to carry out a night raid with the object of depriving 'B' Company of their fat geese. However, despite careful and detailed planning of the operation, fate intervened to deprive them of their prize. Only a couple of hours before the raiding party arrived, 'B' Company's cooks had themselves wrung the birds' necks and taken them into safer custody within the confines of their kitchen to be enjoyed on Christmas Day.

In the Spring of 1942, after Jim's Company had moved to Crownhill Barracks, they were told to make the preparations necessary for receiving officers and troops who had been taking part in a secret raid on the Continent. It transpired that these were members of a task force engaged in the raid on the port of St. Nazaire. During the next couple of days many stories were told of that hazardous but highly successful combined operation of Naval and Commando units against the harbour installations of the port, which were of paramount importance to the Germans. The prime object of the raid was to neutralise the large dock. It was the only one capable of taking the Battleship *Tirpitz*, which was being used to attack Allied shipping in the Atlantic. The raiders had the secondary task of attacking the submarine pens used by the Germans.

Initially the Germans were taken by surprise, but in the later stages they became ruthless in their attempts to thwart the British raiding party. It was reported that they poured oil and petrol into the water of the harbour and set it alight, thereby burning many of the gallant Commandos taking part. Although many of the raiders were taken prisoner, countless acts of gallantry on their part have been recorded, several of which earned the award of the Victoria Cross. Among those who received the supreme award were Lieut.-Colonel A. C. Newman, who was in command of the Commando Force, and Commander R. A. Dudley Ryder of the Royal Navy.

The next large-scale raid was made by a predominantly Canadian Force on the French Coast at Dieppe. It so happened that Jim was on temporary station at Portsmouth at the time. This was less successful, and a very large proportion of the raiding force was either killed or captured. It took place in foul weather and as the remnant scurried back as best they could to Portsmouth, the Luftwaffe strafed them all the way back and then, for good measure, launched several heavy and prolonged raids on the city itself.

Later in that year a directive was received by all field units in the U.K. stating that as many officers as possible should undertake attachments to the R.A.F. so as to give them practical experience in the latter's combat role. As part of this arrangement, Jim was seconded to an R.A.F. Squadron of Coastal Command at Yelverton, fifteen miles north of Plymouth. The

Squadron's primary role was to patrol the 'Western Approaches'. Jim's attachment was to last a fortnight. Although it was not obligatory to fly, he was keen to do so. Initially he was given a local flight in a single-engine 'trainer'. From what happened later it became obvious that the R.A.F. 'type' was determined to give the 'soldier' a 'real run around'. For half an hour he threw his plane around the sky as a display pilot would. He dived, turned, rolled and even looped the loop in an attempt to get Jim to cry quits. Although it was not altogether pleasant, Jim was equally determined not to display any emotion whatsoever and when they landed the pilot actually exclaimed that most land lubbers would have succumbed to a far less exacting flight than that to which Jim had been subjected.

Later in the week he accepted the offer of a three-hour operational patrol flight in a Blenheim twin-engined reconnaissance fighter-bomber. Before taking off he joined the crew for the official briefing and was instructed as to what to do in an emergency and how, if necessary, to man one of the guns. The sky was cloudless as they set off on a triangular course from Plymouth to a point off the South Irish coast, and thence southward over Lorient and Brest on the Brittany coast before returning to base. At the time, the Germans had air superiority over the mainland of France, so that a very real possibility existed of being attacked by the Luftwaffe. Fortunately the flight went without incident except for one small point. As they were de-planing, Jim inadvertently pulled the ripcord of his parachute, which resulted in his having to buy drinks all round for the crew on their return to the Mess. He later learned that a few days afterwards, another Blenheim on a similar mission from the base failed to return due to enemy action. This was understandable in view of the generally recognised fact that a Blenheim was no real match for a posse of half a dozen enemy fighters, any one of which had a far greater speed than that of the British plane.

In August, 1942 Monty was given command of the 8th. Army in Egypt, a job originally intended for General Gott. Tragically, he had been killed in an aircraft accident. As is now generally known, at that time the troops in Egypt had their backs to the wall, and when their new Commander arrived morale was low. It was typical of Montgomery that his first priority should. have been to lift the morale of his men and imbue a spirit of confidence in themselves and in himself as their Commander. It was at this point that he adopted the wearing of the black beret and Armoured Corps badge, thereby associating himself with a Corps which, as he realised, would soon have to play a most important part in the battles before him. Of course that was part of the Montgomery make-up and it obviously succeeded in achieving its intended object. Nevertheless, as one in a position to know, Jim can assert that many past and present members of his own Regiment resented the gesture.

Whilst preparations for the new offensive were taking shape in Egypt, back in England a particular exercise was carried out. It took place on Salisbury Plain and its object was to try out part of the Artillery plan which was to form a prelude to the forthcoming offensive in Egypt. In this exercise the 14th. Battalion, The Royal Warwickshire Regiment played its part. Its task was to construct a 'Battalion Defensive Position' prior to the rehearsal of a massive Artillery barrage against the defences it had put up. The barrage was laid down by guns of all calibres, ranging from 'Field' to 'Medium' and 'Heavy' Artillery. These enacted what was termed a 'gun-fire barrage', and it was certainly the largest of its kind carried out in this country. Thousands upon thousands of shells rained down upon the Battalion position, which had been evacuated just before the barrage commenced. The guns included a 21″ Railway Mounted Gun' firing from a distance of about 18 miles. This was used merely to give the weapon and its crew practice for its own role against the German defences across the English Channel at a later date.

After the shoot had been completed, all the spectators, including many senior officers from the Allied countries together with their advisers, went forward to inspect the results on the target area. The entire area was pitted with craters and, interestingly enough, those of the 21″ gun were all in the area of Jim's forward position, including one immense unexploded shell measuring approximately five feet in length and weighing over a ton. The lessons learned from the exercise were later put into practice at El Alamein.

Chapter 17

In Training with the Seventh Battalion

In November, 1943 Jim went to Northern Ireland to join the 7th. Battalion, The Royal Warwickshire Regiment under the command of Lieut.-Colonel 'Ben' Walton. It was part of the 59th. Welsh Division stationed at Keady on the Border south of Armagh. Ben had the reputation of being a good soldier who had always been madly keen on physical fitness. In the thirties he had played hockey for the Army. As the formation was destined to become part of 21st. Army Group, it was engaged in intensive training, part of which consisted of a twenty-one mile route march every Monday. In the Spring of 1944 a Divisional Route March Competition was held. In the final the 7th. Battalion was matched against the 6th. Battalion, The North Staffordshire Regiment. At the end of the march not a single point separated the two battalions in the judges' marking. In order to decide the winner, the Divisional Commander ordered that the packs of all troops taking part should be inspected to ensure that the regulation contents were being carried. Finally, in the course of examining the kit of one particular soldier of the 7th. Battalion, an umpire noted that one of the soldier's socks had a small undarned hole in it. As a result, a half mark was deducted from the 7th. Battalion's total, which ultimately resulted in a win for the 6th. North Staffs. So infuriated was Ben that he immediately ordered that on return to Camp the erring Private was to 'meet' him at Commanding Officer's Orders. To his utter misery, the foot-weary soldier was incarcerated forthwith, being awarded 168 hours detention – in civilian parlance the equivalent of seven days in jail. It seems a somewhat savage sentence for so seemingly trivial an offence. Such, however, was the standard expected by Ben of all the soldiers under his command. In this case it was his firm conviction that the soldier concerned had let him as well as the Regiment down.

In that Battalion several of Jim's pals of bygone days in India were serving. His predecessor in the Company was Peter Cranmer, who had played cricket as well as rugby for Warwickshire and England. His Company Sergeant-Major, who came from Stratford-upon-Avon, had served with Jim in India. He had the reputation of being one of the best shots in the Regiment. He loved game shooting, and when he could not get hold of a shot gun, he resorted to the use of a rifle and .303 ammunition. On one occasion, when with the 14th. Battalion under canvas near Dorchester, he returned one evening with the brushes of two foxes; he had killed both with a single shot as they stood one behind the other.

Another extraordinary incident involving the C.S.M. took place on a self-made rifle range near Keady. The butts were quite primitive and afforded very little protection to the markers, who had to crouch in shallow trenches with their marking discs and flags. On several occasions when Jim was in the butts, he had cause to warn one particular soldier who seemed to revel in waving the flag when the firer missed the target. In doing so he was allowing his hand to become exposed over the parapet. 'One of these times,' said Jim to him, 'you'll get a bullet in your hand.'

A few minutes later the firer missed the target and the soldier again had cause to use the flag. Then, just as he was violently waving the flag for the second time, he suddenly shouted 'I'm hit!' and clutched his wrist as blood streamed from a wound in his hand. A bullet had passed straight through at the base of his forefinger and thumb. Although there was a formal Court of Enquiry, at the time the accident was attributed to the soldier's own negligence. Later, however, the true story emerged. It transpired that the man firing at the time was none other than the C.S.M. himself, who was trying out a rifle with faulty sights. When he saw the flag waved a couple of times he swore that he had not missed the target and furiously vowed that the next time he saw the flag waved he would 'put a bullet through' the culprit's hand. Such was the accuracy of his shooting that when he saw the flag again he immediately let fly, exclaiming as he did so: 'I hope the bugger felt that one!'. Never for one moment, of course, did he imagine that he had in fact hit the soldier's hand, especially as he was firing at a range of 300 yards. It goes without saying that at the Court of Enquiry the full story was never revealed.

In March, 1943 the Battalion received orders to move to an undisclosed destination. It crossed the Irish Channel from Larne to Stranraer in Scotland and thence moved southwards by train, ultimately arriving at Folkestone. Here, so to speak, Jim knew every blade of grass, having spent years of his childhood in the vicinity as well as commencing his soldiering at Shorncliffe. The Battalion H.Q. was situated close to The Leas, with Jim's

Company billeted in Grimston Gardens. What a surprise he received on his first morning there when he paraded his Company for roll call! Who should come cycling along but his old schoolmaster! He knew that he lived nearby but even so...! Jim took the opportunity of renewing his acquaintance and discovered that Mr. Benson was still making the same journey each day from Folkestone to Horn Street, Cheriton; he had been making it regularly for twenty-five years. Before long Jim had met a fair number of old friends of the Regiment, including some who had been schoolfellows of his at the school at which Mr. Benson taught.

Folkestone was certainly 'in the front line', receiving almost daily bombardments from a German long-range gun across the Channel. These were reciprocated by counter-battery fire from one of our own guns mounted on a railway chassis in the vicinity. Probably it was that same gun which had earlier taken part in the Salisbury Plain 'drumfire' barrage.

During this period Jim's wife visited him for a permitted weekend, and during her stay a warning was given of an impending cross-Channel gun attack. As she heard one of our shells whining overhead she at first became quite anxious, but Jim said: 'Don't worry. As long as you can hear them it's all right, and when you don't hear them it will be too late to worry!'

Whilst standing on the Leas one Summer evening, Jim, together with others, witnessed a remarkable episode and one which was typical of what was happening during those years of the War. As they looked down upon the sea, they saw five planes with Swastika markings flying towards the coast at sea level. Then, without any apparent warning, a single Spitfire swooped out of the sun, straightway launching into an attack upon the German fighter patrol, which attempted to scatter in all directions. Before they could escape, however, three of the intruders were shot down by the brilliant attack of the British pilot. Shortly after this incident Jim was given a lift by a pilot from Hawkinge R.A.F. Station. It transpired that it had been he who had piloted the successful Spitfire in the recent combat. He was a Squadron Leader in his early twenties and already had a D.F.C. on his chest.

As previously intimated, the 7th. Battalion, The Royal Warwickshire Regiment was part of 59 Welsh Division, which had moved to the South-East of England in preparation for the Allied Armies' anticipated return to the mainland of the Continent. As part of this preparation, the C.O. arranged that every platoon in the Battalion would carry out a three-day independent exercise devised to give the troops experience in endurance and survival. During one such exercise Jim's platoon marched ninety miles in three days and nights of fighting. Each soldier had to be content with one pint of water for all purposes for each day and, apart from a meagre 'combat ration', had to live off the land. The last part of the march back to Camp led from St. Margaret's Bay, through Dover, and thence on to Folkestone. It was gruelling indeed! After the extremely long haul from the centre of Dover up to the public house known as 'The Valiant Sailor', the lovely panorama opening up as one looked down on the harbour and the Leas seemed to give added zest for the march in. It was from Capel le Ferne, just a short distance from that same 'Valiant Sailor', that Jim had been accustomed to watch the so-called 'Silver Queen' airships during the First World War. They appeared to slide off the top of the Shakespeare Cliffs. It was in that same neighbourhood, while on leave from India in 1936, that he had seen the German airship, Graf Zeppelin as it glided gracefully down the Channel.

Chapter 18

Instructor at an Officers' Training Unit at Dunbar

Jim was taking part in a large-scale exercise on the borders of Kent and Sussex when he received orders to proceed to Dunbar in Scotland as a member of an instructional team to train officers. It had been foreseen that as the time drew near for the Allies to return to the mainland of Europe, the Infantry would have too few officers while the various Corps would have too many. In consequence, a considerable number of officers from the Royal Artillery, Royal Armoured Corps, R.A.S.C. and other ancillary branches were compulsorily transferred to the Infantry after undergoing a period of nine weeks' specialised infantry training. It can well be imagined how disappointed many of these officers were at having to leave the arm of their original choice. When the first course assembled, the G.O.C. Scottish Command visited them in an attempt to pour a little oil on troubled waters. Despite his efforts, as he left the room after addressing them he witnessed, for the first and only time in his military service, a sign of open rebellion. The large company of officers which formed his audience stamped their feet in unison. Nevertheless it can now be said that once those same officers had joined their new units, not a few of them distinguished themselves as Infantry officers.

As they departed from Dunbar at the end of each course, they were usually in good spirits. Invariably, the Commandant of the Training Unit, together with an entourage of the instructional staff, would gather at the station to see them off and, in response to this gesture, would be given a 'salute' in the form of a fusilade of smoke canisters and thunder flashes. On one such occasion the enthusiasm of the outgoing contingent far exceeded anything of which the Commandant could have approved. In addition to the usual 'small battle effects', a half-pound charge of explosive was ignited and thrown onto the platform as the train was leaving. After this, all departing officers were required to sign a certificate declaring that they were not in possession of any 'battle effects' whatsoever.

The actual course of instruction had its moments too. During one exercise Jim, together with other instructors, was on the edge of the cliffs at St. Abb's Head, where he was initiating some trainee officers into the firing of a 6 pounder anti-tank gun. Jim and some of his colleagues were standing about twelve feet to the rear of the gun's breech. About a dozen shells had already been fired when Jim commented on the considerable recoil of the whole piece every time it was fired. A few seconds later he took a pace sideways so as avoid positioning himself immediately behind the breech as a shell was fired. As he did so, the entire piece, including the barrel, shot right out backwards from the gun carriage and dropped to the ground between Jim and his colleagues. It was one of those miracles of preservation that Jim attributed to his practice of committing himself to God at the beginning of each day.

At Dunbar the instructors used to work together in pairs, and Jim's colleague was a captain in the Royal Norfolk Regiment (9th. Foot), often called the 'Naughty Nineth'. Bill was certainly devoid of fear and there were many times when Jim had to chide him for taking unnecessary risks with explosives. On one occasion he committed the 'deadly sin' of approaching a 'blind' phosphorous grenade immediately after it had been thrown. Jim tried to dissuade him from this course but the warning went unheeded. Just as he was bending down to examine the grenade, it exploded in a shower of burning phosphorous, some of which became embedded in Bill's forehead. Jim had to hold his head in water in a nearby burn whilst endeavouring to extract the noxious material from his pal's head. Jim always maintained that if Bill went into action he would either get the V.C. or be killed. When he did find himself in action, a very short time after the Normandy landings, this prophecy nearly came true, for his gallantry won him the D.S.O.

Another incident with explosives in which Bill was involved appears quite amusing in retrospect, though at the time it might have had the most serious consequences. The student officers had been taken to a remote part of the Lammermuir Hills to be given practice in the planting of 'sticky bombs'. Each student in turn had to plant a bomb against a rock face used to simulate the side of an enemy tank. As beginners are naturally inclined to be apprehensive, one of the two instructors accompanied the student as he planted the bomb in order to give him confidence. The first bomb failed to detonate and Bill, again showing complete disregard of the safety procedure laid down, said that to save time he would plant another bomb beside the first 'blind'. The second bomb likewise failed to ignite and before long a 'nest' had been built up of four unexploded sticky bombs. At that point Bill said to Jim: 'Go on, try just one more'. Having planted the fifth bomb, Jim was, not unnaturally, anxious to regain the cover of the imitation bunker, but as he was in the act of doing so his foot slipped. Quick though he was in regaining his foothold, it seemed an age before he got into the bunker. Even as he did so, with an almighty bang the final bomb detonated the other four.

With such large quantities of explosives being used in the course of realistic battle training – to say nothing of thousands upon thousands of live rounds – it is understandable that some accidents were bound to happen. One such occurred on a Saturday morning, again on the training ground of the Lammermuirs. This time the students were being initiated into the use of electrical detonators. At such times it was imperative always to emphasise the prime safety precaution of keeping the leads of the electrical detonators well away from the batteries which were to be used later. Once again that old adage, 'familiarity breeds contempt', applied, and the attitude it betokens was the cause of the ensuing accident. One of the sergeant-instructors who was making preparations was obviously careless, for he allowed himself to be distracted and transferred a battery into the hand in which he was already holding one of the detonators. A loud bang followed and he was minus three of his fingers.

Yet another incident which remains vividly in Jim's memory involved a young officer. He was firing a two-inch mortar and for some obscure reason he failed to remove his hand from the muzzle after dropping a bomb down the tube. He was left nursing a hand minus two fingers. In neither of the two incidents just described were the effects as grave as they might have been, but another one, involving carelessness on the part of an officer, did have tragic consequences. The officer concerned failed to observe the elementary precaution of taking cover while throwing a Mills grenade. Although he was standing nearly a hundred yards from the target, he was hit in the stomach by a fragment of the grenade and injured so badly that it ultimately caused his death. The golden rule is, of course, that explosives should always be treated with respect.

Another of Jim's colleagues at Dunbar was a major in the North Staffs. whom Jim had previously met while serving with that regiment at Alton Towers. The two had shared what had formerly been the day nursery and, on seeing Jim kneel down beside his bed for prayer at night, Ken Stevens had told him that he too was a practising Christian. It transpired that at the outbreak of the War he had been a clergyman, but that he had immediately approached his bishop to say that he wished to join the Army as a combatant. Despite the bishop's pleadings to the contrary, he had joined the ranks and later been commissioned. Sadly he was killed while leading his Company shortly after D Day, leaving a widow and infant daughter.

Jim's sojourn at Dunbar was a very happy one. Although work was carried out regardless of weather conditions, and sometimes in extremely thick snow, yet the opportunities for Christian fellowship which arose were immensely rewarding. One day each week the Pickerings would hold a gathering in their flat, where as many as twenty or more men and women would assemble for refreshments and Christian fellowship. Among those who regularly met were several young officers, two or three A.T.S. girls, a few men of the permanent staff of the O.T.U., as well as members of the F.A.N.N.Y.

The flat itself was situated on the first floor of an old Georgian building called Cromwell House on the quayside of the ancient harbour of Dunbar. It faced out to the Bass Rock, which stands at the entrance to the Firth of Forth. This is home to the largest colony of Gannets in the world, and as Lynette and Jim looked out of their window they could watch these graceful and distinctive sea birds as they glided between the furrows of the waves. During the breeding season they could be seen diving to catch fish. In general, the bird life in the vicinity was remarkable. In a larch spinney nearby Jim was able to see Long-eared Owls nesting, while near the Barns Ness Lighthouse he could watch Short-eared Owls, which nested on the ground there. Close to the burns there were, of course, always dippers to be seen, as well as the occasional kingfisher, whilst in the estuary just outside Dunbar colonies of common tern, ringed plover and several other waders nested. Facing Cromwell House itself was a potato 'godown' with false windows, and during the nesting season every single window-sill was occupied by two pairs of kittiwakes. During the shooting season it was possible to buy a brace of duck for half a crown from the wildfowlers who engaged in their sport on the shores.

One bird story is interesting enough to deserve mention at this point. Among the student officers on a particular training course was a certain Lieut. Woodcock. During an exercise in the art of 'wood clearing' he, together with other officers, was acting as a 'beater' on the periphery of a small copse. Suddenly they put up a woodcock (the bird!) and as it flew from the edge of the copse it hit Lieut. Woodcock full in the face, almost stunning him.

It was only natural, once the Allied Forces had carried out their assault and landed on the mainland of Europe, that Jim should have taken the keenest interest in the general progress of the fighting, particularly that in which the Regiment was involved. On the early morning of D Day itself, the 2nd. Battalion, then part of the 3rd. Division, landed on the Normandy beaches under the command of Lieut.-Colonel 'Jumbo' Hordern. Tragically, however, on D Day-plus-one this very fine and highly respected officer of the Regiment was killed by machine gun fire. Later The 1/7th. Battalion, as part of the 59th. Welch Division, was heavily engaged in the fighting to capture the strongly-held town of Caen. The Battalion fought with the utmost courage and resolution and not a few of Jim's friends paid the supreme sacrifice. Major 'Tom' Blythe, a Scotsman, who had taken over command of 'C' Company from Jim at Folkestone, was one of these, as also were Second-Lieut. 'Dickie' Dugmore, one of Jim's subalterns, and Lieut. 'Tom' Pritchard. The last-named had joined the Battalion from a reserved occupation. He had played rugger for Walsall R.F.C. Among other casualties was C.S.M. 'Cyril' Deacon, who had played football with Jim in the 1st. Battalion in India.

Later, when talking of the Regiment's exploits during the War, Monty spoke of the heroism and fighting qualities of the men of the 7th. Battalion. At Caen, he said, they had tackled a determined and well-entrenched enemy and, despite having to attack over 3,000 yards of open country and under withering fire, had never faltered in reaching and securing their objective. Jim treasures the memories of times spent with many of those gallant comrades from Birmingham, Coventry and Stratford-upon-Avon.

Chapter 19

Ceylon and India Once More

Just prior to D Day, most of the instructors were recalled to their respective units but Jim, being still of low medical category, remained on the staff of the Officer Training Unit at Dunbar. In the Summer of 1945, however, volunteers were called for to join a pool of staff officers to serve in Allied Land Forces, South East Asia. He saw this as an opportunity to get himself medically up-graded and, if possible, to have a go at the Japanese. The upshot of all this was that he, together with forty other officers, flew to Headquarters, A.L.F.S.E.A. at Colombo, where he enjoyed an all-too-short stay on the lovely island of Ceylon.

Those few days at Colombo, with all its wealth of beauty in terms of scenery and wild life alike, whetted his appetite with a vengeance. They created a desire in him, unfulfilled as yet, to explore all the wonders of that lovely part of the world. His first night was spent in a hutted camp of primitive construction a few miles from the city of Colombo itself. The hut or 'basher' in which he was sleeping was devoid of windows. Hence early in the morning Jim was awakened by the melodious notes of a songbird which was quite unfamiliar to him. It turned out to be a gorgeously coloured Purple Sunbird and as he watched, it hovered collecting nectar from bougainvillea, hibiscus and other brilliantly hued flowers. On the short journey to the city he passed several mud 'tanks', where he saw for the first time the Brown-headed Stork-billed Kingfisher as it perched on a pole in the water in the attitude of a parson in a pulpit.

Outside the main post office of the city professional 'scribes' were squatting, ready, for the sum of a few cents, to write letters for the illiterate and those who could not otherwise communicate in writing. On most of the pavements natives could be seen displaying and selling miriads of semi-precious stones of immense beauty and interest. On the night before his departure Jim spent a memorable evening at that most glamorous and luxurious of all the hotels of that part of the world, the Galle Face Hotel.

After these few unforgettable days in Ceylon, Jim received a posting to join a Commando Brigade H.Q. at Biwandi Camp near Kalyan in the Bombay Presidency of India. When he reported for an air flight, he was told that he would have to do the journey in stages, the first being to Bangalore. What a surprise that turned out to be! His wife's father and other relatives were there, yet for security reasons he was unable to write to Lynette telling her where he was. However, that difficulty was very easily overcome. The moment he spoke of meeting her father and family, she knew exactly where he was! After a couple of days in Bangalore, he was allotted a flight to Bombay in a Dakota twin-engined plane. That was a journey he will never forget. It was undertaken in the teeth of a violent monsoon storm with layer upon layer of dense clouds. As the plane ploughed its way through these towards Bombay, it was being thrown ceaselessly all over the sky. There is little doubt that in peacetime conditions such a journey would not have been undertaken. The fact that the pilot managed to remain airborne at all in such deplorable conditions is nothing short of miraculous. However, as the plane approached Bombay at last, the clouds began to break. On looking down Jim was able to witness the first signs of the fact that 'something big' was shortly to take place. Assembled in the enormous anchorage of Bombay Harbour could be seen the greatest armada of ships of all sizes ever to be found in any port of this part of the Empire. Later Jim was told that these were to be used to convey the main force of 34 Indian Corps in a vast operation to liberate Malaya from the Japanese.

When he arrived to join his Brigade H.Q., he learned that through an inadvertent duplication another Staff Officer had already arrived and been briefed. In consequence, the following morning the Brigade Commander took him to the Corps Headquarters at Bombay, where he joined other officers in the 'pool'. Soon afterwards, however, he was appointed G. III on the planning side of the H.Q. This proved immensely interesting; he was briefed in all planning matters relating to the momentous operation, which was to be launched in a matter of a few weeks.

The Corps Sign, to be worn by all troops taking part in the operation, was a pouncing tiger. The significance of this was that the vast Army assembled in India (represented by the tiger) was to pounce on and seize Malaya, thereby placing Singapore at its mercy so that it would 'fall as a ripe apple'. However, the course of events changed dramatically. Only a few hours after the first 'flight' of Commando Units had left the shores of India, the Americans dropped the first atom bombs on Japan, an act which brought about the total surrender of the whole of the Japanese forces. As a direct result, only a small 'holding force' proceeded to Malaya. The bulk of the vast force assembled in India was ordered to remain there, where they took part in the great V.J. celebrations. It is impossible to believe that Bombay ever has witnessed, or ever will witness, such extraordinary scenes, as the Chinese-Malayan sections of the population went into sheer ecstasy. Short though the time available was, they made a super-dragon of paper. It was several hundred yards long and gyrated round the city accompanied by thousands of happy evacuees, now looking forward to returning to their homeland.

At this juncture Jim was fortunate enough to be offered a Staff appointment at the local Headquarters at Colaba (the place of his birth), and he had to wait only a few months after the end of the War to be joined by his wife, daughter and infant son Robin.

In the course of perusing the shipping list of officers expected to arrive on an incoming troopship, Jim came across the name of his old friend Lieut.-Colonel James (Brasso) Carter, who was returning to India to take command of the 1st. Battalion, The Royal Warwickshire Regiment, then stationed at Avadi near Madras. Knowing that the Colonel would have to spend a day kicking his heels in Bombay, Jim thought that it would be a nice gesture to meet James Carter and put a staff car at his disposal for the day, so that if necessary he could do some shopping before catching the 'Madras Mail' later that evening. It was good indeed to renew the old acquaintance and the two enjoyed a meal together at the famous Taj Mahal Hotel on the sea front, close to the 'Gateway of India'. In the course of conversation the C.O. designate told Jim that he would like him to return to the Battalion as his Adjutant. However, when Jim told him that he had just been appointed to the Staff of Bombay Sub-Area, the Colonel simply said: 'You just leave that to me'.

That evening, when seeing James Carter off at the Victoria Terminus Station, Jim witnessed a typical 'Brasso' incident. Some time before the train was due to depart the Colonel was informed that as the senior officer travelling he was to officiate as 'O. i/c Troop Train' for the journey. He responded by asking for the relevant instructions covering his duties. After reading them he discovered, among other things, that a Medical Officer, as well as other staff, had been appointed for the journey. In his characteristically meticulous manner he sent for the Train Warrant Officer, who immediately thrust the 'Take Over' document before him saying, 'Sir, you just sign here and I'll do the rest'. There was a momentary pause. Then the O. i/c Train replied: 'I'll do nothing of the sort. Firstly, where is the M.O.?'

Stuttering a little, the W.O. informed his new O. i/c Train that it was customary for the M.O. to 'drop off' the train at Poona on its outward journey from Madras and then rejoin it later on the return journey. 'Oh,' exclaimed James, 'is that so? Now you look here, Sergeant-Major. I'm not allowing this train to leave Bombay without a Medical Officer, so you had better get one very quickly. And get this into your head: I'm the officer in charge of this train – NOT YOU! You will simply do what I tell you. Now off you go and get an M.O. as quickly as you can'. The Sergeant-Major shot off with his tail between his legs and from somewhere he did manage to find an M.O. to travel with the train as far as Poona, where the official M.O. re-boarded the train later during the night. Although Jim was not present to witness the latter reporting officially to the Officer i/c Train, he could well imagine that he too 'got a flea in his ear'.

During his sojourn in Bombay Jim had an extremely happy time in fellowship with Christians from all three branches of the Services, ranging from Seaman to Lieut.-Commander of the Royal Navy, from Private to Lieut.-Colonel in the Army, and from Aircraftsman to Group Captain of the R.A.F., together with women from the W.R.A.F. and A.T.S. totalling nearly a hundred. Every Sunday evening members of this band went out 'fishing' on the streets of Bombay to persuade others to join them for the evening service followed by refreshments.

Many instances occurred of men and women of the Services being brought back into the Christian fold as a result of these efforts. On Christmas Day, 1946 many of these, together with Indian Christians, toured the Civilian and Military Hospitals singing carols. One Indian family in particular threw its home open to all Christian members of the Forces. Its members were the descendants of a Hindu priest who was converted to Christianity at Poona in the middle of the last century. He had listened, it seems, to a Christian missionary who used to preach in the open air close to his temple and had been so impressed with what he heard that he had secretly obtained a New Testament from the missionary and had begun to read it. Somehow other Hindus discovered that he was being influenced by the Christian missionary and he was punished by being placed in a small cage in front of a stone monkey god which at some point previously had been broken and repaired. He therefore questioned his captors about it. 'If the stone monkey really is a god,' he asked, 'why hasn't he protected himself?' He then went on to tell his captors about the living God of the New Testament, whom he believed to be the true Saviour of the world. Some time afterwards he openly announced that he was going to be baptised as a Christian, whereupon many Hindus lay in wait to try and prevent him from doing so. However, he learned of their plans and arranged to conceal himself in the small church some time before the ceremony. Once he had been baptised, he went out and openly confessed his conversion to them all. Although he incurred much persecution, nothing deterred him from witnessing to his newfound faith. Jim had the pleasure of meeting many of his grandchildren and great-grandchildren, all of whom had become established Indian Christians.

With the War now over, it was sincerely hoped that a period of peace and stability would prevail in India, as elsewhere in the world. So far as India was concerned, however, few people realised at the time that it was on the eve of a period of tremendous turmoil and change, and that the Indian Continent would be split into two separate nations with the two-hundred year-old British Raj coming to an end. Initially, even a casual observer was able to see that certain political changes were taking place. Even in the villages little groups of people could be seen sitting round a small flag of saffron, white and green, being indoctrinated into Indian Nationalism in preparation for Independence. Certain subversive elements too permeated the Indian Services. Suddenly the flickering spark burst into flame; in 1946 elements of the Indian Navy mutinied at Bombay. They chose a time when no British warship was within a day's sailing distance of the great port. On the morning when this took place Jim was walking to the Headquarters for work. As he passed the Indian Naval Barracks he saw a large gathering of ratings standing about without their head-dress. Later it became known that this was their outward sign of mutiny. When the authorities discovered the trouble, a signal was given ordering all Indian Naval ratings to return to their barracks. A few did, but they immediately seized weapons and ammunition from the armoury, which by that time had been deserted by its usual guards.

Soon all hell was let loose. Outside the barracks indiscriminate firing commenced. Quickly the trouble spread, and a large portion of the Indian Navy in Bombay mutinied. Men began to roam round the streets of the city in large bands, stripping off the uniform of every British serviceman and woman whom they met. This, as so often happened in Bombay, was the signal for the many unruly elements to commence rioting of a communal nature. Buses and buildings were set on fire; looting became widespread and on a major scale. During that period Jim was acting as a liaison officer with the civilian police. With the Assistant Commissioner of Police he visited the market area of the city. Here they came across a large gathering of trouble-makers openly confronting a small detachment of policemen. Realising that it was time for action, the Assistant Commissioner gave a clear warning by loudspeaker that unless they dispersed he would open fire. When there was no immediate response, he stood out in the middle of the road and took careful aim at a group of agitators who, with the typical behaviour of cowards, were pushing and demonstrating from the rear. One more warning was given and then the police officer opened fire. Within seconds the trouble-makers had scurried into the back streets like rats scampering down their holes. On another occasion they came across a group of natives in the act of hurling massive pieces of concrete from the tops of a building down on to their opponents below.

Right at the outset of this period of commununal rioting, a Moslem contractor who was permitted to sell carpets in the Cantonment came to the door of Jim's flat. In response to the question why he had come he replied that because of the trouble he was leaving Bombay immediately and wanted to ask Jim to look after some of his valuable carpets until the trouble subsided. Jim was reluctant to do this. In the end, however, he agreed to put them in his spare bedroom without any obligation. They were all piled onto a sack truck. About two months later the contractor returned to collect his carpets. At first Jim pulled his leg, saying that because of the time he had been away he had disposed of them. When he finally found all his carpets safe the contractor was overjoyed and insisted on making Lynette a present of a small rug.

Because it was Naval mutineers who had made a stronghold of their barracks, in the end a British cruiser was summoned to return to Bombay. When it was within gun range of the port the Captain sent a signal to the mutineers ordering them to surrender immediately. Otherewise, he said, he would shell the barracks from the sea. It was only then that the mutineers laid down their arms and surrendered.

In November, 1946 Jim received orders to join the 1st. Battalion of the Regiment at Avadi near Madras. En route thither he took his wife and family to the home of Lynette's parents at Bangalore.

For Jim himself it was thrilling indeed to find himself back in the regimental fold where he had spent so great a part of his life. There were still several other ranks and a couple of officers who had served with the Battalion before the War. The stay at Avadi was, however, very short, for within a couple of weeks it became known that the Battalion was to move to a camp called Jalahali Camp near Bangalore, which had been built as a huge hospital base for anticipated casualties from Malaya and the Far East.

When the Battalion arrived at Jalahali, another British Battalion was already stationed there, namely the 1st. Battalion of The Essex Regiment (44th. Foot), proudly known to all ranks of the Regiment as 'The Pompadours'. This Regiment had fought with distinction at Badajoz, Waterloo, Sevastopol and the Relief of Kimberley. It is one of the few regiments of the British Army permitted to wear purple facings as part of its full dress uniform.

By this time James Carter was already beginning to shake the Battalion out of some of the lethargy developed by the strain of the War years. On New Year's Eve, 1947 the Sergeants' Mess organised a ball to which officers were invited, and although no wives (apart from Jim's) had yet joined their husbands, a substantial number of local girls came to join in the festivities. The Anglo-Indian girls of Bangalore had a reputation for being the best-looking girls in India. That evening, after both the sergeants and many of the officers had been drinking, it became apparent that some of the officers were using their influence to take far more than their fair share of the 'local talent'. Normally at a sergeants' function, when officers are invited it is customary for them to 'show their faces' for a short while and then retire gracefully. Obviously, however, during the hectic years of war some of the dignity and decorum had been lost and in consequence some of the officers exceeded their welcome. The following morning all officers were summoned to the Mess ante-room by the C.O. When he arrived there were no preliminaries and, as could be seen from the sternness of his countenance, he was not there for pleasure. 'Gentlemen,' he commenced, 'Last night you were the guests of the Sergeants at their Mess Ball. It was apparent to me that some of you more than exceeded your welcome. In fact you made fools of yourselves and behaved in a manner unbecoming to officers of this Regiment. In future when you are invited to any function in the Sergeants' Mess you will behave with dignity and decorum, and after a short while you will retire, as is befitting gentlemen of this Regiment. That is all I have to say'.

Enough had been said, and those few stern words from the C.O. had a profound effect, especially upon those who had not served with him in the past. James Carter always set a high standard himself and naturally expected the same from those who served under him, especially his officers.

An occasion soon occurred to give the C.O. further opportunities to exert his influence upon all ranks. The Battalion proceeded to a Training Camp in the vicinity of the Eastern Ghats. Immediately upon arrival under canvas, the C.O. indicated that it was his intention to give each of the Company Commanders experience in commanding the Battalion on an exercise designed and controlled by himself. He also formed a small unit of selected men to act as the 'enemy' in certain phases of battle. It turned out that Jim was to be the first C.O. on an exercise which was designed to give the Battalion practice in 'Advance to Contact' and also in the procedure of a 'Set piece attack'. Allthough Jim realised that the C.O. would be highly critical, somehow, of all the various phases of battle, these in particular were the ones in which he had had greater experience than usual. This was because of his position as Instructor at the Officers' Training Unit at Dunbar.

The first day little of excitement took place and everything appeared to go as planned. Shortly before dusk, the Battalion prepared for a little respite and a period of rest, prior to continuing the following day. Normal defensive positions were adopted for the night, but Jim realised that the 'wily old bird' would certainly not be giving them any real rest, and he knew full well that the C.O. would be using his 'enemy' to ensure that they would have little respite. Shortly after midnight, when he had inspected the Battalion H.Q. and its defences to ensure that every eventuality had been catered for, Jim thought that he might take 'forty winks' in the back of his 'command truck'. Before doing so, however, he constructed his own 'mantrap' in anticipation of a visit which he believed the 'enemy' might well pay him. It must be said at this juncture that earlier on the C.O. himself had also visited the Battalion H.Q., and as a result he too knew all the dispositions. This information he would, in all probability, have passed on to the 'enemy'.

Jim's intuition was well rewarded. At about 2.30 a.m. a specially briefed enemy patrol managed to penetrate the H.Q. perimeter, having been given the task of capturing the biggest prize of all, namely the Commanding Officer. Jim was not really asleep when he heard a quiet scuffle outside the vehicle and was conscious of someone endeavouring to open the flap at the rear of the Command Truck. However, the attackers were completely unaware of the trump card that Jim himself held.

Before settling down for his nap, he had devised his own mantrap by placing a large camouflage net on the ground to the rear of the truck and then attaching two small lengths of rope to the outside of the net. These ropes were then draped over the canopy frame of the truck to the inside, to operate in the manner of a drawbridge. On hearing the sound of men outside, Jim had already taken up a position and was holding the rope in readiness. Once he realised that two or three of the enemy were attempting to get into the truck, he pulled the rope and quickly secured it, at the same time blowing his whistle to give the alarm. For a few moments pandemonium reigned as the 'enemy' struggled to escape from the trap, which had been well and truly 'sprung'. Before they could get away, members of the Defence Platoon arrived to 'put them in the bag'. The rest of the night was spent in peace. The following day the chief umpire 'painted a picture' according to which the Battalion was held up by 'enemy defences'. This necessitated making preparations for a dawn attack. After all the preparations had been made, however, and the attack was about to be launched, the enemy retreated and the exercise was brought to an end. Before returning to Camp, James Carter reviewed the 'fighting' of the preceding three days and gave Jim a 'pat on the back' for his handling of the Battalion during the exercise.

On their return to Jalahali there was considerable speculation as to the future of the Battalion, with talk of large-scale reductions in the size of the Army and with visions of the Geddes Act after the First World War being repeated. The Battalion received a visit from General Sir Claude Auchinleck, then Commander-in-Chief of the Army in India, and quite frequently Sir Archibald Nye, the Governor-General of the Madras Presidency, popped into the Mess to renew old acquaintances. It was generally considered that had the British remained in India, 'Archy' Nye would have become Viceroy. Later he became Governor-General of Canada, and at the end of a career which had commenced as a Duke of York's Schoolboy, he had the following stars on his chest: G.C.S.I., G.C.M.G., G.C.I.E., K.C.B., K.B.E. These in addition to the M.C. which he had won in the First World War! Thus 'Archy' Nye became one more officer of the Regiment to have distinguished himself during the War years. At the time that Jim joined the Battalion he had been a subaltern.

Early in 1947 an important communique was received by the C.O. and in order to make known its contents to the whole Battalion, he assembled all ranks in a hollow square on the parade ground whilst he himself stood on a small improvised rostrum. His message was grave. As part of the Army's re-organisation, the Battalion was to go into what was termed 'suspended animation'. As almost every regiment in the Army was to lose one of its battalions, it was abundantly clear that in the case of the Warwicks the lot was to fall upon the 1st. Battalion because it was in India and, unlike the 2nd. Battalion, was not part of a regular formation.

After the announcement the C.O. informed Jim that he was to fly to England and, on arrival, report to the War Office so as to be prepared to duscuss the postings of all officers of the Battalion. It was fortunate that at that time John Scott, a major in the Regiment, was G.S.O. II in the branch of the War Office which dealt with officers' postings. He was therefore in a position to ensure that all officers of the Battalion were given favourable consideration as to their future.

This first brief visit to England did not end without incident. Before returning to India Jim was informed that Monty wished to see him and he was told to report to the Main Building of the War Office in Whitehall. At the appointed time Jim was ushered in to the holy of holies, the office of the Chief of the Imperial General Staff. There can be little doubt that it is the ambition of every officer one day to reach the top of the tree, where he would have every officer and soldier of the British Army at his disposal. Whilst Jim was waiting to be taken into the Field Marshal's office he again thought of those prophetic words spoken by Hoppy the Orderly Room Corporal in 1930, 'That chap will go to the top of the tree'. It had taken Monty only seventeen momentous years to reach the pinnacle, going from the rank of Major to that of Field Marshal and C.I.G.S.

As Jim was ushered into the room by the then Colonel 'Ronny' Macdonald (the G.I.), Monty at once beckoned him to take a seat and immediately went on to talk about the affairs of the Regiment, saying that he personally had ensured that the future of every officer and soldier of the Battalion was being taken care of. On this occasion Monty was revealing that facet of his character which perhaps endeared him most to so many of the rank-and-file soldiers of the British Army who served under him – above all to those of the Regiment who had served under him for so many years. To one so subordinate as Jim he showed himself quietly sympathetic and even courteous. The whole interview was in marked contrast to those occasions when he could be cold and calculatingly ruthless in executing his will in order to attain ultimate success as a soldier. There is absolutely no doubt that these two differing sides of his character emanated from those of his two parents: on the one hand his father, the gentle understanding Bishop, on the other his mother with her severe and determined nature. He once said that he idolised his father, who was a saint, but hated his mother because of her domination of his father. So ruthless was this domination that the Bishop had to give an account of every penny of the money allotted to him.

Of the many recollections Jim has of Monty, two in particular stand out vividly in his mind: the first is the confrontation he had with him when he was a lance-corporal in Alexandria, when he told Monty, then his C.O., that he did not keep to his word; the second is the occasion just described, when he visited the 'Supremo' in his den at the War Office. On the first occasion Monty was sporting only five medal ribbons on his chest; on the last, however, he was wearing well over fifty.

That was the first of several missions which Jim undertook in connection with the break-up of the Battalion. Only a few days after returning to

Jalahali, he was ordered to proceed with a party of soldiers to collect the Battalion's baggage, which had been placed in a depot in Meerut at the beginning of the War.

Those conversant with that other turbulent period in the history of the British Army in India during the middle of the last centyry will remember that it was at Meerut that the Indian Mutiny first broke out. Naturally Jim took the opportunity of visiting the famous Garrison Church, and as he walked round that historical building he visualised the scene. After the British soldiers had gone to church without their arms, they were ambushed by the mutinous sepoys in the first of many bloody encounters. Thereafter, when Jim saw the India medal with its red and white stripes, he pictured the scene at Meerut on that memorable Sunday in 1857.

Jim's last mission before departing from Bangalore was to go to Bombay to collect the Regimental silver, which had been stored in the vaults of Lloyd's Bank. It had all to be carefully checked and re-packed for the voyage. Whilst engaged in this task he came across his own father's medals, which had been given to the Sergeants' Mess. He also looked admiringly at many of the magnificent pieces of silver presented to the Battalion over the years, including the lovely tureen presented by William Prince of Orange and the treasured 'Seek Glory' snuff box, both of which can now be seen at the Regimental Museum, St. John's, Warwick.

Almost immediately officers and other ranks began to disperse until all that remained was a very small cadre comprising Lieut.-Colonel Harold Tedder, Major 'Nick' Nicholson, two captains (including Jim) and one subaltern, together with about a dozen other ranks. This cadre was to return to the Regimental Depot at Warwick, together with the Colours, the silver, and other Regimental property.

The departure from India of this small remnant of the Regiment was unmistakably a moment in history. At the same time, however, it was a very sad occasion. Certainly it marked the end of an era in the Regimental history and was one element in the great withdrawal of a sizeable portion of the British Army, which had served in India for about two hundred years. Jim's family, consisting of Lynette, Naomi and Robin Pickering, was to accompany the cadre, and was certainly the last 'official' family of the Regiment to leave India. It is interesting to note that on 12th. December, 1912 Jim had left Bombay with his parents when the 1st. Battalion had left at the end of its previous tour of duty; also that on the 5th. January 1934 he had returned there. As Jim and Lynette walked up the gangway they felt an added sadness in their hearts, for they were leaving behind relatives, including Lynette's father, whom she was not to see again.

Chapter 20

Service in England After the War

The first to greet Jim on arrival at the Regimental Depot at Warwick was 'Pat' Burge, who was then commanding the Infantry Training Centre. He immediately offered Jim a job as Company Commander on his staff, which he readily accepted. It was a period when many changes were taking place throughout the Army. The Training Centre soon became the Midland Brigade Training Centre. A new Midland Brigade had been formed incorporating the 6th. Foot (Royal Warwickshire Regiment), the 10th. Foot (Royal Lincolnshire Regiment), the 17th. Foot (Royal Leicestershire Regiment) and the 45th. Foot (Sherwood Foresters).

Having become Colonel of the Regiment, Monty frequently visited the Regimental Depot. He usually attended the D Day Commemorative Celebrations on the 6th. June each year. On one of these visits the O.C. Depot told Jim that the Field Marshal would like to speak to him in the Ante Room. By that time Jim had been appointed Adjutant of the Training Centre under the command of James (Brasso) Carter. As he entered the room he saw Monty sitting on a piece of furniture known to the officers as 'the bum warmer'. It was a large leather-seated fire surround. As he approached Monty leaned backwards, first looking at Jim's feet and then letting his eyes travel to his upper body with an expression of admiration. He greeted him in the all too familiar Monty manner: 'Well, well... Pickerwing... Adjutant, what?... Big shot... eh?' He then launched into remininscences of past times in which they had served together.

During another of these visits of his Monty faced a different officer of the Regiment in far less congenial circumstances. On this occasion, as part of the annual celebrations, the officers had held a ball in the Mess of the Militia Camp. During these festivities Pook, by this time a Lieut.-Colonel serving at the War Office (and who, it will be remembered, was no friend of Monty's) had enjoyed himself to the full; so much so that in the end he had been 'evacuated' from the billiard room of the Mess by way of a window, away from the view of the assembled guests but not from the attention of the C.O.

On the Saturday morning, after his walk round the Depot, Monty returned to the C.O.'s office to discuss Regimental business and inevitably learned about Pook's behaviour at the ball. It was a red rag to a bull. Monty demanded to be acquainted with all the details of this episode and then, in typical Montgomery fashion, he instructed that the erring officer, then a Lieut.-Colonel, should be summoned to appear before him as soon as possible. As Adjutant Jim was occupying the next office and could hardly fail to hear much of the ensuing conversation. He was instructed to telephone the local hotel where Pook was staying to inform him that the Field Marshal wished to see him at once.

Pook soon arrived, and when he found himself confronted by the then C.I.G.S. he looked decidedly sheepish. When challenged about his behaviour at the ball he denied being the worse for drink. 'A Courts Martial will decide that,' retorted Monty angrily and the crestfallen Pook was ordered to return to the War Office by the next train and to consider himself under arrest. There can be little doubt that Monty had not forgotten his previous encounter with Pook at Poona, and the ultimatum he had then given Pook when the latter failed after attending a course of instruction at the School of Signals. As is usually the case when a senior officer is to face a Courts Martial, the case was widely reported in the press. However, the outcome of the Courts Martial must have thoroughly stung Monty's pride for Pook was acquitted. His defence was that prior to attending the ball he had eaten a meal of shellfish, which had had a detrimental effect upon him. Undoubtedly Pook was extremely fortunate to get away with it. On the night concerned Jim himself had seen him and he had beyond all question been drinking so heavily that he had been carried into the billiard room and passed through a window so that guests would not see him in his inebriated condition. Assuredly for the rest of his service he kept well out of Monty's way.

A situation which was widespread and frequent during the War was for mixed units of men and women to be drawn close together in order to collaborate in their work. Under such circumstances it is perhaps inevitable that occasions will arise when one or other sex, or perhaps both, exceed the bounds of propriety. It so happened that during the time that Jim was Adjutant of the Midland Brigade Training Centre at Warwick after the War, the C.O. instructed him to go through a large file containing details of Courts Martials which had taken place at the Depot during hostilities. One case which he came across concerned an N.C.O. whom he had known in India. It might well have been entitled 'Hot stuff on the Hot Plate'.

The N.C.O. concerned was the Cook Sergeant, who by rank was in fact a Colour-Sergeant. On the material day the dinner meal was ready for serving some minutes before the appointed time. It was a very cold day and, as was the custom, both male and female members of the cooking staff sat on the hot plate to keep their bottoms warm. Among them were several A.T.S. cooks. Obviously a measure of familiarity existed between the sexes. A minute or so before the dining room doors were to be opened the Cook Sergeant looked at his watch and called the cooks, both male and female, to 'stand to' in preparation for serving the meal. Some of the girls, however, were loathe to take their bottoms off the nice warm hot plate. Thereupon, it was alleged, the Cook Sergeant seized one of them by the 'short hairs' in a manner which caused her some embarrassment and to which she took strong exception. As a result of a complaint made by this A.T.S. cook, the Colour-Sergeant was court-martialled. In his defence he produced witnesses who stated that that particular girl was immoral and was on intimate terms with many of the men, including some of the cook N.C.O.s. The Cook Sergeant's version of the incident was that when the girl failed to respond to his order to get off the hot plate, he went to pull her off. As she leaned over backwards he inadvertently grabbed her pants. Her version, he contended, was grossly exaggerated and was tainted with imagined embellishments. It was a view which was obviously accepted by the Court and the case against the N.C.O. was dismissed.

Perhaps the most bizarre posting Jim received during the whole of his service occurred in the second half of 1949, when he was appointed Administrative Officer of a unit at Aldershot called No. 1 Army Basic Trade Centre. The unit was situated in a Militia-type hutted camp called Malta Barracks, only a short distance from the main Farnham-Farnborough road and a mere stone's throw from the Officers' Club. Being almost completely surrounded by trees, however, it was obscured from the gaze of passers by. The unit was commanded by an aged Lieut.-Colonel of The 60th. Rifles who had evidently held the post for several years.

On his arrival, Jim was somewhat taken aback by the almost farmyard atmosphere of the place. Hundreds of chickens were roaming all over the camp. The C.O. lived in the middle of the camp in a bungalow, but the building had been transformed into what looked like a ranch. At weekends, however, he went home to Alton.

The young soldiers under instruction were being initiated into various mechanical trades, the theoretical part being carried out in Malta Barracks while the practical side was catered for at workshops in the old part of the Aldershot Garrison, quite near the Cambridge Hospital. It soon became apparent, however, that the C.O. played very little part in the general work of the unit. He did have the usual C.O.'s Office in the main administrative block. Even there a highly peculiar state of affairs existed, for his 'secretary' shared the same office. It was also apparent that the lady was also sharing the 'Ranch' with him. On one occasion an N.C.O. had to deliver an urgent message to the C.O. and when he knocked on the 'Ranch' door he was met by the lady in question dressed only in a kimono.

It was noticeable that almost every day of the week, at about 11 a.m., the C.O., together with another very aged Major, would proceed by car to the local hotel for drinks, not returning to Camp until about three p.m. There they would find their lunch waiting for them on a hot plate and after consuming it they would retire for a siesta for the rest of the afternoon.

Shortly after his arrival, Jim took his turn as Duty Officer for a weekend, the whole Unit having closed down at 4 p.m. on Friday afternoon until Monday morning. It was then that Jim achieved a greater insight into the farming activities of the Unit. He was told that among his other duties he was to ensure that the chickens were fed by the Cook N.C.O. on duty. It turned out that periodically a batch of about two hundred day-old chicks was purchased and then reared in the Camp, being fed with large quantities of meal prepared in the cookhouse from potatoes, bread and a little bran, most of which emanated not from swill but from the cookhouse larder. When the chickens were nine to ten weeks old they were sold to a local farmer, but no financial transactions whatever were recorded in the Unit's ledgers. Jim also noticed that before the C.O. and other officers departed from the Camp for the weekend, various commodities, including meat from the cookhouse, were placed in officers' cars. One Friday, before he himself left for the weekend, the Cook-Sergeant asked Jim what kind of joint he would like. 'I want nothing whatever from the Cookhouse, Sergeant,' replied Jim promptly. 'It's all right,' the Sergeant protested, 'Even the C.O. takes some home'. This incredible situation created deep anxiety in Jim's mind, for in addition to his other administrative duties he was to take over as Messing Officer.

Jim's family was still occupying one of the Officers' Married Quarters at the Regimental Depot at Warwick, and at Christmas he returned there to be with them, for over the Christmas holiday period the Unit to which he was attached had closed down. On Christmas Day itself there was a heavy fall of snow and after dinner on Boxing Day, as it was a fine afternoon, Jim decided to go for a walk. No sooner had he left the house than he met James 'Brasso' Carter, who was still commanding the Training Centre at Warwick. He too was going for a walk and decided to join Jim. In the course of conversation James Carter enquired how Jim was getting on in his new job at Aldershot. Jim replied that he was extremely worried because of the irregularities that existed there. In fact he opened his heart to his old C.O., telling him as much as he knew. From what afterwards transpired, it became obvious that James had taken steps to make the facts known to a senior officer at Aldershot, although he did not tell Jim that he was doing so.

A couple of days later the situation at Malta Barracks was continuing in its normal way when the tranquillity was suddenly disturbed. Jim was working in his office, which was next to the C.O.'s, when, without any warning, the C.O. was informed that the Brigadier would be arriving very shortly. At that stage no indication was given as to the purport of the Brigadier's visit, but the message still did not give any particular grounds for alarm. However, after the briefest of conversations in the C.O.'s Office, Jim was summoned to accompany the Brigadier and the C.O. round the Camp. There was, of course, no time to warn anyone that the Brigadier intended to make a tour of the Camp. The 'posse' included the Chief Instructor as well as the Adjutant. When they reached the cookhouse, which the Brigadier had said he particularly wanted to see, he told the C.O. to wait on one side of the hot plate. It should be explained that this acted as a barrier between the kitchen and the dining room. Meanwhile the Brigadier himself went to talk to the Cook Sergeant on the other side of the hot plate. The conversation which followed took a highly dramatic turn, for the poor Sergeant was bombarded with questions about the chickens and their feeding and of course the Brigadier asked the crucial question: 'Where does the food come from?' The Sergeant did attempt to cover up by saying that the chickens were fed on scraps from the swill bins, but the Brigadier's reply was: 'Come, come, Sergeant! Isn't it a fact that they are fed on bread and potatoes provided for the use of the troops?' The Sergeant did not know what to say next. By this time he obviously realised that the Brigadier was fully aware of the true situation. The Brigadier then insisted on seeing where the chickens were housed and he soon discovered that as well as chickens, pigs were being reared on the camp site, all being fed in the same sumptuous manner as the chickens, on food provided for the troops. At that point the Brigadier returned with the C.O. to his office without either of them speaking a word on the way. Behind closed doors, however, it was obvious that a great deal was being said.

Once the Brigadier had departed it was unmistakable that the aged Colonel had been thrown into a 'tizzy' with a vengeance. He was walking through the office block repeating over and over again: 'Someone has spilled the beans'. Later it became known that he had been relieved of his post and was to retire; a new C.O. would be arriving soon. Before his departure, however, a massive clearing-up operation took place throughout the Camp. Overnight all the farmyard animals were whisked away and a 3-ton lorry appeared to be ferrying a quantity of stores from the C.O.'s private residence back to Camp. On the Thursday of the following week all the officers were invited to a farewell party for the C.O., which was to be held in an hotel at Alton, well away from the Camp. It was a wild evening indeed, and the C.O. himself truly buried his sorrows. With the exception of Jim, all were thoroughly 'oiled'. It had been arranged that he and three other officers were to return as passengers in the Adjutant's car, but when he saw their state he was highly apprehensive about being driven by any one of them, especially in view of the fact that the car was a small Morris Coupe with a soft top. Strangely enough, the Adjutant, who was driving the car, had only a short time before recovered from an horrific accident. The car in which he was driving had caught fire and he had been dragged from the wreckage with a broken neck, recovering only by a miracle.

On this occasion the drive home was every bit as terrifying as Jim had anticipated. The car was being driven from one side of the road to the other and at the same time went through several sets of traffic lights at red. It was indeed a miracle that it was not involved in another accident. As soon as they reached the boundary of Aldershot, Jim made an excuse to get out, making the rest of the journey on foot. Next day it transpired that the local police had been making enquiries about a car being driven dangerously, but fortunately the culprit was not traced. Under the circumstances it was not surprising that when the Adjutant met Jim he enquired how he had got back from Alton, completely oblivious of the fact that for most of the journey he had been driving him home himself.

Within a few days the new C.O. arrived and in due course summoned Jim to his office. He asked Jim to be completely frank about all the irregularities existing in the Unit. Clearly he had been briefed by the Brigadier, who had assumed that other 'rackets' existed which had so far escaped disclosure. A number of these 'skeletons in the cupboard' had not been discovered by Jim himself but now they were to be revealed. Although by this time the Camp had been 'cleaned up' to a considerable extent, the new C.O. was determined to ferret out anything still undisclosed. He carried out a meticulous inspection of every nook and cranny in the Camp, finishing with the workshop area. Just as he was completing his inspection here, he noticed what appeared to be a basement area underneath the workshops. 'What goes on in that basement?' he enquired. For a moment the Chief Instructor hedged a little, attempting to throw a smokescreen. He said that it was locked and that the keys were kept at the Guard Room. The C.O. was determined to go no further until he had poked his nose into this latest Alladin's Cave, for such it turned out to be. When at last the doors were opened, an incredible quantity of 'jumble' met the eyes of the new C.O. Multifarious stores of every conceivable kind had been accumulated and lay scattered all over the huge room, some being still in crates. There were vehicles large and small, as well as a vast quantity of other miscellaneous military equipment, and it transpired that not a single item had been accounted for in the Unit's store ledgers. Most of it had been 'acquired' during the War years, and all was covered by the general term, 'Surplus Stores'.

To allow such a state of affairs to exist was, of course, a military crime for which there was no excuse. Soon after the War had ended opportunities had been given for accumulations of this sort to be returned to Ordnance Stores. The new C.O., however, lost no time in putting wheels in motion to return this vast quantity of material to the nearest Ordnance Depot, even though the work of transporting it took a number of railway waggons. Thenceforward Jim's job as Administrative Officer was made easy, and he had the full backing of the C.O. in carrying out his duties.

That such a state of administrative chaos should have existed over a long period, and only a stone's throw from the centre of the British Army's principal garrison, is beyond comprehension. One can only assume that during the War years many of the detailed inspections of Units which were periodically carried out had been omitted. Soon afterwards, in order to be given the opportunity of a completely clean sweep, the Unit was moved to Taunton.

It was not long before Jim had another encounter with Monty. By this time he had been granted a regular commission and been appointed Quartermaster at the Regimental Depot. At that time it was customary for the senior Q.M. of each regiment to hold that appointment. Shortly after he had received it, the 1st. Battalion was ordered to go to Korea. Jim was then informed that a Q.M. junior to himself, though nearing retirement age, was to be posted to the Depot, but that Jim was to be offered a Staff appointment elsewhere. Jim was also told that it was Monty's arrangement, made on the grounds that the other Q.M. was too old to go to Korea. Jim asked for, and was granted, an opportunity to discuss the matter with the

Field Marshal, who was also, it will be remembered, Colonel of the Regiment. Accordingly, when Monty next visited the Regimental Depot for the annual Regimental 'At Home', Jim was told that after Monty had finished talking with one of the senior officers, he was to go and see him on the lawn in front of the Mess. As he approached, Monty went straight into the attack. This time there was none of the familiar 'Well, well, Pickerwing . . .'. Instead he opened with a terse 'Well . . . What is this I hear? You are kicking against the pricks, eh?' There followed a pause; he was clearly waiting for Jim to reply. Obviously Jim had prepared his case beforehand and he now explained that he believed it to be War Office policy for the senior Q.M. to serve at the Regimental Depot. Knowing Monty, of course, he did not expect him to become involved in an argument. However, Monty went on to explain that he considered the other Q.M. too old to go to Korea. He should, he felt, be given a couple of years at the Depot so that he could look around for a job in his native Midlands. Monty then added: 'In the meantime I have arranged for you to have a good Staff job and then return to the Depot later.' That was that, and after another typical Monty pause he said: 'If you don't like what I offer, you will have to take what comes'.

Obviously Jim gave the matter long and earnest thought. In the end he came to the conclusion that once again, true to form, right or wrong, Monty was going to stick to his guns. Nevertheless. for the second time in his Regimental career, he was ready for confrontation, believing that as a matter of principle Monty should abide by the rules set by the War Office, C.I.G.S. or not. He therefore decided that come what might, he would seek redress through the normal military channels by putting his case to the Military Secretary. Accordingly, he informed the O.C. Depot of his decision to adopt this course.

As a result of his action, he was later summoned to the War Office and, upon arrival, had to report to a G.S.O.I (Lieut.-Colonel) of the Military Secretary's Department. He, naturally, had already been briefed in the case and had also, perhaps, been instructed to persuade Jim to change his mind before the matter was taken to the Military Secretary himself, who was a Major-General.

In the conversation that followed, the interviewing officer admitted to Jim that it was indeed the policy of the War Office at that time for the senior Q.M. to hold the Depot appointment. However, he went on to remind Jim that after all, Monty was the Colonel of the Regiment as well as being C.I.G.S. and argued that it would be courtesy to accede to his wishes. He pointed out that if Jim persisted with his case, it would be highly embarrassing for the Adjutant-General to have to approach the C.I.G.S on the matter and then, if it were pursued further, for the Army Council to give a ruling. In the meantime Jim learned that the Staff job set aside for him had been given to someone else. However, the senior officer suggested that Jim go back and give careful consideration to the matter, and to this he agreed. That weekend Jim went to consult his brother 'Nank' at Birmingham. Nank's advice was that it would be wiser to accept the Field Marshal's ruling, as any further aggravation would certainly 'put the cat among the pigeons' so far as Jim's future career was concerned. Taking this wise counsel, on the Monday morning he informed the War Office by telephone that he had decided to withdraw his 'complaint'. Within a couple of hours he was told that after all he could have the job originally earmarked for him as Q.M. of the Intelligence Centre at Maresfield in Sussex.

Thus Jim's long period of Regimental service was concluded, though of course this did not mean that he had severed all connections with the Regiment. In any case, at least once a year he would be meeting old friends of the Regiment at the 6th. Foot Dinner Club in London.

During the period before Monty relinquished his appointment as Colonel of the Regiment, it was his custom to preside at the Annual Dinner Club. He would take the opportunity this occasion afforded to give an up-to-date picture of events in the Regiment as well as occasionally talking of his own activities. As he considered these dinners private affairs, he would take steps to ensure that nothing he said at them should be communicated to the press. It was at one such dinner that Monty first disclosed to any outsiders that he was going to China to see Chairman Mao. He went on to give a graphic account of a meeting he had had with Stalin. In the course of it, in typical Monty style, he had suddenly fired a salvo at the Russian leader by asking him whether he was really frightened about the threat from the West or whether it was the Chinese whom he feared. Normally, said Monty, 'Big Joe' would answer questions almost as quickly as they had been put. On this occasion, however, his question was followed by a long and deathly hush. Only after careful and deliberate thought did Stalin reply. 'No,' he said, 'we do not really fear any threat from the West, but we are concerned about the six hundred or more millions of Chinese on our Eastern border . . . They are not so predictable as the West'. Monty went on to say that he did not think that Russia would start another war with the West, but it was his candid opinion that such a catastrophe would only be caused by some trigger-happy lunatic.

Chapter 21

Final Years of Service and Retirement

Jim's last two years as a serving officer were spent as Camp Commandant, Headquarters, South-Western Division, Taunton under the command of Major-General J. H. Cubbon, whom he remembered when serving with the Cheshire Regiment in India. The Deputy Commander was Brigadier George Laing, who ultimately became Commandant of the Duke of York's Military School at Dover. It was at Brigadier Laing's invitation that Jim and his wife spent a most pleasant weekend at the School, where Jim was given the privilege of preaching at the Sunday morning Parade Service. Afterwards he was invited to stand on the dais for the march past of the parade, and was doubly thrilled when the band played the Regimental march of 'The Warwickshire Lads and the Lasses'.

As has been stated earlier, Jim made his debut on the Regimental sports scene when he was only sixteen. The Regimental cricket score-book records the names of Boy Pickering and Major B. L. Montgomery playing in the Regimental team. Jim's principal achievements, however, were in the field of athletics. During the 1st. Battalion's sojourn at Poona he was frequently in contention for major honours in the high jump, long jump, pole vault and hurdles, and at the Annual Athletic Meeting in 1937 he gained the highest number of points and was adjudged Victor Ludorum. For this his name was inscribed on the challenge cup. At the end of his 36 years' service in the Army he was still playing hockey at unit level, and during his final year as Q.M. of the Intelligence Centre at Maresfield he succeeded in winning the Officers' Cup at the Annual Rifle Meeting at Storrington. During his final eighteen years in the Army he also had the distinction of never being beaten in the Old Soldiers' Race.

Jim retired on the 19th. August, 1961 after 36 years in the Regiment, and was privileged to wear his uniform for the last time on that day, which was in fact his daughter Naomi's wedding day.

However, he had not severed all connections with the Service. After only a few months as a civilian he was appointed Deputation Secretary of the Mission to Mediterranean Garrisons, which entailed propagating the work of the Mission throughout England by preaching in churches of almost every denomination. In the course of this work he visited the garrisons of Gilgil in Kenya, and also Aden and Cyprus, thereby finding an opportunity to obtain up-to-date news of work in the field. It entailed seeking to bring men, women and families of Service personnel into lively Christian fellowship. It had been in a Soldiers' Home in Jerusalem when he was a young soldier that Jim had received much spiritual help. This work continues today under the wider name of 'The Mission to Military Garrisons', with centres in Cyprus, Benbecula in the Hebrides, Antwerp and the Falklands.

Shortly after visiting Aden, Jim learned that his old boss, General Cubbon, had been appointed G.O.C. Aden, which had become a focal point in that part of the world. Shortly afterwards a British officer disappeared whilst on active service and some open criticism was levelled at the General for his handling of the affair. When Jim read about this in the National Press, he at once sent a cable to the General quoting Romans 8, verse 28: 'We know all things work together for good to them that love God'. Jim knew that the General had high Christian principles. Not long afterwards, when fuller details of the affair became known, the General was fully vindicated in the action he had taken. He wrote a letter to Jim saying what an encouragement it had been, in a time of adversity, to know that Christian friends were supporting him both in prayer and by letter.

Much has been said concerning the distinguished officers who served in the Regiment during the two World Wars. Since then, however, at least one officer has risen from the rank of 2nd. Lieutenant to that of Lieutenant-General. Jeremy Reilly, who is the present Colonel of the Regiment, was awarded a D.S.O. while commanding the Battalion during operations in Northern Ireland and later received a knighthood, being made a Knight Commander of the Bath. Although he has recently retired from full-time service in the Army, he still takes an extremely active part in the affairs of the Regiment, and for those officers of the Regiment who meet annually for the 6th. Foot Dinner Club at the Mayor's Parlour of the County Hall at Warwick, Jeremy's quiet account of current affairs in the Regiment is always of great interest.

Because of Jim's long association with Monty, it is understandable that he should have written at some length about this famous, though often controversial, soldier. Whenever Monty's name cropped up in conversation Jim would be questioned about him, and scores of times he was asked for his own candid opinion of the great soldier. In reply he would always declare that in his opinion Monty was the greatest and most brilliant field commander of all time, excluding no one – not even the legendary Wellington. Many of the uninitiated, who had perhaps only read about him, branded him as a mere showman. That he certainly was, but that aspect of his make-up played a highly significant and valuable part in his overall qualities of leadership. It was an integral element in an aspect which he himself always maintained to be of paramount importance, that namely of man management. To be successful, he would say, the men must always have complete confidence in their commander, and the commander in those under him. After all, Mohamed Ali, the greatest pugilist of all time, was also recognised to be the greatest showman. Those of the Regiment who had known Monty from his earliest days as a soldier were not surprised at his achievements and his success as one of the greatest soldiers of all time. He was a dedicated professional soldier who had supreme confidence in his own ability as well as in the British soldier with whom he served.

Twice during the War Jim met and spoke to senior officers who, on noticing his 'antelope' cap badge, were prompted to speak of their own experience of serving under Monty. The first was General Tuker, who had commanded the 4th. Indian Division in North Africa. He said that Monty's tactical handling was simply brilliant; he was a master of appreciation and application and no matter how great the task, he was always able to analyse the situation with such clarity that he could clearly see what were the prime factors. It was this that enabled him to formulate his plans with such outstanding success. In the heat of the battle he remained unruffled. During the Battle of Alamein at least one Divisional Commander began to get anxious and attempted to contact Monty in the middle of the night. The reply that he received through one of the Army Commander's Staff Officers was that he was to get on with the job and not 'belly ache'. Again, after the Germans' last desperate fling in the Ardennes, Jim met a Gunner officer who had been a G.I. on Monty's Staff. He described an occasion when the American troops were being hard pressed and General Eisenhower, in a moment of desperation, had telephoned Monty asking him to go over and discuss plans. Monty's reply is said to have been: 'I have made my plans some time ago and see no reason why I should change them.' After a very brief exchange Monty stayed where he was to carry out what he was doing.

One aspect of Monty's character always made Jim a little sad. It was his particular brand of Christian faith, which appeared to be centred only on the Old Testament. Whilst he unquestionably honoured the Law, he appeared to lack the spirituality, freedom and grace of the New Testament. This was reflected on many occasions in his dealing with his fellow soldiers – officers in particular. He undoubtedly had his favourites. If he liked a particular officer he certainly graced him with favour; contrariwise, if an officer fell out with him, he might as well go to the farthest corner of the earth to get away from Monty, for he showed no mercy. Although Monty's father had been an Evangelical, little sign of this attitude appeared in his own way of life. This was sad indeed because his influence as a Christian could have made a tremendous impact on Service personnel, as did that of General Dobbie of Malta fame. The latter officer sought every opportunity to encourage Christian men in their faith, whatever their rank. Nevertheless, it must be said that in Jim's case, even though he had crossed swords with Monty in at least two instances, Monty bore him no malice. The fact that this was so is borne out by the following inscription, which the great Field Marshal wrote in one of his books when he presented Jim with a copy: 'Major Pickering – who was a brother officer with me in The Royal Warwickshire Regiment many years ago, from the author'. It is signed 'Montgomery of Alamein, F.M.'

Not long before he died he invited Jim to his home at Isington Mill near Alton in Hampshire. The two spent a couple of hours together, and the Field Marshal indulged in reminiscences of the years they had spent together in the Regiment. Jim was deeply impressed by the clarity of his mind, especially his capacity to recall relatively insignificant incidents which had occurred when Jim's own father was in the Regiment with Monty over sixty years before. A typical instance of this trait occurred when, in the context of the Regiment's service on the North-West Frontier of India in the reign of King Edward VII, Jim happened to mention the name of a certain officer who had been awarded the D.S.O. during operations. Immediately Monty retorted: 'Useless officer . . . quite useless.'

During that same meeting Monty commented on the fact that the night on which his Field Marshal's baton had been stolen happened to have been that of his eightieth birthday. He had gone to London for a special celebration and obviously the occasion had been given advanced publicity. As so often happens, the thieves had had their ears to the ground and, having obtained some prior information about the geography of the house, had entered through an internal garage door. Apart from the baton, they had taken a quantity of silver and also one of the Field Marshal's most coveted decorations, one which had been given him by Stalin. It was the 'Order of Victory of the Soviet Union', which Eisenower had also received at the same time and which had never before been given to any foreigner. It was shaped as a five-pointed star set with diamonds and rubies, so the intrinsic value of it was naturally considerable. The old boy was deeply hurt to feel that after all that he had done for the nation, men with no pride whatever had robbed him of two of his most treasured possessions.

In the Spring of 1976 Jim had written a letter which he had intended to give to the then Colonel of the Regiment at the Annual Officers' Dinner of the 6th. Foot Dinner Club. In it he proposed that in view of Monty's association with the Regiment, his name should be linked with it perpetually; henceforth it should be known as 'The Royal Warwickshire Regiment (Montgomery's Own)'. In the meantime, however, Jim had learned through one of the Field Marshal's household that he had had a severe stroke. In fact he had sent a copy of Monty's latest book, 'The History of Warfare', for him to inscribe as he had inscribed his previous books. Through illness, however, there had been a delay. In the end it was sent back to Jim with a note dictated by the Field Marshal to his housekeeper. It said: 'You will observe that my signature is not as it used to be'. Jim believes that this may well have been the last time that he inscribed any of his books, and it completed a collection of all Monty's books inscribed by himself.

It was as Jim was listening to the radio in his car on the way to the annual dinner of the 6th. Foot Dinner Club that he learned the sad news of a deterioration in the Field Marshal's condition; he was now 'very poorly', stated the bulletin. Later that evening the information was confirmed by the Colonel of the Regiment, Brigadier 'Harry' Illing. It was therefore suggested that at that juncture the contents of Jim's letter should be held in abeyance. Within two days the nation was informed of the passing of this very great soldier. Naturally, Jim's immediate reaction was that he wished to attend the funeral, which was to be held at St. George's Chapel, Windsor. When he telephoned the Headquarters of the Guards' Brigade in London he was told that whereas the available seats numbered four hundred, some four thousand applications to attend had been received. Nevertheless, when Jim informed those in charge of the arrangements of his long association with Monty, he was allotted a ticket for the ceremony without further ado.

On the morning of the funeral Jim set out by car very early so as to avoid a possible hold-up round Windsor. Even though he arrived some hours earlier than the ceremony was due to start, however, he found the streets already lined with thousands of people, many of whom had obviously been associated with Monty in some way or other. Many of them, Jim noticed, were wearing the familiar Royal Warwickshire Regimental tie of orange and royal blue. Once they had been shown to their seats, many of the mourners went outside the Chapel to inspect the vast number of floral tributes which had been placed on the lawns. Jim's own tribute, in the form of a cross of flowers in the Regimental colours, bore the inscription, 'Monty, a revered Officer and Friend – You have earned your Master's 'Well done thou good and faithful servant'. We shall meet again – Lynette and Jim Pickering.'

The scene was unforgettable. Officers and men of all three Services, as well as statesmen from all over the world, had gathered to pay their last respects to one of the greatest soldiers of all time. The Guard of Honour lining the steps of the Chapel consisted of young soldiers of the Field Marshal's own Regiment. Flanking the aisle of the Chapel were nine Field Marshals, one Admiral of the Fleet and one Air Marshal of the R.A.F. The coffin was preceded by two officers, one carrying a baton, the second his medals, while Monty's famous black beret was laid on the coffin itself.

As the cortege moved into the Chapel Jim's heart was full of emotion. In his mind's eye he could see the familiar face of his old boss, his blue eyes at once soft and piercing, and he could almost hear that long familiar voice saying: 'Well, Pickerwing... what?' Among those attending was Lady Clementine Churchill, the widow of that other great Englishman. Because of her age, she had been brought to the Chapel in an invalid chair. Jim also noticed the sad figure of David, the Field Marshal's only child.

All this time Jim had been retracing in his mind the events and the associations of the years that had passed. This, he concluded was truly the end of an era – surely one of the most memorable in the annals of the British Army and nation, and most certainly in the history of The Royal Warwickshire Regiment. He reflected upon the bond of comradeship, so marvellously deep and strong, which united all the members of that Regiment; a bond which had been fashioned in peace and war and nurtured by imperishable memories of times spent together on the field of sport and around the barrack scene; a bond which spanned countries and continents, the fellowship which it created embracing officers and other ranks alike. Yet to Jim at least this was no last farewell; as fellow Christians, he was certain, another great re-union awaited them.

After the funeral it was no random chance that constrained Jim to call upon his dear friend, Erica Evans, whose father, George Kingsbury had met Jim's own parents seventy years before on that far-off occasion when George had black-leaded the wooden training horse at Budbrooke Barracks.

As he arrived at Erica's house, she was just taking off her coat, having that moment returned from attending Monty's funeral. Her first words were: 'Jim, we thought that you would be there'. So ended a remarkable era in the lives of two soldiers who, as Monty put it in the inscription he wrote in the book he had given to Jim, '... were brother officers in The Royal Warwickshire Regiment many years ago...' As he looked back on it all Jim said: 'I thank God for the wonderful way He has led me, kept me and provided for me over my many years in the Army. God grant that many more of those who serve in the Services may be granted the same experience.'

Some time after his retirement from full-time service in the Army, Jim was employed in a civilian capactiy as Quartermaster of the City of London Territorial Association, being based at Finsbury Barracks, London. Although this again brought him in touch with the Service life he had always known, yet he had the ignominious task of closing down many of the T.A. Centres in and around the City of London as a result of the then Labour Government's policy of slashing the size of the Territorial Army. It was a task which he found deeply saddening.

Even now, however, it was not to be the end of Jim's active life. In 1962 he was invited to become a member of the local Village Council at Buxted in Sussex, where he lived. After a short time he became Chairman of that Council. It was the beginning of fifteen years of active involvement in local government. For ten of those years he served as the County Councillor for Uckfield on East Sussex County Council, and for a time he also represented the town as a District Councillor. Besides all this, he was a Conservator of Ashdown Forest.

His experiences during this period were intensely interesting and often entertaining as well. In the field of Secondary Education the Government of that time had determined upon a policy of creating Comprehensive Schools, and in the course of its implementation of this Jim accused his own Party of merely 'rubber-stamping' the Government's policies in the matter. In fact, when the question was debated in full Council, he rose to his feet and accused his fellow Councillors of swallowing whatever was put before them hook, line and sinker. He even called them 'a lot of gullible goldfish'.

One incident that caused some amusement occurred at the first meeting of the new Council following the re-organization of East Sussex County Council in 1973. A motion was brought forward by a Left-wing Labour Councillor to the effect that in future Councillors should not be addressed by any title they happened to have, but should always be addressed as 'Councillor'. During the debate, one of the younger Socialist Councillors rose to inform the assembly that during his National Service he had been a mere corporal – never a major or a squadron leader. Jim let him have his say and then caught the Chairman's eye and rose in reply. 'Mr. Chairman,' he said, 'I'm sure you will realise that when I joined the Army the King did not put a crown on my shoulder straight away. For the benefit of the previous speaker, it will interest him to know that I started in the Army about four rungs lower than a corporal – in fact as a "Boy".' Then turning towards Brigadier Dame Jean Rivett-Drake, who was sitting on his right, he continued: 'Dame Jean, the next motion will be that you should be called "Sister" and I "Brother"!' It goes without saying that the Left's motion was defeated.

One quite exciting episode in Council took place at a particular meeting, especially well attended by the public, at which a determined demonstration was made against one of the Council's motions. Suddenly, during the debate, a number of the younger demonstrators, including several women, ran to the front of the Council Chamber and lay on the floor. Naturally this led to some considerable commotion. When no other member of the Council took any positive action, Jim felt that this undemocratic behaviour was more than he could tolerate. He quickly left his seat and went to the front to assist some of the officers in ejecting the interlopers. Finally one young woman was left clinging onto the floor in a defiant manner. At this point Jim said to her: 'Young woman, if you do not leave the Chamber in a dignified way, then I will see that you leave in an undignified one.' When she still made no effort to move, Jim seized her by the feet and dragged her outside on her bottom – splinters or no splinters!

By the end of his time as Councillor, Jim felt that he had found the experience both enlightening and rewarding; certainly he was a better citizen for it.

During that period there were two more occasions of Regimental interest which Jim will always remember. The first was the unveiling of the statue of Montgomery on the lawn opposite the Ministry of Defence in Whitehall. The ceremony was performed by the Queen Mother, who had stood by her late husband, King George VI, during the momentous years of World War II and was there to do honour to the country's great hero of that war, Field Marshal Lord Montgomery of Alamein. Later, in a B.B.C. programme, Jim was given the opportunity of speaking of his association with Monty, which spanned a period of about 65 years.

The other memorable occasion was the funeral service of Colonel 'Pat' Burge, who was perhaps the most universally loved officer of the Regiment. Officers and other friends had come from all over the country to pay their last respects to this fine officer in the small village of Ashton in the picturesque Teign Valley of Devon.